THE ULTIMATE GUIDE TO SELLING ON ETSY

How to Turn Your Etsy Shop
Side Hustle into a Business

by Noelle Ihli and Jeanne Allen

CONTENTS

A QUICK NOTE

At the very end of this book (page 264), you'll find a link that will direct you to an offer page for the University of Etsy (our video courses!) exclusively for our readers.

The University of Etsy (by yours truly, CraftRanker!) is made up of **more than 90 in-depth instructional videos and worksheets** that enhance and reinforce book learning and help you apply what you've learned about starting a successful Etsy shop.

These standalone video courses are $247 at full price on our website. We're offering them as a learning companion to our readers at a price we don't advertise anywhere else (19.99).

We created these classes as a way to help friends and family who asked for help with their shops but had trouble digesting some of the concepts in book format ((It's kind of like we're sitting right next to you by the computer, taking you step by step through each concept).

While you can absolutely get everything you need to know to start a successful Etsy shop from this book (or from the University of Etsy video coursework; either is meant to be a complete resource!) many of our readers find that the video instruction is a helpful companion. If that's you, we invite you to take advantage of this offer for our readers!

INTRODUCTION

When I opened my Etsy shop almost ten years ago, the gig economy was just a twinkle in a bunch of baby hipsters' eyes. You either had a cute little side hobby on Etsy, or you had a "real" job. And all I knew for sure was that I didn't have a "real" job. I was a mom with two little kids, screen printing designs I came up with in my basement in the butthole of Utah.

I started my Etsy shop as a way to carve out something that was just mine. Something that I loved to do, even if I was tired after a long day of tricking my kids into liking vegetables or later, when I was back at a full-time job writing about candle wax for a company that shall remain unnamed.

I tell this story often, but I have this vivid memory of sitting at my desk, writing an article about why a particular wax was really amazing and wouldn't poison your house with VOCs. It was like 8 am. I was really tired, I felt so unmotivated, and I had the sudden realization that my kindergartener's music program was that afternoon—and I hadn't asked my manager for time off. I was just kind of burned out. And I felt stuck.

When my coworker and longtime friend Anna and I talked about our dreams for the future, I always told her that if I could do anything—money didn't matter—I would run my little fledgling Etsy shop full time. I had no idea how to do that. Or what that would really look like. I'd seen a few sales trickle in since I launched, but those earnings were nothing compared to what I was making writing about candle wax. But Anna, who has always been very wise, looked me dead in the eye and said, "I bet you could do it."

And I found I couldn't stop thinking about it.

So little by little, I started researching. And planning. And I started throwing spaghetti at the wall. I connected with other shop owners and learned what I could from them. I pored over the forums on Etsy. I experimented. I had some failures. But I also had some successes.

I did more of what worked. I took what I could from the failures. And I kept learning.

. . . Until I was so busy, that I had a decision to make. I couldn't keep my full time job and my Etsy shop because I was getting home at 5, spending time with my kids, and then working until midnight. So I made the leap. I quit my job and became a full-time Etsy shop owner. And it was the best decision I ever made. Or at least in the top five, sorry kids.

Etsy is an incredible platform. There's so much potential there. And if you know what works, you can be successful. I know because I did it.

If you're like me, you're probably wondering if you have what it takes. If your product is good enough. Even if you've seen some success, you may still think of your Etsy shop as your "little hobby." And I want you to knock that off right now. I've found that the people who run Etsy shops are some of the most creative, tenacious people I know. And I have no doubt that you are one of them. You can do this. You DO have what it takes.

And that's why Jeanne and I wrote this book (Remember when I told you I found what worked? Well, Jeanne's brilliance and insight into the SEO/keyword/algorithm aspect of Etsy has worked magic in my shop. I'm going to let her introduce herself in just a bit). Jeanne and I are going to help you take your basic Etsy shop, and make it into something that gives back to you what you're putting into it.

Real talk. No BS. No secrets. Just what actually works.

We've broken this book into three sections:

→ Foundation work. First things first, let's get you set up correctly and optimize your Etsy shop. Even if you already have an Etsy shop you feel is doing well, I'd recommend you at least skim this section. There are tips and suggestions throughout that can really help take your shop to the next level.

➔ Marketing and advertising. In the next section of the book we'll cover everything you need to know about marketing your product within Etsy and across the web. Marketing and advertising are how you get the sales that push you over the edge from hobby to business.

➔ Building and expanding your business. The last section of the book is all the details about building and expanding your business from filing as an S-corp to how and where to get your own website (and still keep your Etsy shop). This is where we put everything together and help you reach your goals so that (if you want to) you can turn your hobby into a legitimate business.

Crafting is not for losers. Handmade doesn't mean cute (I mean, it can). Handmade just means that you know how to roll up your sleeves and turn something ordinary into something incredible.

And that's exactly what we're here to help you do. No matter where you are in your Etsy journey, we're here to help you succeed.

~Noelle and Jeanne

A LITTLE ABOUT US

Before we dive in, we want to introduce ourselves. We hope the advice in this book feels like pointers from a good friend: tips and advice from someone who will give the good stuff to you straight. To that end, we want you to know a little about who we are as people.

Noelle

I just told you part of my life story (the one that involves my success on Etsy), which is arguably the most important thing you need to know about me (since you're reading a book I co-wrote called "The Ultimate Etsy Guide.")

But again, the whole point of this book is avoiding BS and getting the real scoop on Etsy. So in that spirit, here's a little more about me:

First of all, I'm a mom. A boy mom to Luke and Max, and a cat mom to Michelle. When I'm willing to wear pants (which is less often than I aspire to wearing them), I can be found in mom jeans.

My husband Nate is the best person I know. He's hilarious and sweet and has an adorably bald head.

The two things I love most (in addition to Etsy and the aforementioned children and husband) are murder and horses. (Separately, never together.) I'm the weird horse girl you knew in elementary school who never grew out of that phase. And I'm the person Netflix is targeting when they roll out a new serial killer documentary, which is also the reason I have a keyed lock on my bedroom door.

My degree is in Spanish translation, which I don't use but don't regret because it opens up an entire world of television to me. In addition to being a mom and Etsypreneur, I've worked "traditional" jobs in marketing, social media, writing, and editing. I don't regret them either, even though I've never looked back from my decision to pursue Etsy as my full-time job. (And I'll be sharing plenty of helpful information about marketing, writing, and design that will help your sales later on in this book!).

That's me. I'm an introvert, which means that if you ever see me on a coaching video or webinar, I am definitely sweating. But I learned a long time ago that regularly doing scary, worthwhile things is a smart way to live. So here I am.

Jeanne

Like Noelle, I'm also a mom—to Kaylee, Eileen, and Tober. (Yes, Tober. The short story is that I let Kaylee name her baby brother when she was five. I swear I would have stepped in if she'd added too many Xs or Zs, but luckily, she hadn't learned those letters yet). And my husband Bryan is, like Noelle's Nate, adorably bald and pretty dang awesome and supportive. Especially when I decided to veer off a more standard career in technical editing and jumped headfirst into the world of Etsy selling.

As for pets, our family's latest foray is to adopt two mini rex bunnies, Ginsburg and Rocky Balboa. Who knew bunnies could be such great pets or that they have such big personalities? Rocky is in the habit of picking fights with animals much bigger than himself (chickens, cats, raccoons), and I'm pretty sure Ginsburg has clinical anxiety (possibly because of Rocky. Sorry Ginzy…). I've fallen in love with them both, surprising myself, since I've never been a huge animal person.

I thrive on political podcasts, fantasy novels, and group exercise classes (I'm 100% unmotivated to move my body without someone telling me what to do). And I really, really love coffee.

My degree is in Editing and SEO, and I started out in technical editing after college. I've edited everything from textbooks to computer manuals to journal articles on aerospace engineering (a.k.a., rocket science) and earthquakes. Technical editing has its perks (it definitely pays well), but one thing it's not is very exciting (at least, not for me). Working with Noelle the last three and a half years in the Etsy shop has been so much more fun. The work we do pulls from all the technical training I've had and has given me opportunities to learn a lot of new things as well.

I'm a numbers person more than a creator, so I never thought I'd end up as a partner in an Etsy shop, but it turns out there's a lot of technical and marketing expertise needed to run a business no matter what kind. In this book, I'll share with you tips for Etsy SEO, data analysis, pricing, ROIs, ecommerce platforms, and troubleshooting among other things. I love our Etsy shop, and I love Etsy as an ecommerce platform. We're here to help you feel the love (and success) on Etsy too!

SECTION 1: FOUNDATION WORK

Setting Up and Optimizing Your Etsy Shop

Whether you're new to Etsy or have already launched your shop, taking the time to cover the fundamentals—shop components, listings, keywords, graphics and design, pricing, etc.—is VITAL to laying the foundation for a successful Etsy shop with lots of growth potential.

So whether you're new or simply aren't seeing a lot of success yet (or want to feel confident that you've mastered the essentials before moving on to next-level strategies for growing your Etsy shop), let's talk fundamentals. We'll walk you through each critical element of your shop so you can feel confident (and so you can start seeing those sweet sweet sales come in!)

CHAPTER 1

The Anatomy of a Good Etsy Shop

We're going to kick things off with an anatomy lesson. Don't worry, you're still reading the right book. But just like med students need to get familiar with the individual parts of a human body before diving into surgery or physical therapy, you need to get familiar with the different parts of your Etsy shop. You need to know where the heart is, what keeps it healthy, what different parts need to work correctly, and what could go wrong.

Much like a human body, each Etsy shop is unique. But they're also quite similar when you peel back the branding.

Even if you've already set up your Etsy shop, it's important that you DO NOT SKIP this chapter. You'd be surprised how many Etsy sellers are unaware that they've missed opportunities and left shop components half-baked in their rush to get selling. So, let's start with the basics of setup and continue with the anatomy of a healthy shop.

Setup: It's Really, Really Easy

Getting started on Etsy is extremely simple and honestly not worth a step-by-step here. You've got this, because Etsy has done a fantastic job of guiding you through the setup process to get your shop up and running as quickly as possible. It's possible to get a shop up and running in about five minutes with their walkthrough wizard.

Basically, Etsy strives to make setup super user-friendly. You can open and even run your entire shop on a phone or go seamlessly back and forth between your phone and laptop. Etsy's seller app for mobile is called "Sell on Etsy," and you can download it and start your shop by clicking "Don't have a shop?" right below the sign-in in the app.

All you really need is a product to sell and a niche that product fits into (which includes a pool of customers who would be interested in your product). Of course, zeroing in on how customers are searching for your product (through keywords), and which keywords fit your product best isn't quite so simple. But we've got your back, and we'll get to all that in good time.

As for the nuts and bolts of your actual Etsy shop setup, you'll need to create a Shop Name, Shop Policies, a logo, an About Section, a profile photo, and of course product LISTINGS. All of these components are important. But listings are the true lifeblood of your shop (the heart, if you will.) And because of how Etsy is set up—as a giant online craft bazaar—some people will purchase your products directly from your listings without ever clicking through to your shop itself.

This leads a lot of new sellers to focus only on listings without circling back to really hone their other shop components. If, during setup, you need to put "real good earrings" in your shop's About Section and come back to it later because you aren't sure what to write yet, do that. But remember to come back and give each part of your shop the love it deserves. Each of the aspects of your Etsy shop matters to potential customers and contributes to the overall impression you'll make: sloppy and rushed, or streamlined and professional. Basically, your Etsy shop is the sum of its parts. And the work you spend to strengthen each aspect of your shop strengthens the image you project as a whole.

Anatomy 101 of Your Etsy Shop

The following is an overview (anatomy 101) of an Etsy shop. You'll want to return to this section at different points throughout your journey to hone your Shop Name, About Section, Tagline, etc., as your shop grows and evolves. But for now, here's what you need to know about each major part of your Etsy shop and why it matters:

Shop Name and Title/Tagline

Your Shop Name and Tagline are closely tied with marketing and branding. But don't stress, because we'll cover all things marketing in Section 2 of this book. For now, suffice it to say that your Shop Name and Tagline make a big difference to the first impression you cultivate for customers and even for SEO/search engine optimization (not just on Etsy, but on Google!). Choose something creative, intuitive, and make sure your Shop Name is available as a URL in case you decide to also open a Pattern by Etsy site (do a "domain name search" to find out if your Shop Name is available as a web domain). Etsy allows you to change your name if you want, so if you've made a horrible mistake you aren't doomed.

Your Shop Name should reflect what you do. "Earthling Cards" or "Cathy's Cards" are much better names for an Etsy shop that sells greeting cards than, say, "Cathy Creates" or "Greetings Earthling" (even though it's clever and I'm proud I thought of it). You want someone who hears your Shop Name for the first time or glances at it on google (and decides whether to click or not) to immediately have a solid idea of what you make. This helps google sort you out, it helps your customers connect with and find you, and it makes for a great first impression.

This can be tricky. Good names (and their corresponding URLs) are often taken. Be creative, but don't be weird. Be as clear as you can. And don't use weird cutesy spellings if you can help it. "Kathy Kreates" isn't going to do you any favors in Etsy or beyond. Shop Names have to be somewhat short, no longer than 20 characters. Your name can't include spaces, just be aware that you need to use capitalization to separate words (e.g, CathysCards, InspireArtwork, FourthWaveApparel).

Your Shop Tagline (or title) is a short (55 characters or less) blurb that should share briefly what you do. Your customers will see it just beneath your Shop Name, and Google may also display it in search results next to the name of your shop. So be keyword conscious without stuffing things in that don't fit. If you make greeting cards, stencils, and name tags, say that. Don't be coy. Keep it simple, and focus your Tagline around at least one great long-tail keyword (a phrase of two or more words) you can find.

For example, "handmade silver necklaces" is SO much more specific and useful than "necklaces." You're trying to imagine what your buyer would type into Google or Etsy that you provide. This can take some trial and error. Make it sound natural, do your best to think what ONE long-tail keyword phrase your customer would search to find your shop, and model your Tagline around that phrase or a series of phrases. A great example is "Small-batch jewelry: Handmade silver and quartz necklaces."

If you're too broad, you'll be easily forgettable and lost in a sea of competitors. It's a big ocean of shops and keywords out there. You want to hone in on what YOU have to offer. And you want to speak directly to those customers who are trying to find you. It's like your mating call (ew).

About Section

If a customer clicks through into your shop, the About Section is often the first place your buyers will click to see what kind of vibe you project into the Etsyverse. After all, Etsy is a handmade marketplace. It only makes sense that people want to know a little bit about the hands that made their product!

Your About Section tells who you are, where you came from. It humanizes you and connects you with your potential buyer (not to mention media outlets or social media collabs).

Aside from a good header image and a carefully curated first page of listings, your About Section is about as important as it gets to how customers will perceive you and your products. Here are the components of a really good About Section:

1. **Share your origin story.** It doesn't have to be epic. It just needs to be heartfelt, human, and explain in a satisfying way to your customers why you sell custom pickle dishes or felt hats or whatever you sell. Did your mom teach you to sew when you were younger and that was when you realized you were born to do creative things? Did you craft a pickle dish at a ceramics workshop and become the talk of the neighborhood after a backyard barbecue? SHARE THOSE THINGS. Humanize yourself. Endear yourself. Do you have family or employees involved in what you make? Make them part of the story too.

2. **Set yourself apart.** A lot of people make similar stuff on Etsy. Before you dive into your About Section, take a few minutes to write down the top three things that set you apart from the crowd. Do you use a special kind of ink? Are you a person of color in a white-dominated industry? Do you paint with your toes? Lead with this information proudly instead of

burying it at the end of your About Section. What makes you unique makes you human and connects you to potential buyers.

3. **Use all five photos.** You have the option to include up to five high-res photos in your About Section. USE THEM. Each one is worth 1,000 words (at least). Etsy is about buying from a human, remember? And what medium best tells the story of a human, relatable shop owner? Photos. Use natural lighting and a variety of compelling, interesting photos that show yourself, your shop members, and any aspects of how you make or create your products. Think of it as a "behind the scenes" photoshoot that shows who you are visually. If it makes sense, include kids, animals, family members, and pets (everyone loves these things). Avoid straight-to-camera shots in all of the photos. You want this to feel like a glimpse into your world.

4. **Make a shop video.** This one is daunting for most people. But armed with a smartphone and free video editing software (OpenShot is a great option), you too can have a shop video. Keep it simple. Show footage of your studio, your workspace, your employees, your product. Again, probably don't shoot stuff straight-to-camera or you'll look like a used car salesman. Make this a "behind the scenes" glimpse, as if your potential buyer just opened up a little portal to your shop. Pair it with neutral, positive music (but nothing copyrighted—you can find free tracks in a variety of places like the Free Music Archive or Jamendo.com).

5. **Include photos of each shop member.** In addition to your About Section's five photos, you can upload a photo and an "about" description for each person in your shop (including yourself). Keep these descriptions concise, upbeat, warm, and relatable. Not everything you share has to be about your business, but at least some of it should be. You've already told everyone why you started your shop: Focus this blurb for each shop member on personal details. Do you have five kids and an obsession with hot hula dancing? Do you have a raccoon for a pet who sometimes accompanies you to the studio? Share these details.

Remember, keep everything as professional, tight, and human as possible. Ask several trusted friends to look at your photos and read your About Section copy (text) and offer critiques (use that word, you're not asking for a pat on the back). If you can't find someone to do this, join a seller's forum on Etsy and offer to exchange feedback. This is well worth your time.

Don't have the money for professional photos for your About Section? No problem. Student photographers often offer discounted rates. You can also do a lot with your smartphone, a little patience, and a willingness to learn some tips on lighting and composition (check out chapter 3).

Shop Sections

Shop sections are like the skeleton of your shop. They help keep your shop navigable and organized for both you and your potential customers. You're allowed to have up to 20 shop sections, which will appear on the left side of your shop. These sections help organize your shop into categories that either help or confuse the crap out of your customers.

Do some serious thinking about how you want to organize your products. Is it by color? That might make sense if all of your earrings are quite similar and differ mostly by color. Is it by theme (e.g., ocean paintings in one category, and forest paintings in another)? Decide on the factor that's most important to your buyers that intersects with what sets your listings apart from each other, and divide things up that way.

Keep your section names simple and short (as with your Shop Name, you've got 20 characters to work with). Etsy will automatically create an "All Listings" section for you that you can't remove, as well as an "On Sale" section that shows what you've got on sale. The rest is up to you.

Listings can only be added to ONE section (unless they're on sale, in which case they'll appear in the On Sale section and whatever other section you've assigned them to).

TIP: If at any point you decide you hate your shop sections or want to shift things around, that's easy to do en masse from your listings manager. Within the Listings section of your Shop Manager, you can select (check the box in the bottom left corner of a listing) as many listings as you like, click "Edit Options," and swap them into a new shop section in one fell swoop.

TIP: Once in a while, I forget to assign a listing to a shop section when it's created (this isn't mandatory. You can have listings with no shop section). These listings will appear in searches, and in your "All Listings" section, but nowhere else. This is a bummer for visibility. Don't do this.

TIP: Keep it simple, try to make things intuitive for your buyer, and use sections to keep your shop organized and navigable. This makes you look smart, savvy, and on-top-of-things to buyers.

Shop Announcement

Your Shop Announcement appears prominently right below your Shop Name and logo. You can change this as often as you like. And you can add quite a lot of text (but you probably shouldn't. Only the first two sentences or so show automatically without the buyer having to click "read more"). Keep this short, to the point, and personable. I choose to tell buyers that if they sign up for my newsletter, they'll receive a code for 15% off their order (we'll talk about why you want an email list and how to do this later in Chapter 11). At other times, I've chosen to relay information about holiday shipping cutoff dates, a fun quote that appeals to my buyers, or a sale announcement. Use concise, tight copy ("copy" in this case and throughout the book simply means "writing"), and let your personality shine a little without being unprofessional.

Etsy will show your buyers how recently you updated this announcement, so make sure you tinker with it regularly to cultivate the impression of a doting shop owner who is heavily invested in their craft (because that's probably highly accurate, but it's easy to forget to update this section!).

Shop Updates

Shop Updates work as both free advertising and another tool to help you create a good impression on potential buyers. They get sent via notifications to anybody who has favorited your items, your shop, or made a purchase from you. Pretty cool, huh? These updates are sort of like Etsy's in-house social media tool. You have to make updates from your phone (it's hidden under the marketing tab on the Etsy Seller's App), and ideally these posts are quite similar to your social media feed with updates, announcements about sales, and general frivolity and behind-the-scenes goodness.

Posting Shop Updates regularly shows that you are an engaged shop owner (and Etsy loves engaged sellers!). If you make one Shop Update in 2016 and never again, people may worry that you are dead or just a deadbeat. Post regularly to show that you are IN THIS. Sparse or nonexistent updates can make customers worry that you might not really be active in your shop—that you might not respond to questions promptly, ship items on time, or keep up with current trends. And that kernel of worry can quickly translate into clicking away from your shop (especially for larger or important purchases).

Your updates appear on your shop homepage, toward the bottom underneath your reviews. And your customers can peruse old shop updates to get an idea of what you've been up to over time. While you have the option to cross-post shop updates to other social media platforms like Instagram, I wouldn't recommend it. Cross-posting too much too often teaches your audience to ignore you on most of your channels, since you post the same stuff there anyway.

TIP: Shop updates are clickable! And you can link products to each shop update. Aka, if you have a brand new purse and you share the news with your fans, they can click the shop update to be taken directly to the purse's listing. Amazing, amirite?

TIP: Don't use photos that are already part of your listing images. Show your product being made, behind the scenes, interacting with a customer, a sale or coupon announcement, or "coming soon" teasers about stuff you have in the works so your customers know to stay tuned.

Shop Banner, Shop Icon, and Profile Photo

Your **shop banner, shop icon, and profile photo** combine to create the face of your shop.

Your shop banner is the big banner image that covers the length of your Etsy shop homepage at the very top. In the past, Etsy used a more narrow banner—which you still have the option to use, but I wouldn't recommend it because it doesn't show up on mobile.

This shop banner should set the tone for your shop visually, since it's one of the first things a buyer sees when exploring your shop. Keep it simple, make it beautiful, and include some of your favorite products. You can create a basic collage of cohesive photos of your products (Canva is a great way to do this easily). Or you can show one fantastic "lifestyle" image of people using your product (we'll talk about photography in more detail in Chapter 3). Whatever you do, make it beautiful, impactful, and keep it simple. Don't try to cram in a lot of text. In fact, I prefer not to use any text because your buyer's eye will move right along to your shop icon.

I'm not going to give you the exact dimensions of your shop banner, because Etsy keeps changing this and they will inevitably make a change as soon as I publish this, which will leave you feeling confused and distrustful. SO. Do this. Google "Etsy shop banner dimensions." It will take you three seconds or less. Make your shop banner this size, and make it a 75-dpi JPEG (for some reason, Etsy freaks out about pngs a lot of the time).

If you're stumped as far as what you want your shop banner to look like, browse through other Etsy shops that catch your eye and you'll start to get an idea of what looks nice to you. Do this until you get a sense of what you're after. Don't snag anybody's idea wholesale, but inspiration is always kosher.

Your **shop icon** is a small image that appears underneath your shop banner, to the left. This should, in most cases, be your logo (and yes you DO need a logo, even if you're a newbie. You can create one for free or very inexpensively, just hop on over to Chapter 8 to find out how). Your Shop Name will appear right underneath your logo, and visually it just makes sense. Having a logo as your shop icon projects legitimacy, professionalism, and the idea that you are highly invested in creating your products and running a top-notch shop. Make sure you have one.

Your **profile photo** (or shop owner photo) appears beneath your shop banner on the right. This should be a close-up of you (don't make your buyer squint, this photo is already pretty tiny).

Your shop banner, shop icon, and profile photo should look COHESIVE. Don't include an edgy, avant-garde banner with a cutesy logo and a serious black and white photo of yourself. You want your buyer to say "Ahh, all the pieces here fit together" instead of "What is going on, did three different people put this Etsy shop together?" (Maybe they did, but you don't want your buyer to think that.)

The result of a beautiful shop banner with a smart and cohesive logo, along with a photo of you, and the name of your shop (this will automatically populate from Etsy's info) is that your customer has a LOT of information at a glance about you. And a budding sense of trust that you know what you're doing.

Listings: The Heart of Your Etsy Shop

Congratulations! You're cruising through Etsy Anatomy 101. Drumroll, please. Because ladies and gentlepeople, we have reached the HEART of your Etsy shop: Your LISTINGS.

The truth is, the vast majority of Etsy users won't ever see inside of your shop. Which means that while the individual components of your Etsy shop (the ones we've just covered in Anatomy 101) are very important and can have a big impact on your growth and how potential customers view you, some components of your Etsy shop are more important than others. Think of your Shop

Name, About Section, and Updates like your Etsy shop's mouth. Your shop can survive even if they aren't doing much talking (it's not ideal, but you get my point!). But you can't survive without your heart: listings.

Here's the thing: Most of the traffic to your Etsy listings will come from Etsy users who don't know you exist a full-blown shop (yet) and are scrolling through MANY different listings (often very quickly) that populate after they type a query into the Etsy search bar —until something catches their eye. Your goal is to make sure that it's YOUR listing that catches their eye.

Not to mix too many metaphors (actually that's one of my favorite things), but think of your individual listings as your shop's ambassadors. Each one is an opportunity to catch a buyer's eye and entice them to click into your shop or simply buy without ever knowing much about you.

Imagine the moment your buyer clicks on a listing, or clicks on your shop from an ad somewhere as a "first impression." Of course, in Etsy as in real life, first impressions will only get you so far (see the rest of the chapters in this e-book on customer service, listings, tags, and so forth!), but first dates can often mean the difference between a sale and a hard pass.

That first impression determines whether a buyer is interested in continuing the conversation by reading more of your listing description, adding stuff to their shopping cart, "favoriting" a listing for later, checking out your shop and other products, or making a purchase.

Basically, you want to turn your Etsy listings into the Brad Pitt of e-commerce shops—highly likely to make a good impression and spark interest and interaction. And happily, you are the god of your Etsy shop. You determine whether you end up with Brad Pitt or Brad from next door. Or Frankenstein's monster (don't worry, you won't end up with that. I've got you).

Creating listings that make a good first impression and entice buyers to click is the first big hurdle toward earning a customer (Chapter 2 is actually all about listings, so I won't delve into the details here). For now, what you should understand is that we have reached a VITAL organ when it comes to your Etsy shop. Listings are the lifeblood of your shop. And for that reason, they deserve the bulk of your attention and time.

Reviews

Reviews aren't quite heart-level anatomy. But they are pretty darn important. Like … maybe the butt. Not always pretty, often overlooked, but HIGHLY important.

Your shop reviews show up under ALL of your displayed listings, within any given listing a customer clicks, as well as on your shop homepage. These reviews are often the VERY first thing a buyer will check (and may even be the reason they click (or don't click) on your listings. Across the board, surveys show that 97% of Etsy customers look at reviews before deciding whether to make a purchase. That's almost every single potential customer.

So reviews are arguably one of the most important parts of a healthy Etsy shop. They are highly visible in multiple locations, and they can either signal major confidence to potential customers—or major red flags. We'll talk more about reviews and customer service in Chapter 6, but reviews are such an important part of the first impression you create for buyers that we need to talk about them here, too.

You should aim for five stars whenever possible. A shop with many five-star reviews gives your buyer confidence that other people have been in their shoes (making a decision about whether to click "add to cart"!) and they don't have any regrets.

The importance of good reviews can't be overstated. The more the better. Do everything possible to ensure that the reviews you DO have are stellar. I know what you're thinking: Are reviews really something I can control? I can't do anything about it if a customer decides to go all Rambo on me and hit me with a 1-star. And you're a little bit right. But you actually have more control than you think. You CAN heavily influence whether or not people leave five-star reviews. And you can help avoid (and soften the blow) of the negative reviews. We'll get to all that in Chapter 6. For now, just remember: Reviews are IMPORTANT. Don't neglect them, even if you sort of want to.

Featured Listings

In our Magic School Bus journey through your Etsy shop anatomy, another very important part is your **featured listings.** And yes, these are just your listings, four of them. But these particular listings are extra important and have a prominent and visible place in your shop. They're kind of like beckoning hands that say, "If you like these, there's more inside!"

Featured listings appear right below your shop banner and icons. You get to pick four listings you love the very most and that you feel will speak to your potential buyers. Anyone who clicks on a link to your shop will see these listings first.

Switch up your featured listings depending on holidays and what seems to be selling well. Etsy shows buyers whether or not a listing is a "bestseller" or "in 25 people's carts" or "on sale!" Stack some if not all of these hot-sellers in your featured listing bracket right up top. This acts as compelling social proof for potential buyers. Basically, "Whoa, look at how many other people love this! I love it a little more too now."

It can be a little confusing to swap and update featured listings. At the bottom of your Shop Manager, you'll see your Etsy shop listed under "Sales Channels" (see image below). Click the "pen" icon next to your Shop Name and you'll be taken to an editable version of your shop as your customers see it. You'll see your Featured Items section with another pen icon in the bottom right corner. If you click that and then "edit queue," you'll be able to choose which four listings you want to feature and see how they look to customers.

TIP: Try to show a good variety in your featured listings (price point, type of product, color variety, etc.). Customers often eyeball these as a way to gage what else they might find in your shop.

TIP: If you're pushing a sale item or something important on social media, feature it as a featured listing as well. This helps your buyers make an immediate connection with the product upon visiting your shop.

Things I learned the hard way: I'm guilty of forgetting to make key changes to my featured listings during busy seasons. At one point I looked at my shop in February and realized I'd forgotten to swap out my Christmas seasonal featured listings. That looked SUPER professional to buyers (eye-roll).

First-Page Listings

Moving right along from Featured Listings, of major importance are your first-page listings (there are 36 per page). These listings create a strong visual story of your Etsy shop as a whole and are going to be the most-seen listings (right after your featured listings) in your shop.

You should know that you have the option in Etsy to arrange your listings in a custom order or "newest first." You can rearrange listings by clicking the pen icon next to your Etsy shop at the bottom of your Shop Manager (under "Sales Channels") and selecting "Rearrange Items" (top right of "All Items"). Most of the time I'd strongly recommend choosing a custom order. It gives you significantly more control over the impression you create for your buyers. Unfortunately, any time you create a new listing for a product, it's going to appear at the top of your page until you move it around in editing mode. Make sure to edit your first-page listings regularly, since best-selling listings change throughout the year and holiday seasons, and any time you add a new listing it'll change the look of your first page (since it appears at the top).

Since I don't create brand new listings that often (maybe twice per month), I like to maintain a lot of control over how my first-page listings look. Like my featured listings, I try to show a good mix of products in different price tiers, styles, and colors. I want this first page to be as visually interesting as possible and encourage my customers to click one or more of those listings and see my shop as an oyster of possibilities. I also like to include a lot of my best-sellers and shirts that seem to be perpetually in "10 people's carts."

If not much appeals to a buyer on the very first page, they're not super likely to keep clicking through in hopes that you have good stuff buried in page 4. They're gonna click out of your shop and your life. Page 2 and 3 are of secondary and tertiary importance, because if an eager buyer loves what you show on page one, they'll likely keep clicking.

TIP: I don't worry that much about page 4 onward. Most people just DON'T click that far. Those listings WILL be seen when they come up in search for your buyers who type in relevant search queries, but it's only really essential to order pages 1-3.

The Knee Bone's Connected to the Leg Bone: Creating Synergy in Your Shop

Synergy is the phenomenon that happens when something becomes greater than the sum of its parts. And that's exactly what happens when you spend the time to create an Etsy shop in which each aspect of your shop's anatomy pulls its weight.

The more cohesively the different parts of your Etsy shop work together, reinforce each other, and complement each other, the more you'll appeal to your customers (and even earn repeat customers). You're aiming for tight listings that sell your brand as a whole (along with individual products), a Shop Name that strikes just the right balance of informative and creative, a visually appealing first impression with a cohesive shop banner and photos, and copy that reinforces the vibe and products you're peddling.

Here's a high-level overview of what you're trying to accomplish with that synergy:

- Your shop banner, listing images, and featured images are clear, beautiful, and cropped properly. **What buyers take away:** This person is a professional. What I see is what I get, and I anticipate a beautiful, interesting product.

- Your shop looks organized and professional (e.g., no spelling errors).**What buyers take away:** This person knows what they're doing. They're going to take care of me.

- Your shop sections are concise, descriptive, and intuitive. **What buyers take away**: It's fun and interesting to explore this shop—instead of confusing or annoying.

- Your "About Section" includes helpful, interesting information about your business origin, you as a person, and what you sell (instead of being sparse or blank). **What buyers take away:** You're a real person! I feel connected to your story and have a better understanding of why your product differs from something I could buy with two-day shipping on Amazon.

And that's your Etsy shop anatomy! Strut your stuff with confidence, you sexy animal. You're well on your way to becoming a self-actualized Etsy shop with a killer bod.

CHAPTER 2

All About Listings and Search Algorithms

Like we keep saying, good listings are your key to success as an Etsy seller. You may be selling the coolest, most unique product, an item that sells like hotcakes at an in-person event, but on Etsy your product is doing virtually nothing. The big difference is that in-person sales connect you and your customer directly while online sales take place through an intermediary, in this case, *Etsy's search algorithm.*

All this is to say that your listings need to deliver the right signals to Etsy's search algorithm. It's the gatekeeper between your product and your potential customers. If you don't know how to speak the algorithm's language, you'll have trouble selling even the best products.

How Etsy's Search Algorithm Works

So, how does Etsy's algorithm actually work? The basic process goes like this:

- Step 1: A potential customer types what they want into the search box, say "birthday gift for mom."
- Step 2: Etsy's algorithm pulls all the listings containing this search phrase and similar *keywords* and displays them in order based on *certain ranking factors* (which we'll discuss in more detail below).
- Step 3: Your customer sees your product, clicks on it, places it in their shopping cart, and buys it.

Like Google's search algorithm, the details of how Etsy's algorithm works are a closely guarded secret. However, Etsy has been pretty open in recent years about many of the factors they use to determine a listing's rank.

We've been around the block enough times (and experimented enough with different factors) to tell you with a high degree of confidence that the following factors are absolutely key to communicating with Etsy's algorithms. Now, some things are going to change over the years. The algorithm is going to get smarter. But these lynchpin factors aren't going away anytime soon. Because they're important to customers, and therefore they're important to Etsy's algorithm.

Fundamentals of a Listing That Speaks to Etsy's Algorithm

Remember at the beginning of this book when we told you that your Etsy shop is the "sum of its parts"? Well, here's why that's true from a search algorithm perspective. Etsy's algorithm gives each shop a score internally based on how professional and complete that shop is, the quality of its listings, and customer experience (largely shop reviews and shipping accuracy). We're going to refer to this score as your "shop quality score." You won't be able to find out exactly what this number is (that's the secret part), but it greatly influences the rank your listings get in search, and it's constantly changing based on how you and your customers interact with your shop. So it's pretty important.

When a buyer types a search query into Etsy, the algorithm first pulls all of the relevant listings—ones containing the customer's search phrase and similar keywords. And then the algorithm ranks these listings based on the shop quality scores. Even if you sell exactly what the customer is looking to buy, if your shop has a low quality score, your relevant listings will rank too low to be found.

Chapter 1 talked about how to optimize the various parts of your shop. This is the first step toward raising your shop quality score. The second step is creating consistently good listings. In this chapter, we'll be talking about the main factors that Etsy's algorithm cares about when it comes to listings—titles, tags, attributes, and descriptions—as well as ways to engage with your listings that send positive signals to Etsy's algorithm and are guaranteed to raise your shop's quality score.

High-Quality Images

Since it's text-based, Etsy's search algorithm doesn't directly interact with or evaluate your images, but it does take into account how often customers click on and engage with your listings, and these factors are often a direct result of having high-quality thumbnail images. (We'll talk about thumbnail images specifically in much more detail in Chapter 3.)

Here's what Etsy's search algorithm considers when it comes to images:

- You've used all 10 images. Using all 10 images seems to give you a tiny edge in rank, so if you can, use all the image slots available even if you fill the extra slots with images that don't directly relate to the listing (like pictures of you in your studio, promotional, or brand images).

- You've linked images to all of your variations (e.g., different colors and styles), and link each variation to the related image. This is a cool new feature that Etsy recently (in early 2020) added, and it's super handy for customers who want to see exactly what each variation looks like. It'll also give your listing a tiny boost in rank, but it's not something to stress about, especially if you have a lot of variations or your variations don't look much different visually.

- Use simple, clear, correctly sized images (we'll talk ALL about images in Chapter 3). Like I said before, while Etsy's algorithm won't be evaluating the actual QUALITY of your images (i.e., how appealing they actually are to a person), your customers will. And how often your customers click on your listings because they LOVE your images will send strong signals to Etsy's algorithm.

Properly Crafted Listing Titles

Listing titles are arguably one of the most important ways you communicate with Etsy's algorithm. Specifically, the first **keywords** you use in your listing title.

I want to take a slight diversion here to define some terms. There are two types of keywords I'll be talking about in this chapter. The first type is **short-tail keywords**: these are words or phrases that describe general categories of products, e.g., women's shirts, silver earrings, blankets. You can recognize a short-tail keyword on Etsy by how much competition it has—do a generic search for "women's shirts," and you'll see that over 5 million listings come up (Yikes!). Any keywords/phrases that bring up more than 50,000 listings are considered short-tail keywords (and saturated markets). Generally, you'll want to avoid most short-tail keywords in listing titles and tags.

Instead, try to use **Long-tail keywords**: these are more specific phrases that describe niche products, and they're much more effective at bringing in sales. Why, exactly? People typing long-tail keywords into Etsy's search box are usually the customers that know what they want. They have something specific in mind and are ready to buy it as soon as they find what they're looking for. It may feel counterintuitive to use long-tail keywords that attract a smaller crowd, but the truth is that more eyes on your listings doesn't necessarily translate to more sales, especially if the people seeing your listings are just there to browse rather than buy.

I'll also be mentioning **queries** throughout this chapter. Queries are the keywords or phrases customers on Etsy are typing into the search box—queries ask the algorithm, "Do you have any listings offering 'hand-stamped silver necklace charms'? Or 'dinosaur baby blankets'?" And the algorithm answers the query, "Why yes, here are 6,000 or 10,000 or 5 million results you might be interested in."

All right. Now that you understand the terms I'll be using in this chapter, let's get back to the topic at hand: Listing titles. A truncated form of your title appears under your thumbnail image in search results, and your full title appears next to your image after someone clicks your listing. In its official guidelines, Etsy encourages sellers to write titles for their customers (as opposed to trying to game the algorithms). After all, titles are the first text your prospective buyers will encounter when visiting your listing.

However, in reality, Etsy's search algorithm doesn't distinguish between a human-readable title and a long list of keywords separated by commas. In fact, Etsy actually rewards *keyword stuffing* in titles, which is why most sellers do just that. If you've spent any time studying Google SEO, you'll balk at this. Google doesn't reward keyword stuffing. But Etsy does. (Although Google seems to have accepted that Etsy sellers are going to stuff keywords in their titles and doesn't punish individual listings for this. Whew!)

Here's how to write listing titles the algorithm will understand:

General Good Practices

- Put your BEST keywords first. Don't bury the lede. The very first keyword you use in your listing title is given the most weight by Etsy's search algorithms. Try to put your very best keywords within the first 40 characters of your title.

- Use a mix of descriptive long-tail keyword phrases and short-tail, generic keywords. In those first 40 characters, focus most on finding really good long-tail keywords. For example, lead with "abstract acrylic pour painting on canvas" instead of simply "acrylic art" or "abstract painting." Place shorter, more generic keywords further down your title. This will help you connect with customers who want exactly what you're selling, a.k.a., the kind that actually buy stuff.

- Describe your item precisely and with as much detail as possible within the 140 character limit.

- Use as many keywords and keyword phrases as possible, and separate these with commas (again, keyword stuffing is perfectly acceptable in Etsy titles).

- Avoid whimsical product names, the name of your company (unless it's super well-known and associated closely with your product), and any other fluffy, non-descriptive phrases in the title. If you want to include any of these, place them as close to the end of the title as possible. (Better yet, put those fun, creative product names in your description and keep your title focused on keywords.)

- Once you find a good long-tail keyword, repeat it throughout your listing using different variations as many times as possible (But don't bother with plurals or misspellings, Etsy's algorithms view them the same way so you'll be wasting valuable title space). This is especially important for tags, which I'll discuss in a bit.

Tools for Picking the Best Keywords and Phrases to Use in Your Title

Finding the BEST keywords can feel like throwing darts in the dark. But you don't have to endlessly guess and hope you hit the target. The following tools will tell you exactly what customers are typing into the Etsy search box so you know exactly which keywords to use in your.

- Use the **Etsy search box** to type in keywords you'd use to describe your product and see if Etsy autofills phrases that describe it. This strategy will definitely give you ideas, and it *does* represent what customers are typing into the search box. However, keep in mind that Etsy's autofill phrases are taken from the most *recent* searches rather than the most popular. So if you use this method, you'll have to watch how your keywords are performing using Etsy Stats and adjust accordingly.

- **Mimic other sellers' titles**. Do some searches for your chosen keywords, and see if products similar to yours come up. Craft your title based on what seems to be working for others.

- **Use Etsy Stats**. Once your product has been listed for at least a month, Etsy stats can be a very powerful tool. You can view your shop data by clicking "Stats" in your Shop Manager. Or, in your "Listings" section, click on the arrow below each listing to see stats for that listing. Etsy will show you a list of keywords and phrases that have resulted in people visiting (clicking on) your item. These keywords and variations on them are great to include in your title if they're not already there, because they represent what actual customers have typed into Etsy's search box in searching for your product.

- **Using a Keyword Tool (Marmalead or eRank):** If you're ready to go a step beyond the free tools, a paid service can make writing titles and tags a lot easier and more efficient. These tools will show you how competitive a keyword is (how many other listings are using it), the search volume for each keyword (the number of people typing it into Etsy's search box each month), and the amount of engagement a keyword receives (how many people searching for that keyword or phrase actually click on listings and buys stuff).

- **Sign up for a Google AdWords account.** You don't actually have to USE Google Adwords. Just sign up for an account (it's very straightforward and easy) but don't create any ads. You'll have to put in payment information but you won't be charged. And then play around with the keyword tools within Google AdWords. You'll often find a whole slew of new keyword ideas this way that you hadn't thought of, and you'll be able to see how popular and competitive these keywords are.

The Bottom Line: Put your best keywords at the very front of your listing titles. Write straightforward titles using as many keywords with high engagement and low competition as you can fit within 140 characters.

Compelling Listing Attributes

When you go to Etsy.com, you'll notice that just under the search box are nine clickable categories—Everyday Finds, Jewelry & Accessories, Home & Living, etc. These are just the first level of categories that Etsy uses to divide and group the products across its enormous site. And there are hundreds of subcategories under each one. From a seller's perspective, these categories and subcategories are known as **attributes.**

In addition to browsing by category, customers can narrow their search results using **filters**. Here's how it works: After typing in something generic like "cool women's t-shirts," customers can check boxes listed down the left side of their results page. Like "blue," "free shipping," and "crew neck."

From a seller's perspective, you'll absolutely want to specify as many of your listing's attributes as possible. Why? Because you want your listing displayed in as many search categories and within as many filters as possible. Because each attribute you specify is a box that a potential customer may check when searching for a product *just like yours.*

Can you offer free shipping? *Check.* That's an incredibly valuable attribute because customers LOVE it and will often narrow their search just to find products that have it. Can you ship in one business day? *Check.* Is your product a specific color that fits into an attribute in Etsy's dropdown menu? Take advantage. Instead of listing your item's color as aqua, choose blue (because your potential customer doesn't have a filter option for aqua!). Another *check.* The more of these attribute filters you can feasibly pass through, the more likely you are to connect with the customer who wants exactly what you sell.

While Etsy's algorithm doesn't care how many or few attributes you list, it will still reward you for using them by putting your product in increasingly narrow search results (with less competition) if your product meets a customer's specific needs.

Choose the Right Product Category

Perhaps the most important attribute you'll select is your product category and subcategories (which is why they deserve their own subhead). When you do this, more attribute options related to this category will populate. It might look overwhelming to select all these attributes, but it's worth it! Painstakingly go through each set of options and select the ones that describe your product—but ONLY the ones that actually describe it. You don't have to, nor do you want to select an attribute for every single category proffered by Etsy (more on that in the next section). For now, just know that if an attribute definitely applies to your product (e.g., if you're selling a crew neck t-shirt and Etsy allows you to specify that), DO IT. However, hold off on any categories or attributes that are confusing or ambiguous.

TIP: Follow Etsy's instructions for selecting a category by typing in a few descriptive words about your product, but don't just pick the first category Etsy suggests. Make sure you click the "manual" option, especially if you're a new seller. This will give you the option of selecting more specific subcategories related to your product. Fourth Wave's T-shirts, for example, are technically "women's t-shirts," which is the category Etsy always suggests when I create a new listing. However, manual selection allows me to choose a subcategory one level deeper, "women's graphic t-shirts," that better describes what I'm selling.

TIP: If you're not sure which category to pick or if more than one seems to fit, take a peek at what your top competitors are doing.

There's a simple trick to spying on the competition—simply go to a listing that's similar to yours and also ranking well. Right-click anywhere on the page and select "view page source" from the dropdown menu. This will open up a new window with the html that makes up the page. If you "control + F" (find) and search for "tags" (with the quote marks), you'll be treated to a list of all the attributes and tags your competitor is using. The first of these will be the category.

Ignore Attributes That Don't Quite Fit

Some attributes are better than others. In fact, some attributes can actually hold you back and keep you OUT of search results.

Only select attributes that actually describe your product. For example, I have no doubt your crocheted cat sweater would be a really amazing Christmas present, but unless it's specifically a Christmas item, selecting "Christmas" under the holiday attribute list can end up limiting the number of people who see your item. It works like this: Customers have the power to limit the types of listings displayed to them by checking a box, and if that person has checked "Easter," Etsy will stop showing any item with a holiday attribute other than Easter. It will, however, keep showing items that have *no attribute* selected under "holiday," presumably because non-holiday specific items may still make great Easter gifts.

The Bottom Line: Carefully selected and accurate attributes are the clearest signals you can send to Etsy's search algorithm about what your product is and who your customers are. This process may seem tedious, but it's vital to a listing's success on Etsy's platform.

Include Variations When Needed

You can send positive or negative signals to Etsy's algorithm depending on how you use variations (if you use them, that is). Variations are very similar to attributes from Etsy's perspective. They make it easy to offer different sizes, colors, and styles of a product without listing each option as its own separate listings (saving you money!). However, if you do use variations, don't make them too complex, especially as a new seller. Your customers can be overwhelmed if you offer too many options. And like I mentioned before, if your variations are too unique, your listing will be thrown out of results any time a customer sets a filter.

But as with attributes, using Etsy's variations CAN help you rank higher in search if you use them properly. If you sell your product in several colors, make sure to use Etsy's "Color" variation option and pick the colors Etsy lists as options instead of creating your own (i.e., select "green" from the dropdown instead of creating a new variation called "forest"). That way, Etsy will show your product to the customers searching generic terms like "green women's t-shirt" as well as to customers who check "green" in the color filter.

Variations can be complicated to work with at first. Here's a step-by-step of how to set them up:

- Click on the variations button, and a pop-up will open. In this pop-up, you'll have the option of selecting a variation from a list provided by Etsy or creating your own.
- Depending on the variation you're using, you may also need to select a scale, for example, "US women's letter sizing."
- You can then add the options your customers will see by selecting from Etsy's generic list or by creating your own.
- You can choose two different variations and as many options under each as you want. (You'll only be able to link images to the first 10, though, and frankly, I'd recommend not offering more than 5-6 different colors or styles so as not to overwhelm your customers.)

Use Tags Wisely

Like titles, tags are a keyword-centric way to communicate with Etsy's algorithm. Etsy allows sellers 13 self-chosen tags per listing. Each tag can be a maximum of 20 characters in length. Because these tags are hidden from customers, it's tempting to treat them carelessly, especially since they're toward the bottom of the listing and decision fatigue is kicking in. You just want to be DONE.

Trust me, I know exactly how this feels. But remember, with online sales, you have to interact with customers through that pesky intermediary, the search algorithm, and tags are critically important to this. BUT, I have good news. You can use the same keywords (like the EXACT same ones) in your tags that you used in your title.

Here's how it works:

- Use all 13 tags available.

- As with your title, you'll want to use long-tail keyword phrases with high engagement and low competition whenever possible, and add generic, short-tail keywords if you have exhausted that long-tail list.

- Repeat the keywords from your title **exactly**. And use variations on the same keywords when you run out. Tell Etsy in your tags that your item is a "feminist shirt" and a "feminist t-shirt" as well as a "feminist tee shirt." (Remember, you're trying to think like a customer. How might different customers search for this item?)

- Within reason, the more times you include a certain keyword or phrase in different forms in your title and tags, the more convinced Etsy will be that your item fits that category and the higher it'll rank your item in results when a customer searches for the phrase "feminist shirt."

- The order of your tags doesn't matter. All 13 will be considered equally by the search algorithm.

- **Avoid** repeating the attributes you selected in your tags. Etsy gives extra ranking points to keywords repeated in both the *title* and the *tags*, but it sees tags and attributes as essentially the same thing, so repeating *attributes* in tags is wasted space.

- Recently, Etsy announced that its algorithm recognizes plurals, regional spellings, and misspellings in search queries, so including these variations in tags is also unnecessary. While I believe this is true for plurals ending in "s," well-recognized regional spelling differences (color vs. colour), and common misspellings and typos (coffe instead of coffee), if your product is quite unique or your industry very niche, you might want to include these keyword variants in your tags to be safe. In other words, it's not a hard "don't," but it might save you some space in your tags for more important keywords.

- Don't adjust tags more often than every 30 days. It takes about this long for changes to take effect and for sellers to see results in Etsy stats.

TIP #1: If a long-tail keyword phrase is too long to fit in one tag, it's perfectly acceptable to split it across 2 or more tags. Just repeat the most important keywords. For example, Fourth Wave get's a lot of traffic from the long-tail phrase "trendy plus size clothing," which doesn't fit in a single tag. I break it into two tags "trendy plus size" and "plus size clothing."

TIP #2: Tags are hidden from customers, so you can include loosely related recognizable words and phrases here that might get you views but that you might not want to have in your title (cheat words). Examples include Shop Names of your Etsy competitors who get a lot of views for similar items, pop-culture references and hashtags that a customer might type into a search box when they don't know exactly what they're looking for product-wise, and trademarked words and phrases (be extra careful with this last one).

WARNING! The practices mentioned in Tip #2 technically fall under the category of black hat (or at least gray) SEO—basically, they try to trick the search algorithm into displaying listings it wouldn't normally display for a particular search. And just as Google is cracking down on the black-hat SEO techniques used in the early 2000s, Etsy's algorithm will probably get wiser in the coming years. In other words, manipulating your tags *does* work in the 2020s (I confess, I do it), but it may not work forever.

The Bottom Line: Fill in the tags as much as possible with the best keywords from your title. Then wait 30 days, and hone the tags to reflect what your customers are searching for that gets them buying your product.

Finding the BEST Tags

The process for finding the best tags is the same as choosing keywords for your title, so you can use all the tools we talked about in the Title section. These tools will help you get inside the minds of your customers, to know exactly what they are searching for and what they're actually buying.

I highly recommend using a service like Marmalead or eRank to make choosing tags as painless and efficient as possible, but you can absolutely create an amazing listing without a paid service. It just might take a little more work and experimentation.

Etsy's Obsession with Seasons/Trends

Along with choosing tags and keywords that describe your product, you'll want to choose some tags and keywords related to the "season" in which you think it'll most likely sell. "But my product isn't seasonal," I hear you say, "It's popular year round." That may be technically true in the real world, but Etsy has an obsession with seasonality. They refer to it as "trends," but I prefer the term "seasons" because that better describes the search algorithm's behavior.

Etsy's algorithm gives boosts in rank to listings that were trending during certain weeks or months in previous years. Thus, you might discover an old listing is doing really well again in the fall of 2020 even though the trend for that product really happened in the fall of 2019.

As far as I can tell, seasonality is a ranking factor that is unique to Etsy, at least to the degree that it affects ranking. At the tip of the iceberg, seasonality is just what it sounds like: At Christmas, Etsy gives a ranking boost to listings with "Christmas" tags, attributes, and titles. This makes sense—more people are searching for Christmas items—but Etsy goes even further and ranks Christmas items higher during the Christmas season even for searches that don't relate to Christmas. For example, if you sell a Christmas-themed baby blanket, and someone searches for "baby blankets" in December, Etsy will boost your listing right to the top because of the season, even if it wouldn't rank high normally for such a generic keyword.

Etsy also uses your sales data from previous years to determine when your listings might be popular again in the current year and gives them an automatic rank boost during those same days or weeks they sold well in years past. What this does is it gives "seasonality" to listings that aren't seasonal at all. For example, after the 2018 State of the Union Address, Fourth Wave sold a shirt depicting Nancy Pelosi clapping with the phrase "Clappity Clap" above her head. The shirt got picked up by BuzzFeed in an article on the "most sarcastic shirts of the week." We sold over 600 shirts in a few short weeks in June that year. This incredible conversion rate sent a lot of positive signals to Etsy, and the next June, 2019, Etsy bumped that listing to the top again for searches like "Feminist shirt" and "trendy plus size clothing" and other more generic keywords. We joked that the shirt was selling well again because it was "Nancy Pelosi season."

In practical terms for your shop, the concept of seasonality can be used to make sure you have a steady flow of items selling throughout the year, even if your stuff isn't particularly seasonal in the traditional holiday or weather sense. Take a listing that's not already selling super well at a particular time of year, and think outside the box—would your item be a good Mother's Day gift? Change a tag or two at the beginning of April to "Mother's Day gift" related keywords. If an item really takes off during the "Mother's Day buying season," don't change the tag. Etsy will still display your item throughout the year, but it'll give it an even bigger boost in ranking next Mother's Day. If you can make sure you have items that fit a "season" throughout the year, you'll have a good steady flow of income even if it looks like certain items have stopped selling while others are taking off. Seasons can be anything—graduation, summer, winter, pop culture references (e.g., Fortnite season, Joe Exotic season—we had a lot of fun with that one).

The Bottom Line: Over the course of your first year selling on Etsy, keep track of which items sell well at certain times of the year. If you sell a lot of a product in the spring and summer, consider adding listings specifically targeted to fall and winter seasons so you have steady product sales all year round. Read over Etsy's yearly "Trend Report" for ideas on seasons to target (Google "Etsy Trend Report" for the current year's findings).

Hone Your Listing Descriptions

Etsy's search algorithm doesn't currently look at the listing description at all when determining where your listing should rank for a given search. This means that if your goal is to sell your product on Etsy's platform only, you can keep your description brief, geared toward your customer, and focus your SEO efforts on your title, attributes, and tags.

So, are listing descriptions unimportant? Nope! Here's why:

Anatomy of a Good Listing Description

A good description is still important.

1. It can help your customers connect with your product or shop —Etsy customers don't just want to know about the item they're buying, they want to know about you. As a small seller on Etsy's handmade mom-and-pop online platform, you have the opportunity not only to offer a one-of-a-kind product but to build up a base of customers loyal to you and to your shop. You also have the opportunity to fully describe your product and preemptively answer your customer's questions (We'll talk about the importance of copy and good listing descriptions more in Chapter 9).

2. While Etsy doesn't look at your listing description, Google does. Google's search algorithm "reads" the first 150 characters of your listing description to determine when and where to rank it. This means that a well-written description can help your listing rank in Google search results and reach a much wider audience.

The First 150 Characters of Your Description

Unlike Etsy, Google does not look kindly on keyword stuffing, so write your description in readable sentences as you would if you were writing directly to your customer. Make sure to include relevant keywords within your beautiful prose, especially in the first 150 characters. Just as you did in researching keywords for Etsy search, researching high-volume, low competition keywords for Google will give your listing the best chance at ranking in a Google search. Tools like Google AdWords' "Keyword Planner" and the Chrome extension "Keywords Everywhere" can help you do this.

Don't copy and paste the same or a very similar description into several listings. Come up with something fresh. Google's search algorithm flags and penalizes duplication when it finds it, so even if you sell many products that are very similar to one another, write a new description for each one focusing on different keywords in each.

If you're finding your listings are so similar that it's difficult if not impossible to come up with varying descriptions, you may want to consider consolidating all of these products under a single listing by taking advantage of the Etsy's options for listing variations.

Additional Product Information

After the first 150 characters (usually the first sentence or two (if they're short)), give customers more information about your product, stuff that's not obvious when looking at the listing images. Do customers have the option to get the item monogrammed? Does your product have a scent? Tell customers about the history of your product. What inspired the design? Are you donating proceeds to a cause? This is the kind of information that makes a great description and connects you to your customers well beyond a single sale.

Information about Your Shop and Yourself

After giving a description of your product, give your customers some basic information about your shop. Hit the highlights. Your shop's "About" and "Shop Policies" sections are better places for lots of details. Direct customers to these sections and to your FAQ if they have questions. You can even include links to these pages. Etsy doesn't currently allow linked text, but you can shorten extremely long links using Bitly.com and paste the shortened links into your description. You can also link to similar products if you have any. And ask customers to sign up for your mailing list if you have one (which you should—see Chapter 11 to learn how).

Direct Them to Your Social Channels

Either just before your shop information or at the end of your description, direct customers to your social channels: "Find us on Facebook and Instagram @YourCompanyName." I'll talk about how to maximize the benefit from social channels in Chapter 13, but for now, let's just agree that advertising your shop via social is a must in today's world.

Example Description

First 150 characters ⌐

Rhinoceros grocery tote, "Head up, stay strong." Great gift for that friend having a hard time. Help save the planet one shopping trip at a time with this large, reusable 100% cotton grocery tote. © Design by Fourth Wave Feminist Apparel

Useful information

Totes are 11 x 13 inches and sturdy enough to hold a lot more groceries than plastic bags.

Looking for something a little different? Explore the rest of our grocery totes!

Link to our homepage

https://www.etsy.com/shop/fourthwaveapparel

Fourth Wave feminist apparel makes a great gift for your favorite sister in the resistance, ally, friend, or partner. Or, you know, yourself.

Where we donate

5% of all profits are donated to the Thurgood Marshall College Fund, which earns an incredible 100% rating on Charity Navigator for its effective work in helping students at HBCUs (historically black colleges and universities) and predominantly black institutions through leadership, lobbying, job recruiting, and scholarships.

We have a FAQ

Check out our FAQ for more information on custom order, organizations we donate to, sizing, materials, shipping, and wholesale opportunities.

Find us on social channels

Find us on Facebook, Pinterest, and Instagram! @FourthWaveApparel

Etsy's Point System for Listings

It's important to understand that Etsy's algorithm is always at work. And it's always evaluating your shop as a whole as well as your individual listings. Remember that "shop quality score"? Well, Etsy also gives a point value to each of your listings, and this "listing quality score" has far-reaching effects. It impacts where each of your listings rank individually, and the average of your listing quality scores is also a factor Etsy uses to determine your shop quality score. This means Etsy's algorithm punishes (drops in rank) poor listings twice over—once for the low quality of the listing and again for a low shop quality score. But this also means a shop full of awesome listings will be rewarded handsomely.

Here's the details. For each listing in your shop, Etsy awards an ever-changing number of points (the listing quality score) that determines where it ranks in comparison to similar listings. New listings start at zero points and, as time goes on, earn or lose points depending largely on the *conversion rate* (the ratio of views to sales) of the individual listing.

Imagine you've listed your item as a "dog sweater" because it's an adult-size sweater with a picture of a dog on it. The problem is that most people searching for "dog sweater" want a sweater *for a dog* rather than one for a human. Your dog sweater listing will likely get a lot of *impressions* (views) at first, especially because Etsy gives a boost in rank to new listings (more on this later). But as time goes on, and almost nobody searching for "dog sweater" *engages with* (clicks on) let alone buys your sweater, your conversion rate will drop and Etsy will punish the listing with a negative listing quality score.

Listings with negative scores rank more poorly in search results for all relevant searches. And this listing can drag your shop down with it. It might only be one tag that's causing you problems, but if you have one problematic tag, none of the rest of your carefully chosen tags will be serving you fully. In this case, the best strategy is to deactivate (remove) the listing and relist the item (as a completely new listing) without the problematic keyword, in this case "dog sweater."

Some Etsy sellers are rumored to repost *many or all of their listings every day* in order to "reset" them and take advantage of the temporary boost in rank given to new listings. This seems more like rumor than fact to me, and it's certainly not necessary or even advisable for a seller trying to do well on Etsy. Plus, who has time for that? Not me.

Guidance for When to List, Renew, Edit, and Take Down Listings

Etsy loves sellers who are highly involved. Good sellers (aka, involved sellers) give Etsy a good reputation as a platform, which is why Etsy has written its search algorithm to reward sellers who interact regularly with their shops.

New and Renewed Listings Get a Boost in Rank

New listings and renewed listings tell Etsy a seller is engaging with her shop. And the algorithm gives a temporary but significant boost in rank to all new and renewed listings. This doesn't mean that your new listings will automatically appear on the first page for those high-competition keywords. Etsy still places a listing in results based on other ranking factors first (including relevancy and shop quality score); then, from there, it bumps it up a number of positions (it's impossible to give an exact number here, so let's just say a *noticeable* number, sometimes a full page or more!). This is also true for renewed listings, by which I mean listings that have been automatically renewed by Etsy (which happens every four months), manually renewed by the seller, or renewed after a sale (on items with a quantity of more than one).

What does this look like exactly? For Fourth Wave, the temporary rank boost for renewed listings means that certain designs sell in waves. A customer will purchase our "phenomenal woman" shirt after a general search for "feminist shirts," and because a sale causes the listing to renew, Etsy's algorithm will temporarily boost that shirt for all searches related to "feminist shirts," which means more customers will see it and buy it. That week, we'll have an unusual number of sales of the "phenomenal woman" design before it drops back down in the results.

TIP: Remember that this boost in rank is only temporary (1-2 hours if that), so if you plan to add a new listing, try to do it when the maximum number of your customers will be online. For Etsy's overall platform, this is 9:30–11:30 am Eastern time, but it will, of course, vary seller to seller, so be sure to check your stats and post new listings during the hours your customers are most likely to see them.

The Bottom Line: Etsy rewards sellers who regularly add new listings and renew old ones.

Deactivating Listings for a Better Conversion Rate

| Last 30 Days: Feb 28 - Mar 29 ▼ | ⏱ 4 hours ago |

Visits	Orders	Conversion rate	Rever
7,185	233	3.2%	$5

In the Tags section, I discuss how Etsy uses the *conversion rate* (number of sales divided by the number of views) of a listing to determine that listing's rank in search results. In addition to looking at the conversion rate of the individual listing it's displaying, Etsy's algorithm also looks at a shop's overall conversion rate for the last 30 days and rewards or punishes all the listings in a shop based on that number.

A good conversion rate on Etsy is about 3-4%, so we're not talking very big numbers here. The amazing news is that it's shockingly easy to improve your conversion rate. We've done it with great success. If you're in the 1% range, you may want to try some of the ideas below to bring it up just a few percentage points. Credit for many of these ideas goes to Joanna Vaughan, a writer for the Marmalead Blog and an absolute wizard at Etsy SEO. Definitely check out her tutorials for more tips and ideas.

- Deactivate listings that aren't selling well. The criteria for "not selling well" will be something you'll want to determine up front. For Fourth Wave, I decided to flag all listings that had had fewer than two sales in the last year. I also flagged low-margin items (aka, we don't make much from a sale anyway) that had fewer than six sales in the same time. With these items gone from the shop, customers more often saw and purchased the already popular listings, and our conversion rate jumped.

- Set up a "Last Chance Sale." Thanks Joanna for this brilliant advice. Instead of immediately deactivating all the items you flagged as not selling well, place these items into their own section called "Last Chance" or "Clearance," and discount them at least 25-30% for a month before deactivating them. This can really get sluggish listings selling again. Customers *love* a sale as does Etsy's search algorithm (more on this in Chapter 10), and the "last chance" element also prompts customers to impulse buy, since they know these products are disappearing after the sale.

The Bottom Line: Keeping a close eye on your stats can help you see which listings are selling and which aren't. And either getting rid of or discounting listings that aren't selling can really bump up your shop's conversion rate, which improves the rank of all the listings in your shop.

Regularly Rotate through Your Listings, Making Small Edits

Another great way to send "involved seller" signals to Etsy's algorithm is to regularly interact with your existing listings. This can be in small ways—changes like swapping out an image, replacing a keyword with another, or editing your listing title or description. You'll want to rotate through your listings when doing this; Etsy recommends you leave a listing alone for 30 days after any changes to give the algorithm time to recognize the changes and recalculate the listing's rank in search results. And don't ever make any major changes to your best sellers. You don't want to break what's already working. The goal with regular fine-tuning is less to achieve the PERFECT listing and more to show Etsy that you're a good investment because you really care about your shop and are highly engaged in its success. After all, your success is Etsy's success as well.

Stuff We Learned the Hard Way

When it comes to creating superb listings, I've learned more than I'd like to admit the hard way. I started out using whimsical product names in my titles, picking unrelated tags that felt right just to fill space, copy-pasting my listing descriptions, and so much more. I'd like to list some of my biggest ah-ha moments, so you don't have to make the same mistakes I did.

Keywords: When I first started making listings, I used as wide a range of keywords as you could imagine from "feminist shirt" to "hipster tee" to keywords related specifically to the design like "steamroller" and "bloomers." I used up the title space and continued filling the tags with ever more obscure words and phrases. My listings definitely got a lot of views that way. The problem was that the people seeing my listings were usually looking for something else entirely, so I had a terrible conversion rate.

I finally discovered that I should have been putting the *exact same keywords* in both my titles and tags. And I should have picked the strongest 5-6 keywords and filled in the rest of the space with variations on these same keywords.

Cannibalizing an old listing for a new product: Just don't do it. I'll tell you I used to do this all the time simply because it saved me time. Because creating new listings takes a LOT of time. There are two main problems with just recycling an existing listing for a new product. One, the new product will be "tainted" by the sales (or lack of sales) from the old one. (Remember Etsy's point system and the listing quality score?) Odds are, if you're replacing one product with another, the old product wasn't selling very well, which means it has accrued a lot of negative ranking points from Etsy's algorithm. This starts the new listing off at a huge disadvantage, and you miss out on the rank boost Etsy gives to new listings.

Two, your stats for that listing have become largely worthless. The conversion rate over time is meaningless because it averages the sales and views of both products, and the keywords the listing is being found for are mixed between the old and new products. It's not impossible to separate, but it's way more trouble than it's worth. Trust me on this one.

Selecting attributes that don't exactly describe your product: For at least a year, I had our "phenomenal woman" shirt listed as a Valentine's Day item (E.g., I checked this box as an attribute). The design is in the shape of a heart, after all, and the shirt did sell in February. But it completely stopped selling the rest of the year until I finally unchecked the Valentine's Day box. All of a sudden, the shirt started showing up in searches throughout the year. I honestly had no idea how detrimental limiting my listing in that way would be. The takeaway is that if you're unsure an attribute really describes your product well, it's probably wise to leave it blank. Your item may still experience seasonal highs and lows—and certainly don't be afraid to list season keywords in your title and tags! But be VERY careful about checking those holiday boxes. Go ahead and experiment but make sure you do some A/B testing (more on this in Chapter 14) over several months to see if the listing actually benefits from being categorized a certain way by Etsy or not.

CHAPTER 3

Product Photography and Listing Images

We've already established that LISTINGS are the heart of your Etsy shop as far as Etsy's algorithm is concerned. And as far as your customers are concerned, too. Because without listings, you can't make sales.

Product photography and listing images, then, are one of the most critical parts of your listing. Because overwhelmingly, Etsy customers report that they determine whether or not to click on a product based on its image. And you'd better believe that those customer signals are important to Etsy's algorithm (not to mention your own sales).

What I'm trying to say is this: I can't really overstate the importance of good product photography. The image your buyer sees as they scroll through Etsy search results is often your one shot at a first impression. Think of it like Tinder. Your goal is to get your potential buyer to STOP scrolling, forget the competition, and think, "WHOA, I want to get to know THAT soap dish/custom ant farm/ pair of socks better.

Much like Tinder, if you don't stand out, have boring or off-putting listing images, or don't represent yourself accurately and favorably, you're not going to get a second glance, let alone a date.

And at this point you might find yourself thinking "But I'm not a graphic designer, I don't know how to use photoshop, I only have a basic smartphone, and I should give up because I don't have the technical skills to do this." I want you to stop it right now. We're going to talk about graphics and design (and the tools you can use and master and look like a legit PRO even if you don't know what a pixel is yet). That's coming up in Chapter 4. For right now, let's talk about best practices for the images you're going to create with your blossoming photography skills.

First, Let's Get a Few Things Straight

If you're new to Etsy (or if you're just new to Etsy lingo), it can get a little confusing when we talk about different image types. So let's start with a few definitions.

Some of the tips I'm going to share with you are specific to **main images.** (I'll also refer to them as **"thumbnail images**.") Main images are the very first image any buyer will see BEFORE they click on your product in an Etsy search. That main image will appear as a little thumbnail image alongside competitors' items when your buyer is scrolling through Etsy search results, looking for something that meets their needs. If a buyer clicks on the thumbnail image, they'll be taken to your product page, where they'll see an expanded/larger version of that thumbnail image. In other words, main images/thumbnail images are extra important.

When I talk about **listing images**, I'm referring to all ten images that your potential buyers will see when they click on a particular listing. There's your main image and nine **product images**. These ten images are important and help seal the deal with a buyer. But remember, your buyer will only be able to scroll through all ten photos AFTER you've successfully enticed them to click on your product through that all-important main image.

Best Practices for Photography on Etsy

Remember how I told you that Etsy buyers consistently point to images as the most important factor in whether or not they engage with your products? Well, here's some data: In a survey conducted by Etsy itself, 9 out of 10 Etsy buyers indicated that listing images were the main factor that determined whether or not they made a purchase. That's a BIG deal.

So, what goes into good images on Etsy? Whether we're talking about a main/thumbnail image or a product image, there's some very important best practices that apply to any image you use.

First, a few boring technical tips:

- **Your listing images should be 2,000 pixels wide.** This size looks best for desktop and mobile users. Etsy WILL let you upload images that are narrower than 2,000 pixels, but they aren't going to look nearly as good.

- **Images should be 75-dpi JPEGs**. Do take the time to set your image resolution to 75 dpi so your images are both screen viewable and not too large to upload. And make sure they're in .jpg format. (Etsy will accept PNGs and GIFs, but doesn't upload these as reliably.)

- **Make all of your listing images the same shape.** Use a 4:3 ratio (basically a fat rectangle) for optimal viewing experience (this also allows you to zoom and crop your thumbnail preview for buyers, but shows the entire product with some white space once the buyer clicks on it.)

- **Include your logo and Shop Name in a visible but unobtrusive place in each photo.** This helps your potential buyers recognize your shop as a distinct entity. (Sometimes folks tend to see Etsy as one big store instead of many different small shops.) Some people also choose to watermark (overlay a transparent logo) over their photos to deter copyright thieves from stealing their photos. (We'll talk more about copyright in Chapter 7.)

That's the technical stuff you need to know. Now on to the fun stuff:

- **Make sure your photographs are in focus.** This might sound like a no-brainer, but if it was so obvious, I wouldn't see so many slightly blurry photos on Etsy. Take your photos in good lighting, and prop your phone or camera up with a stand or against a solid surface to minimize jitter from your hands. Don't tell yourself it's "not a big deal" if the image is just a LITTLE blurry. Blurriness equates with sloppiness and amateur hour in your buyer's mind. Use crisp photos.

- **As Lizzo puts it, you need the "bomb lighting."** Natural light (from the sun) is ideal, but that isn't always easy. You're looking for soft, diffused lighting that you find in the hour before sunset or after sunrise. Avoid harsh shadows and blown-out highlights. If natural lighting is too difficult to achieve, take your photos indoors in a well-lit room (from natural sunlight).

Experiment with different angles and different times of day to get the best results. The time you spend will be worth it.

- **Invest in basic equipment.** If you're selling small items, do yourself a favor and purchase a cheap light box (you can find one easily on Amazon). It'll give you perfect lighting and excellent results with minimal effort. If you have larger items, invest in a lighting kit and photo backdrops. If you have the perfect natural environment that you can use as a backdrop with excellent lighting, that's amazing. But consider whether that natural photo studio will be available to you year-round whenever you need to photograph. If it isn't, create a photo nook that will allow you to replicate your listing photos (particularly your main/thumbnail images) year-round, with a consistent result.

- **Don't be coy with your buyers.** Show exactly what the product is, and keep it very simple, e.g., if you are selling ceramic pots, don't show a ceramic pot sitting in a saucer beside a cute watering can. Keep the main focus on your product. If you have too much going on in your photos, you're going to confuse or annoy your buyers, who imagine they will have to do some digging to figure out what you're actually selling.

- **Use props wisely and sparingly.** Despite the importance of keeping the focus on your products, props can be an invaluable tool to show size and context. Make sure your props serve a purpose and don't distract from your product but instead give additional information about your item (like how it's used, its relative size to something your buyer will be familiar with, or how it might look displayed).

- **Give your buyers accurate, easy-to-interpret information.** This should include information about color, size, shape, and texture. You don't want to send mixed messages about any of these things. Back this visual information up with your listing description.

- **Define your shop's holistic style.** You might want to create a vision board on Pinterest or just cut photos out of magazines that appeal to you and deliver the tone and feel that you want your buyers to see when they look at your images and your shop as a whole. This is hugely important to creating a cohesive shop (your buyers will interpret this as professionalism and skill in your craft). For instance, if you have some photos that are peaceful, with white backgrounds and succulents, don't suddenly throw in images that are filled with splashes of bright color and funky wallpaper. This creates a disjointed feeling when a buyer looks at your shop as a whole or peruses through additional listings. Here's some ways you can achieve that consistency:

- ○ **Use simple, consistent backdrops for your products.** I recommend choosing 3-4 backdrops and reusing them over and over again. These backdrops can be different and unique, but they must look cohesive and beautiful next to each other.

- ○ **Come up with a color and texture palette that you adhere to in your images.** This doesn't mean everything you post HAS to be in those colors. But hone in on a few key colors and textures that you tie into everything you do, whether that's whitewashed fences, neutral burlap, rustic brown wood, leafy green plants, neon vases, etc. Keep it consistent, and be intentional about the colors and patterns that appear throughout your shop.

- • **Consider seasonality and style trends**. If you have a big shop, it may be a lot of work to update listing photos with seasonally enticing colors and options. However, it may be worth the effort to essentially put a big red bow on your best sellers that shine during Christmas or to have summer and winter photos of your product that you change out twice a year. This will communicate relevance to your buyers. I tend to choose a somewhat neutral palette for most of my image backgrounds and color palettes, but I do update these images every year or so to help my shop look fresh instead of dated.

Main images (Thumbnail Images): Your First Priority for Photography

If you get only one listing image perfect, make it your thumbnail image. I know you have limited hours in a day, and you're likely juggling a lot of roles as a shop owner. So, it's important to prioritize your efforts. Main images (thumbnail images) deserve your first priority. Main images are the image buyers will see as they scroll through your shop, or more often the wild world of Etsy search results when they type in a query.

For the most part, your thumbnail image should be a simple, clean studio shot that shows the product itself up close. A white background or very clean, simple background is optimal. This image should show your buyer exactly what they will be buying. The image should be clean and bright, crisp and beautiful. This is the virtual equivalent of your buyer seeing the product on a shelf and saying, "Oooh, look at that!"

Product images

In addition to your main image are the nine product images in any given listing.

All of the product images you include in addition to your main image/thumbnail image are important to sealing the deal with a buyer and communicating proficiency and thoroughness to Etsy's algorithms. Which is why it's critical that you maximize all ten listing images to give your buyer a complete picture. Etsy shows you different thumbnails in the open image slots, encouraging you to show your product from different angles, illustrate its size and texture, where it was created, who might love it, and how it might be used. Here's a breakdown of the image shots I recommend you include:

- **Lifestyle:** Include one or two shots that look like a sneak peek into someone's home or life after purchasing your product. These lifestyle shots may show your product being displayed (on someone's wall, shelf, or closet), enjoyed, or interacted with (e.g., children playing with a toy, people having a snowball fight in your hat, or a couple cuddled up under your minky blanket reading a story). Lifestyle photos allow your buyer to see themselves using and interacting with your product.

- **Genesis and creation:** If you make your product by hand (or someone else does), lean into that handmade vibe (remember, your buyers are on Etsy for a reason), and show the product being created. Show your buyer the thing that you'd show them if they came to visit your studio—the most interesting and fun-looking aspect of creation, e.g., you working with fire, or saws, or inky screens, or sewing in your amazing artsy craft room.

- **Options:** If your buyer will need to make choices about color, size, style, etc., it's a really smart idea to show those variations side by side in a matrix-type image. This helps your buyer feel prepared to make these choices when they add your product to their cart instead of wondering, "Wait, what is blue vs. aqua? What sizing scale is this?" While you should certainly communicate information about options and sizing in your listing description and variations, many people will look at images for this kind of information without reading your descriptions very thoroughly. Use this opportunity to instill confidence and provide details visually.

- **Model shots:** If your product can be worn or displayed on a person, FIND YOURSELF A MODEL AND PHOTOGRAPH THEM. This doesn't need to be an expensive endeavor. You may have friends or family willing to model, or you may be able to find models who are excited to be part of your shoot in exchange for products, etc. You can also model your products yourself, as long as you can find someone to take the photo for you (or use a self-timer on your phone). Choose models that resemble your target market and customer. Play around with different poses and backgrounds for your model shots, and pay attention to the way an urban, natural, or indoor setting jives with the vibe and colors you're working toward cohesively creating in your shop.

- **Visual scale shot:** For most products, your buyer will want to have a very clear idea of exactly how big it is. While this information should be provided to your buyer in exact measurements in your listing description, you should also give your buyer a clear idea of scale by showing the product in context and next to easily recognizable objects, e.g., show earrings next to a quarter, in the palm of your hand, or on someone's earlobe.

- **Accessories and companion items**: Do you sell accessories or companion items that your buyer might love (if only they knew about them?!). Use one of your listing photos to advertise to an interested buyer (who is invested enough in your products to spend time scrolling through your listing) additional products they might love. Buyers who are ready to make a purchase are likely to add an extra item to their cart from your shop if they're inspired by what they see/encouraged to explore the rest of your shop. Since many buyers will be introduced to your shop by a single listing they click on in Etsy search (and may not even see your shop as a whole), it's important to entice them to look around.

- **Fine details and textures:** Don't count on your buyers to zoom in to inspect tiny details, textures, and other little things that they might easily glance past on their phone. Zoomed-in images help you avoid returns and surprises for your buyer that can result in bad reviews. It also helps you show the fine craftsmanship and detail that sets your item apart from other competitors.

When to Use Variation Photos

Do you use one listing to sell a product that comes in several colors, sizes, or varieties? If so, you can add variations for up to two attributes (e.g., size, dimensions, color, or style).

Once you've set your variations, you can link photos from your main 10 to those variations. This functionally means that your thumbnail/main image will vary depending on what your buyer searches for (i.e., if they search for a blue dress and you've listed "blue" as a color variation and linked a photo, that photo of your blue dress will show up in search for your buyer instead of the red dress you've set as your main image).

Taking advantage of variation photos can help you connect with motivated buyers who have something very specific in mind. For instance, if a buyer is searching for a red dress and your image of a white dress appears in search, that buyer may scroll past (even though you have a red dress available). An immediate visual match to a specific search query helps snag a motivated buyer.

Stuff We Learned the Hard Way about Photography

Because images are so important and so unique to each business, there's going to be some trial and error. We certainly have had our share of lessons learned, and I'm sure we'll continue to refine. Here's some of the big stuff we learned the hard way:

Zoom Issues: For a while, I operated under the impression that buyers needed to see every single inch of my product—which meant that my thumbnail/main listing images looked small. And as it turns out, we got a LOT more sales once we zoomed in a little bit more so that buyers could more easily see our designs (the most important part of a shirt in many respects) clearly and easily as they scrolled. Once the buyer clicked, of course, they were able to see my main image in all its glory and white space. But to entice that click, I needed to zoom in more. Experiment with zoom, and you might be surprised by how it affects your sales.

Using lifestyle shots as the main image: Lifestyle shots are so beautiful and so compelling. They just FEEL like Etsy, right? So we used them as our main images for way too long before realizing that those clean, bright studio shots sold way more stuff. Why? Probably because they weren't as busy; it was clear to someone scrolling past what we were selling. And maybe those clean studio shots are more similar to what a buyer is used to seeing in other online shopping venues. Those lifestyle shots are very important. But use them as your main image with caution, and don't say I didn't warn you.

Being inconsistent in our global presentation: As our shop started to grow, it felt hard to wrangle that overall aesthetic—which meant that sometimes, because of entropy, our shop didn't look very cohesive. Colors weren't harmonizing, some photos looked like they belonged in an entirely different shop, and so on. It took some TIME to get this right, but it was worth it. We have a far more professional presentation and aesthetic nowadays, and we're taken more seriously because of it.

Not communicating enough visually: I'm a reader and a detail person. When I personally purchase something, I read every single word of the listing description. But that's me. And it was a hard lesson to learn that not everybody does this. Most scan through photos, scan for any questions they might have, and make a purchase. I've learned not to assume buyers will read my listing descriptions, and to communicate a lot of info about sizing, color options, fit, etc., in one of my listing images to increase the chances that buyers will order the correct item that meets their needs (and not return it to me or give me a negative review).

CHAPTER 4

Graphics and Design

Not all of the images you use in your shop will be plain photographs. Often, you'll want to use photographs with text, images with text, graphics, and infographics to communicate information with your customers visually. You'll use design elements in your shop banner, shop updates, social media, and within your listings. In other words, it's pretty important to understand the basic principles of design and how to create graphics.

If you haven't already read the previous chapter about listing images (Chapter 3), go back and read it first, even if you have no idea what a pixel is and you're feeling ANXIETY because the idea of trying to create beautiful images and graphics for your shop seems beyond your grasp. Don't worry, we've got you covered.

That's what this chapter is about. You don't need to have a degree in graphic design or even an artistic predisposition to create beautiful images for your shop. (But for real, go back and read Chapter 3 first. You need to know where you're headed before we talk about how to get there.)

We'll be covering best practices for design in your Etsy shop, advice for beginners, tools that are easy for just about anyone to master, and color theory too (how to use colors to appeal to your customers). We'll also touch on photographs again since they play such an important role in many design elements you'll create for your shop.

First, Some Advice for Noobs

If you're just starting out on Etsy (or haven't really dipped your toe into the designable elements of your shop just yet), let me offer a few bits of advice about design before we dive right in:

Figure Out Your Style

Spend a lot of time looking at other Etsy shops, other online shops (not necessarily Etsy), and the types of images that grab your eye when you're cruising through social media. Start a Google drive or a private Pinterest board of the ones that stand out to you. You don't have to know why they stand out to you yet, you just need to recognize that someone did a fantastic job of catching your interest, drawing your eye, or making you think, "Oooh, I need that in my life!" This is going to give you a much better idea of your own personal style. Do you gravitate toward bold colors and fonts? Feminine, delicate details? Playful images?

Put Your Style into Words

After you've gathered your collection of images, create a style sheet for your shop. Include your five favorite images (basically, make yourself a little collage of the stuff that appeals to you the very most), and then write keywords that describe the style that you want to embrace, e.g.:

Bold, dramatic colors, serious models, cacti accents.

Or

Playful, rainbow colors, silly models, lots of polka dots

This might sound like a school assignment, but it'll help you nail down your style in words so you can duplicate it across your shop.

Choose a Color Palette

If you're not sure what to do here, google the phrase "color palettes," and then pull a few that you like. These are colors that look good together/complement each other and can be used over and over in elements of your images and photos to keep things cohesive.

I'd recommend you choose about five or six colors that look great together. That's not to say you can't incorporate other colors into your shop—but make these colors the meat and potatoes of your appearance and your design elements.

Join a Facebook group or Etsy Forum for Feedback

Find a group that's supportive, intended for Etsy or small business owners to bounce ideas off each other, and share your ideas. Don't worry about sounding silly. But as you create initial attempts at cover photos, social media images, and product main images, you'll be amazed by how useful feedback from your peers can be—and how little feedback you actually need to get a good consensus of what a larger audience might think. Five to ten people's opinions, and you'll get a good idea of whether something is working or not (and why). This feedback is an extra step in your process of creating graphics, but it will save you time in the long run as you hone in on what works (and why).

Elements of Successful Graphics and Images

So, what makes a good graphic or image? The first element is CONTEXT (Which is why I'm going to again recommend that you go back and read Chapter 3 on listing images). The most technically beautiful photo of a bunch of employees enjoying their morning coffee isn't going to sell your office humor mugs. A simple studio shot is (as your main image, anyway. You should definitely include that employee photo as one of the other nine!).

That said, the other half of a successful photo or graphic is the technical stuff. The stuff that, if you saw the photo or graphic outside any kind of context would make you either nod your head and say, "That's a good photo," or shake your head and think, "Amateur hour." In this chapter, we're mostly dealing with the technical aspect. So, let's talk about what makes a good photo or graphic:

Elements of Successful Graphics

You'll use graphics heavily in your social media channels (more on this in Chapter 13) to communicate with customers and potential buyers about your brand, your style, news from your shop, etc. You'll also use graphics on Etsy when you post shop updates, and sometimes within listing photos to communicate details about sizing, color options, etc.

Good graphics vary in style, color, font choices, and composition. But good graphics all follow these design rules:

Keep it Simple

The number one mistake of new designers is using too many different fonts, too many images, and too much text. Basically, too much clutter. Most of the time, you have one fleeting moment to attract your buyer's attention on social media, ads, or your news feed on Etsy. Don't confuse or overwhelm them with too much information or the equivalent of a confetti cannon.

The Less Text the Better, Generally

And the fewer fonts the better, generally. If you're new at this, some of the tools listed below (in "Tools You Should Master") include templates meant just for you—basically, someone else has already done the work of pairing compatible fonts, colors, and layouts.

Take a Page from the Pros

Stick closely to the templates in graphics programs like Canva until you understand better why certain formats and fonts work well together, a.k.a., don't trust your eyes at first. Starting out in graphic design can be a lot of fun, and once you know enough to be dangerous, you may be tempted to ride without training wheels a little too quickly. I made the same mistake, and I look back on some of my earliest creations and … they weren't awesome.

Keep it Balanced

Does one side of your image have a lot of text while there's a lot of blank space on the other side? In other words, is it too heavy or light on one side or the other? You want to create a feeling of balance within your graphics.

Keep it Aligned

You also want to create a sense of alignment by positioning design elements like text, borders, and blammies* in relationship with one another instead of haphazardly. Alignment creates a sense of order instead of chaos. The basic types of alignment include left or right alignment (elements that align along the left or right side of the image) and centered alignment (elements that are centered in the middle of the image). Basically, create an imaginary line running along the left, right, or center of the page and make sure the edges of your text and images touch that line to create a feeling of order. It's okay to use a couple of different types of alignment in one image, as long as you're consistent. For example, you might center the heading and subheading, and left-align thumbnail images that show your product, while right aligning the details of your sale or promotion.

A "blammie" is like a graphic sticker that overlays your image and highlights key text. It might be a circle, star, or rectangle shape with the words "Sale!" or "50% off!"

Embrace White Space

Don't try to fill every single inch of your image with text or graphic elements or "stuff." Let your graphics "breathe" with plenty of white space to create an image that feels clean and purposeful.

Stand out from the Crowd

While it's a good thing to sift through other Etsy shops and online stores, the last thing you want to do is look just like your competition. Once you've identified which style elements appeal to you in terms of colors and composition and feeling, hone in on what makes you unique—and highlight that visually. Let what makes you unique and interesting shine. Let it shape your images into a visual voice that's all yours. I can't tell you exactly how to do this—it takes some time—but you'll find it as you continue to work at articulating what you're trying to communicate and what makes you and your products special.

Read the Room

Appeal to YOUR customers: Don't try to appeal to everyone. In fact, if you try to make your images appealing to everyone, you'll find the approach counterproductive. What images and text speak to YOUR customers? (Hint: It might annoy or turn off people who are NOT your customers.) You don't need to sell your product to the world. You just need to sell it successfully to the people who are looking for your product and are aligned with the type of Etsy shop you want to create. If you're selling to nerds, embrace nerd lingo and images. If you're selling to moms, embrace mom talk. Find your demographic and speak to THEM.

Keep a 70/30 Ratio of Images to Text

Don't be tempted to overuse text. Images are what will catch your customer's eye for the most part. Use text as a secondary element, and use it sparingly (most of the time. If you deviate from this rule, go big with simple text and keep design elements minimal).

Match your Images to Your Text

Ask yourself, what is it I'm trying to communicate? What do I want my customer to feel when they see this graphic? Inspired? Comforted? Amused? Choose an image and text that both align with the message you want your customer to receive.

Be Intentional

Don't just include elements because they're cute, or a font because it's cool. Choose elements, fonts, and text because it complements your aesthetic, communicates key information to your customer, or showcases something about your product. Remember, the goal is for your customers not to be distracted by your design, but rather to entice them to take action or feel a certain way about your business.

Color is Important

While there aren't any hard and fast rules of color theory (because your culture, audience, and country will make a big difference in how your audience responds to different colors), you shouldn't choose colors randomly. Because people DO respond to color! Here's a few generalized principles of color theory that apply most of the time. Experiment, and dig in to figure out which colors your audience responds to best. Remember, seasonality and trends will play a role in which colors look best together. Keep your color palette fresh, and update it regularly.

- Red: Power, passion, speed. Commonly used to advertise food.
- Yellow: Your brain processes this color first, so it's an attention-grabber. Yellow communicates joy, happiness, and warmth.
- Orange: Playful, teasing, warm
- Gold: High end, expensive
- Silver: Refined, distinguished
- White: Clean, professional
- Pink: Sweet, feminine
- Green: Natural, fresh, cool
- Black: Strength, sophistication, elegant
- Blue: Calming, trustworthy
- Purple: Dignity, LGBTQIA+ ties

Contrast, Don't Clash

Without contrast, it's difficult to make elements of your images and graphics stand out. Take a look at the color wheel, and use colors that are opposite one another (e.g., red and green, yellow and purple, blue and orange). Contrast (including elements that are different from one another in shape, size, and texture) adds visual interest and keeps the eye moving across your image. However, using too many contrasting colors next to one another, in large amounts will create disorder and chaos to the eye (or clash).

Your goal will be to include enough contrasting colors elements in your images for visual interest, while using enough harmonious shapes, fonts, and color pairings (e.g., colors that are next to each other on the color wheel) for order and balance.

Elements of Successful Photos

In the last chapter, we talked about the different KINDS of photos you should include in a successful image. Now, let's dig a little deeper into what makes an individual photo appealing.

Thankfully, the elements of successful photos will include all the same elements of successful graphics that we covered above (e.g., contrasting elements, balance, color theory, alignment, standing out from the crowd) with a few key extras:

Models Matter

Who are you selling to? That audience needs to see themselves (or more accurately their aspirational selves, the people they WANT to be) in your photos. Choose models that appeal to your demographic (or whoever that demographic will be buying for) in terms of age, aesthetic, posture, styling, clothing, facial expressions, etc.

Setting Matters

Where you take your photos matters as much as who and what appears in them. Choose a setting that complements your models or product and appeals to your audience. A pristine, pinterest perfect house might look beautiful, but if you're selling counter-culture t-shirts, it's not the right environment. Your setting shouldn't distract from your product or your models, but rather enhance and support both. Remember, you need to look at the frame you'll be capturing when you determine what settings you'd like to use. A cool urban environment might be just the right setting, but if you need a lot of product close-ups, you might just get a lot of cement. Choose your setting with the types of photos you'll be taking in mind, and choose backgrounds that will complement your shot list.

Find that Perfect Lighting

This really can't be said enough: Filters and contrast settings can cover a multitude of minor sins in lighting, but they can't ever replace the beauty of really good, natural lighting. And they certainly can't correct bad lighting. Choose natural lighting whenever possible. The "golden hour" right before sunset is ideal and will give you that perfect diffused sunlight instead of harsh highlights and shadows. When shooting indoors, take the time (and invest the money as you are able) to create bright, beautifully lit photos indoors. Remember, photography is your Etsy shop's first impression. If the photos don't look beautiful, you'll sell far less than you could.

Pay for the Really Important Photos When Possible

Sometimes it's worth it to get your photography done professionally —particularly when you're after lifestyle photos with lots of moving parts (models, setting, lighting, vibe) or when you're after photos that will be highly visible (like your banner photos or main listing images). If budget is a concern (and of course it is, you're paving your own way here!), reach out to photography teachers at local Universities to connect with students who may want to build their portfolio.

Design Tools You Should Use and Master

Let me reassure you one more time: You don't need to be a graphic designer or photographer to succeed on Etsy. You just need to use the right tools. These are my favorites because they're easy to use, free or low cost, and they're confidence builders: even if you're new to design, you can create beautiful images using them.

Canva

Canva is the #1 tool I would recommend for non-designers. Why? Because it's a huge collection of very user-friendly, pre-designed templates, images, fonts, and layouts for you to access. Best of all? The free version has everything you need to succeed. The paid version (about $12/month) is worth it to me (you get access to even more features, like additional illustrations and the ability to download images with a transparent background).

I consider myself an intermediately skilled designer, and I plan to use Canva for the foreseeable future. If you have zero skills in design, you can search through templates until you find something you like, then swap out text and images. As you gain more skills and an eye for design, you can start to play with creating your own images. You'll find templates for Instagram, Facebook, banners, letterhead, business cards, you name it: It's on Canva.

Freelance Photographers

I already talked a bit about this earlier, but it's worth mentioning again. Freelance photographers are absolutely worth it for the crucial photography for your business. Learning the skills required to take a truly beautiful photo is hard, and it's worth your time to outsource this skill selectively to get that professional, beautiful touch to your business.

Photoshop and Lightroom (Adobe)

If you do delve into learning how to take your own photos, you should really subscribe to Photoshop and Lightroom (there's also Open Source software that's free and mimics these programs, but I prefer the real thing for usability. (You can get Photoshop and Lightroom for around $10 a month).

While Canva is wonderful, it'll only take you so far in being able to adjust and manipulate images and fonts (e.g., you can't create an arched font in Canva). These two programs are also great for your resume if you ever decide you want to branch out to a new career path. I taught myself how to use both of these programs. And it took a while. But I went a step at a time, focusing on specific tasks I needed to learn and gradually becoming familiar with how to use different tools and features to make my photos and *mockups look good.

 *When I talk about "mockups," I'm referring to images of full-sized product models that you can purchase and use in place of your own product photos.

Placeit.com

If you sell T-shirts, sweatshirts, leggings, iPhone cases, pillows, greeting cards (basically anything that you can loosely classify as "merch"), you'll find an entire database of models and staged mockups on Placeit.com. If you don't want to spend much on models or your own photography, Placeit allows you to create convincing mockups by uploading a .png (with a transparent background) that looks like it's been printed on the T-shirt/sweatshirt/leggings/iPhone case in the image.

Placeit continues to aggressively expand, adding more diverse models, some really pretty staged mockups, and even videos to showcase your products. It's super easy to use, and for less than $20 bucks you can download as many images as you want a month (and if you ever stop using the service, your images are still stored in your account).

Other Etsy Sellers

Other Etsy sellers are a WEALTH of resources for mockup photos, design help, and artwork elements. Just search for what you're seeking and see what comes up. For instance, for a long time I had no idea there were Etsy sellers who created beautiful flat-lay mockups of the exact blank tees I used—for a price that was way less than what I'd pay in time and energy and resources to take the photos myself.

Stuff We Learned the Hard Way about Design

I'm not a graphic designer by trade. I hadn't heard of Canva before I started my business, and I had never touched Photoshop. To be honest, I was really intimidated by the whole thing, and my first efforts were fledgling to say the least. So I guess it's fair to say that I learned everything the hard way!

Here are my biggest mistakes:

Getting too complicated: A lot of my initial efforts were full of too much text, too many fonts, and were just generally a little confusing. They weren't very successful, and it makes sense why.

Trying to do my own photography: I've learned that this is just one area of my business that I want to outsource, especially when it comes to the highly visible and important stuff. I've spent some time learning how to use Photoshop to edit my own photos that appear within listings, etc. But for those main images and for my model shots, I tap my favorite freelancer. It saves me so much time, stress, and energy.

Using blurry images without realizing it: It's really important to follow Etsy's sizing guidelines. Otherwise (especially if you're doing a million things at once), it's easy to think a photo looks good—without considering what that photo will look like when a customer zooms in. (And sees a blurry mess. TURNOFF.) I uploaded images that were too small and too low resolution far too often before I realized what I was doing in the early days.

Jumbled/clashing aesthetic: As my business started to actually take off, I failed to pay attention to the overall aesthetic of my shop. It ended up looking really disjointed with a lot of different types of photos and styles. That didn't necessarily hurt me when buyers viewed individual listings, but it did hurt my credibility as a business and wasn't exactly impressive to buyers who took a big-picture look at my shop as a whole.

I hope you're feeling more confident about graphics and design. You've got this. With some practice, an understanding of the fundamentals of good design, and what you just learned from my mistakes, get out there and take some pictures.

CHAPTER 5

How to Price Your Stuff

One of the top questions Etsy sellers (new and experienced alike) have is, "How should I price my products?" It's a good question, and it plays a pretty important role in your sales. Many sellers automatically assume that the answer is "as low as possible"; however, that's one of the biggest misconceptions about pricing. In fact, a race-to-the-bottom pricing approach can actually HURT your sales.

In this chapter, we're going to give you a solid foundation for how to price your products. And to do this well, it helps to understand how Etsy is positioned in the global ecommerce marketplace.

First, a Little Context

As a platform, Etsy is growing. It's becoming quite well-known and supports sellers across the globe. Etsy's performance is similar to the other large online sellers like Amazon and Walmart, Overstock.com and Wish. And because of this, far too many sellers try to compete in price with similar products outside the Etsy universe.

BUT, and this is vital: Etsy is not Walmart or Amazon (more on that in just a bit). Etsy has a reputation as a market of mom-and-pop shops selling handmade goods. And because of this reputation, customers go to Etsy looking for something they can't get on Amazon or Walmart—high-quality, handmade, unique items from sellers they can connect with in a personal way. And (this is the important part for pricing), *they'll pay for that.*

So, how exactly can you figure out the perfect price for your item? Let's get to it!

Do Your Research

To get your bearings, it's always a good idea to check out what other Etsy sellers are doing. This can at least give you an idea for the right price range to shoot for. But, as I said above, some sellers are selling themselves short or are selling cheaply made, mass produced products that really belong on Amazon and are often a turnoff to Etsy customers. So don't set a price as low or lower than the lowest you see. I promise, it won't work.

When you're looking for comparables, make sure the shop vibe and aesthetic line up with your own (or your aspirational vibe!) Choose four or five comparable shops that appear to have the same product quality, product type, and aesthetic. Create a price range based on those comparables.

A Formula for Success

Once you have that range determined, the next step is to determine your set costs (the costs you'll need to subtract from the price you charge your Etsy customers, a.k.a., your profit margin). Here's a basic formula for calculating how much you need to charge in order to make a profit.

- Calculate the cost of your materials and fixed expenses per item as accurately as possible (including Etsy fees, packaging, and shipping costs if you offer "free" shipping). We'll talk about Etsy's fee structures more in the next section.

- Add up any yearly shop expenses and divide by 12 to portion those expenses out monthly (e.g., any equipment or materials you purchase infrequently, yearly subscriptions, insurance costs).

- Add up all your average monthly expenses (e.g., rental space, utilities, and those portioned out yearly expenses) and divide those expenses by the average number of products you sell per month.

- Figure out exactly how much time you spend creating your item (labor) and pay yourself for your work (I usually estimate around 10-12 dollars an hour).

- Add everything up and multiply by 1.15 for wholesale (15% profit margin) or 1.30 for retail (30% profit margin). For newbies, wholesale is the price you offer for someone who wants to order in BULK then turn around and sell your products in their own venue. Retail is the price you'll charge to an end-consumer who is purchasing your product to enjoy themselves.

You'll generally offer your *wholesale price* only if someone wants to buy 50+ items. Your *retail price* should be the displayed price on your typical Etsy listing. Use this formula as a starting point, and compare it with the price range you calculated after looking at your #shopgoals competitors.

If your production costs mean that you would have to charge more than your competitors by a significant amount, it's time to look at your materials and sourcing (and check out Chapter 18). If your number is significantly lower, congratulations! You might have a high-margin item. Some products are very easy and cheap to produce, but people will pay significantly more than 30% markup. Don't be afraid to charge what the market will pay, if the situation allows.

Accounting for Etsy Fees and Ad Charges

To accurately determine your profit margins, you need to understand Etsy's fee structure for listings, transactions, and ads. Here's what you need to know:

Listing, Transaction, and Processing Fees

Like I mentioned earlier, you'll need to consider Etsy's fees when you determine your pricing because these fees apply to every sale you make.

Here's the breakdown of Etsy fees.

- Etsy charges $0.20 to post a listing for four months. (And if you offer a quantity of more than 1, you'll be charged $0.20 each time your product sells and your listing renews automatically.)
- When your item sells, Etsy charges a transaction fee, which is 6.5% of your sale price (including shipping costs). This fee increased from 5% to 6.5% as of April, 2022.
- Etsy also charges a payment processing fee when an item sells— 3% + $0.25.

So, let's say you list a handmade coat for $100, shipping included. You'll be charged $0.20 when you list the item. When it sells, you'll be charged $6.50 in transaction fees, and $3.25 in processing fees. So, you need to account for $9.95 in Etsy fees for each $100 coat you sell.

Fees for Offsite Ads

In addition to these basic fees, small sellers have the option to participate in Etsy Offsite Ads, which comes with fees of its own (don't worry, we'll tell you ALL about offsite ads in Chapter 12). Sellers who make more than $10,000 a year in sales are actually automatically enrolled in this program (but it's not a bad thing, really).

But back to the fees. When a customer buys a product from an offsite ad, Etsy charges you 15% of the sale price. (Sellers making more than $10,000 a year are charged a discounted rate of 12% of the sale price for offsite ads.) So, if you're small and want to participate or if you have to participate like us, make sure to take these higher fees into account. These are sales you likely wouldn't make without the ad (Etsy is fronting the cost of advertising your item beyond Etsy's marketplace), so any profit you can glean from them is something to celebrate!

So, back to that $100 coat you sold. If the coat was sold as part of an offsite ad, you're out an additional $15. So, in total, your fees before shipping would weigh in at $23.45 even before you calculate for the cost of materials and shipping.

Fees for Native Etsy Ads

All sellers also have the option to participate in Native Etsy Ads. Somewhat confusingly, this program is different from Etsy Offsite Ads. Like the name implies, these ads are shown within the Etsy universe, instead of offsite on Google or other websites.

With Etsy Ads, there is no set percentage in fees. You decide how much you want to spend per day between $1 and $50 and Etsy will advertise your listings each day until your budget is gone. More on paid advertising later in Chapter 12. Just know that the fees for Native Etsy ads will depend on how heavily you want to hit them.

Etsy Pricing Strategy: Don't Be Walmart/The Dollar Store

One of the most important parts of your Etsy pricing strategy (after you've accounted for all your fixed costs) is this: You are a handmade goddess/god. You are NOT Walmart. And you should price accordingly.

In other words, don't price your stuff too low. Now, Walmart and The Dollar Store definitely have their place in our culture, but there's really no place for cheaply made, disposable, mass-produced items on Etsy. Don't undercut yourself. Most sellers find that they make *more* sales if they up their prices a bit. For each product, there's a sweet spot, and once you find it, I guarantee your sales will jump considerably. Here's why:

Customers not only *don't mind* paying a little more on Etsy (than they would at Walmart or the Dollar Store), they actually *expect* to pay more, which means you can actually do your sales a lot of harm by pricing your items too low. Because if customers see you acting like Amazon or Walmart in terms of price, they'll often associate you with lower quality, mass-produced goods in a race to the bottom. Don't undersell yourself. Price your products with pride, while taking into account solid principles of pricing.

Finding the Pricing Sweet Spot Through Testing

Okay, so you've taken a good look at your fees, your production costs, and you've seen what your competition is doing. You feel the power of being a handmade creator running through your veins and you know you shouldn't undersell yourself. How do you find that exact pricing sweet spot, though?

There's always the "pick a number that feels right and see how the item sells over the next 30 days" method, which is what a lot of sellers do and what I did at first too. You can look at that list of comparables you made earlier and see where the TOP sellers are pricing their items and just go with that. This works pretty well for niche products, but less so for broad category items like earrings or abstract art, where pricing can be all over the place.

While both of the above methods will likely land you eventually on the right item price, you can get there faster by using Marmalead's price tool or by doing A/B testing within your shop (more on A/B testing in Chapter 14). Marmalead offers a free 14-day trial and then charges month-to-month ($19/month) after that and is worth it for the hours it'll save you, especially if you're just starting out.

When you type a keyword into Marmalead, it will give you the average price across Etsy of items ranking for that keyword. For example, Fourth Wave largely sells "feminist shirts," and Marmalead's price tool gives me a good idea of what the average "feminist shirt" is selling for on Etsy.

A/B testing within your shop is also a good way to test prices more quickly than the "guess and wait" method. Duplicate a listing (Etsy will allow you to copy a listing exactly) and list it twice, changing only the price and then watch both listings for 30 days to see which sells better. If the higher-priced listing is selling better, you can adjust both listings up and watch for another 30 days. This will help you hone in on the pricing sweet spot more quickly.

Warning! There are some downsides to duplicate listings. Customers may see both side-by-side in search results, which looks a little strange and can make customers see your shop as less professional. Also, if a customer does venture into your shop proper and sees a lot of the same listings over and over, they might be turned off by that as well. Once you start seeing views and sales for a listing, it's probably a good idea to get rid of any duplicates and focus on whichever (A or B) listing is performing better.

The Big Question: Should You Offer "Free" Shipping?

Etsy's big thing in 2019-2020 was offering free shipping site-wide. They really really want to compete with Amazon on this. And it's a little frustrating, because, as I've said before, Etsy is not Amazon or Walmart or the The Dollar Store. It's supposed to be more like a craft bazaar or an art fair. Nonetheless, Etsy is really encouraging sellers to offer free shipping, and they'll reward you for it not only with a boost in rank for listings with free shipping, but with a label across the bottom of your listing that says "free shipping" to entice buyers.

That said, Etsy's push for "free" shipping is rooted in sound psychology. Buyers are more likely to purchase a $30 product with "free shipping" than they are to purchase a $25.50 product with $4 shipping. Something about skipping that extra step, feeling like they got a freebie, and the simplicity of the price is enough to tip the scales.

So, here's what you do. Go ahead and offer free shipping to domestic customers, but raise your prices to cover the average shipping cost. For us, this meant pricing our shirts up about $3-4. It ended up being a good move—our number of sales didn't drop (or go up) despite the small price hike and we've had fewer abandoned carts. Chapter 17 talks in detail about the logistics of shipping and product fulfillment, so definitely jump over there if you want to learn more!

Staying Competitive on Pricing as the Market Shifts

It's important to remember that Etsy is an ever-changing marketplace. Shifts in the economy, the job market, and other trends affect how likely someone is to buy on Etsy (and at what price). So your perfect pricing sweet spot won't stay the same forever. When I started Fourth Wave, there were approximately zero other shops selling feminist shirts on Etsy, and my products sold no matter how I priced them (within reason, of course). But as the market shifted, feminist and political shirts became much more common, which means I've needed to be more competitive in my pricing.

Regularly Pretend You're a Customer Visiting Your Shop

Etsy is constantly changing how it sorts and displays items to customers. I mention this because a little over a year ago, Etsy added a checkbox under the search criteria for "items under $25." I had been pricing my shirts at $25, so to qualify for this box, I set my shirt prices at $24.99, and, you guessed it, my sales jumped. With a click of a checkbox, a customer could eliminate a large portion of my competition, making it much more likely that person would find and purchase a shirt from my shop. So, it's a good idea to role-play a customer coming to your shop and see what options they have for weeding out competitors based on price.

Etsy adds new checkboxes all the time, to encourage buyers to hone in on the exact product and price range they want. Make sure you stay in the loop on these changes that can drastically affect your pricing strategy.

Estimating Shipping Costs

Shipping costs are going to differ depending on where your shipping *from* and *to*. I'm only going to talk about shipping from the US or Canada because Etsy has specific tools for both countries, so if you're not based in one of those two countries, this section may not help you much. You'll pretty much need to calculate your own shipping costs through whatever carrier you use in your country.

If you are a US or Canada based shop and want to know exactly how much it will cost to ship a single item, you can use Etsy's handy "Price Your Postage Tool."

It's a great tool for getting an idea about your shipping costs, but you don't want to have to use it for every item you ever ship. It's easier to estimate the average you'll be spending on shipping in future weeks or months in order to get a good idea for how much to budget for shipping. Here's what you need to know:

- Etsy gives sellers who ship through their platform a discounted rate (somewhere between 15%-30%), so **it's almost always cheaper to create your labels and ship through Etsy** rather than take everything to the post office.

- For USPS, package **shape will affect your shipping cost**. There are three categories: Letter, Flat, and Parcel. Etsy-calculated shipping pretty much assumes everything is a parcel, so if you sell cards, posters, or something like face masks that can be pressed flat inside a mailing envelope, you will need to use the custom shipping option or take stuff to the post office for accurate pricing. I've found that for cards and flat (squashable) items (like face masks), it's cheaper for me to use stamps rather than purchase labels through Etsy. Canada Post doesn't have a flat-parcel option, but if you sell cards or something similarly flat, definitely check out the pricing options for letters vs. parcels to decide how best to send your items.

- Etsy costs for parcels are largely dependent on weight, **approximately $0.30-$0.40 USD per ounce** (the price per ounce goes down as the item gets heavier). The heaviest package you can ship is 70 lbs through USPS and 30 kg through Canada Post. (If you sell really heavy stuff like furniture, I'll give some suggestions for cost-effective shipping below.)

- **Package size** can factor into the cost if your box or mailing tube is very large or unusual in shape. If your packaging is unusual (say, very long and thin or very large and flat), use the

Price Your Postage Tool I mentioned above to get an idea of your shipping costs.

- **If you sell educational materials** from a shop in the US, you can take advantage of Media Mail prices.

Takeaway: For averaged-sized items, you can estimate your shipping costs at $0.30-$0.40 per ounce (under a pound is closer to $0.40/ounce and 3 lbs or more is closer to $0.30/ounce). These are better prices than you will get at the post office because Etsy shipping gives you a discount of "up to 30%" (again, larger items get closer to the full 30% while items under a pound get closer to 15% discount).

Shipping Really Large Items

Furniture is probably the most common example of the large items available on Etsy, and as you can imagine, shipping it can be daunting. Here are some tips if you ship furniture or something else too large to use Etsy's calculated shipping options:

- Keep in mind the type of customer that shops on Etsy. This person wants a very specific custom or hand-crafted piece, something they can't get at their local furniture store or on Amazon, and they're not only willing to pay more for it, they're happy to pay the hefty fees to have it shipped to them. In other words, if your shipping costs are in the $300's, don't freak out. Your customers will be okay with that.

- Get quotes from several carriers. Fast shipping carriers (FedEx, UPS, etc.) will generally charge more and slower carriers less. It's nice to offer customers options when you can: "Pay more to get the piece right away or less to receive it a few weeks out." For example, there are services like White Glove Shippers that offer shipping discounts but may only pick up items once a month for shipping, meaning money savings but shipping times of 5-6 weeks.

- Another tip is to use Etsy's option "fixed shipping costs" to enter an average price, but ask customers to message you for a precise shipping quote before they purchase. That way, you can adjust the cost based on where you're sending the item and charge the customer accordingly.

- Or offer free shipping, and adjust your price up $300 or so. You may want to wait until you've sold several pieces before trying out the free shipping option. The potential for losing money on shipping is a lot higher with very large items.

Stuff We Learned the Hard Way

Don't set your prices too low: Like many Etsy sellers, I priced my stuff WAY too low at first. I was so worried about turning off my potential customers that I didn't realize I was turning them off through the very way I hoped to win them.

When I finally raised my prices (and improved my shop aesthetic and keywords to match and inspire customer confidence that my prices were well-warranted), I saw my sales increase significantly.

Do the math: I also (like many Etsy sellers) have made the mistake of choosing pricing points on new products without doing my due diligence by looking at comparables first. It can be really tempting to choose a "gut-based" price, but if you choose wrong (and you probably will unless you are a genius), you'll send bad signals to Etsy's algorithms and your customers. Which means that your listing will earn negative points that aren't so easily erased even if you update your pricing strategy. Start things off on the right foot with your listings and price smart from the START.

CHAPTER 6

Customer Service

As an Etsy shop owner, you wear a LOT of hats. You are CEO, CMO, the design team, and the customer service team. If you don't approach this last role with the right mindset, it can cost you significantly and even slow your shop's growth. Here's what I mean:

You can have a truly amazing gem of a product, but if you treat your customers with a hit-or-miss bedside—or I guess *web-side*—manner, you're going to earn yourself bad reviews. And I won't sugarcoat this: Bad reviews will kill your business in the short and long-term.

Remember, part of the reason your buyers come to Etsy in the first place is to have a more personal, human experience and to support a smaller shop that feels more human than corporate. If you seem annoyed by messages, don't respond to people promptly, or craft automated messages that sound, well, automated, you're going to turn people off.

The bottom line? Good customer service equates to five-star reviews. And five-star reviews are a powerful signal to buyers that your shop can be trusted. They also raise your shop quality score significantly and help your listings rank higher in Etsy's algorithms.

Let's explore a few key best practices in customer service that will help you earn those sweet, sweet five-star reviews (and possibly a new Star Seller Badge).

Best Practices in Customer Service

These best-practices are the end result of my ten years of customer service experience in Etsy. The more closely I adhere to them, the more five-star reviews I get.

Promise with Precision, Over Deliver

You know that saying, "Under promise, over deliver?" I'm going to recommend a bit of an alternative: "Promise with precision, over deliver."

Promise with Precision

Your sales will suffer if you sandbag your product or include mediocre descriptions. You need sparkling, clean, beautiful, compelling images and text to catch a potential buyer's eye and encourage them to add your product to their shopping cart. Use your photos and listing descriptions to highlight every single amazing feature of your product, and don't hold back! But you need to be absolutely accurate in your descriptions and images. Don't use super-saturated photos that distort colors. Don't try to make something sound bigger, softer, brighter, etc. (you get the idea) than it is to make a sale. You'll only set your buyers up for disappointment, which will show in your reviews.

Do your handmade items vary somewhat from the listing photo, by nature of being handmade? Tell your buyers! Do you need a little longer to ship everything? Tell your buyers why, and create accurate shipping profiles.

Over Deliver

Okay, now for the fun part: Over deliver in ways your customer won't expect—so usually in some way that's related to but not directly involving the product you've sold. Surprise and delight your customer with something a little extra.

When our expectations are met, we feel pleased. When our expectations are met and we get a little surprise or thrill we weren't expecting, we feel delighted. Aim for giving your customers that feeling of delight in as many ways as you can without slowing down your process or adding a lot of extra expense. These are all ideas that have worked well for me, but I'd encourage you to combine your creativity with what you know about your target audience. Don't be afraid to play around a little bit and think outside the box.

- Use fun packaging that makes your customers smile. This packaging usually doesn't cost much more than the plain stuff, so why be plain? Some of my personal favorites are poly mailers with unicorns, donuts, or flamingos. (Check out Chapter 17 for more info on where you can cheaply and easily source packaging, notes, stickers, etc.)

- Include a handwritten note. It doesn't have to be long. It just has to be handwritten. I prefer writing these notes on stick-on kraft gift labels since I sell t-shirts. That way my note doesn't get lost in the packaging when it's opened.

- Buy custom bulk decals or bumper stickers that include a fun message your buyer will want to display (and include your company logo or name very unobtrusively in the corner).

- Add tags or labels to your product with a humorous or inspirational quote. You can also buy custom stamps to add a special touch to the outside of paper packaging.

- Create a lighthearted, fun purchase confirmation. Etsy allows you to customize the message that gets sent to buyers any time they make a purchase. Don't be shy about using humor and down-to-earth language in this message. For instance, here's what my purchase confirmation message says:

  > *Please stand by as your order from Fourth Wave is infused with solidarity, a feminist fist bump, and, well, ink and stuff. I hope wearing it reminds you to "Let the beauty of what you love be what you do."*
  >
  > *If you would, take a moment to double-check that you entered the correct shipping information, to avoid possible delays (Etsy's system can be a bit confusing!) Thank you again for your order!*
  >
  > *Get 15% off when you sign up for our newsletter! Click here to subscribe: https://bit.ly/2LWYYEh*

  A bit of humor, a helpful reminder (that helps catch a surprising number of incorrect shipping addresses), and a plug for our newsletter that adds value.

- Use your shipping message as another way to thank your buyer for shopping with a small business (this feels good!), and tell them that you hope they love their product.

Notifications and Communication

In today's fast-paced, web-based world, people expect a response to electronic queries pretty promptly.

What does that mean? For a while, I kept my Etsy notifications set to alert me any time I received a message (or "Convo") from a buyer. But to be honest, that stressed me out, and I wasn't crafting the best replies because inevitably those convos came through while I was working on something else.

I've found that a more sustainable system is to set aside two different times per day when I will check my Etsy convos. I make sure I'm in a good headspace, I'm not hangry, and I'm not feeling particularly stressed out by anything. And then I check out my Etsy convos and respond to them all. I've never had anyone express irritation for slow responses; on the contrary, we've gotten lots of comments about prompt replies and helpful responses.

Make sure you check over weekends and holidays, but I usually decrease my response frequency to once per day. You don't want to burn yourself out or add too much stress. As your shop grows, consider adding a part-time freelance position that's just a few hours a week to help you respond to messages.

If you're on vacation and want to unplug (and you absolutely should do that!) You have the option to set an away message in Etsy. Make sure to be thoughtful (your buyer's questions are important, and if they aren't answered, you may lose a sale), and to reassure buyers that you are taking a bit of much-needed time away from your computer. Then let them know exactly when they can expect a response (and follow through!).

You can also choose to provide an "emergency" email where you can be reached if someone simply must talk to you. Most people won't use it, but the ones who do are the same ones who will leave you a poor review for not responding to them—so bite the bullet and respond!

Don't Make It Personal

This sounds easy but is actually really hard. On Etsy more than any other platform or marketplace, you ARE your product. As a handmade item, it's an extension of you. If a customer sends a message complaining about quality, the fact that it didn't ship with Amazon-Prime warp speed, or simply doesn't appreciate it as much as you think they should, it's all too easy to respond with a defensive, curt, or snarky reply.

The brief satisfaction of sending back the perfect zinger will be short lived. Most people who complain are looking for validation and want your help solving a problem. They're not out to hurt your feelings or your shop's success (even though it may feel like it at the time.) Respond with compassion, validate their feelings, and make it all about them (not you). How you choose to respond will depend on your product and the particular complaint, but it's my policy to do whatever it takes within reason to create a happy customer and a great review. Those good reviews are worth far more to me than a partial loss I'll take by sending a replacement, allowing an exchange (even if it's not allowed in my policies) or sympathizing with someone who didn't get their product immediately.

Outsource If You Can

I'll say it again: It's really freaking hard not to take things personally sometimes. As my shop got bigger, I felt burnt out by dealing with customer questions and complaints. There were relatively few (maybe a couple out of every hundred orders I sent out), but most of the time you don't hear from the happy folks (except in your glowing reviews, read those often!) but rather the folks with a bone to pick.

I decided to outsource my customer service to a freelancer who would spend just a couple hours a week answering my questions and dealing with customer issues. It was one of the best things I've ever done for my shop. Not only is Leesa cheerful, helpful, and my customers love her (after all, it's not personal to her when someone doesn't cherish my hard work), but she has a background in hospitality and is incredibly good at making my customers feel heard and appreciated.

If you work with a partner, take turns doing customer service if you can to give each other a breather and enjoy tapping out of the constant stream of questions and comments for periods of time.

Take the Loss and Assume the Best

As much as you're in the business of creating t-shirts, artisan jams, princess dresses, or decals, you're in the business of making your customers happy. Your shop can't succeed without them. Any one negative review your shop receives hurts you more than any one positive review helps.

So what does that mean? Take the loss. Especially if it was your fault anyway (in the customer's mind, not yours). If your customer feels unhappy, your response should proportionally reflect the feelings they're projecting at you—no matter how justified or not you feel they are. Their reality is their reality, and to succeed you'll need to meet them where they're at. Take the loss to keep a happy customer. This doesn't have to mean a total loss, but it usually means giving up something extra for the long-term goal of your success. Taking the loss for the greater good looks like this in my shop, depending on the particular complaint or the customer's demeanor (I don't do all of these every time a customer complains—I pick the one that I think will best satisfy the unhappy customer):

- Sending out a new product completely free of charge.

- Offering a special discount for future orders.

- Including a unique goodie or note in an order (for example, if the order hasn't arrived on the customer's timeline).

- Offering to cancel the order and refund the customer (if I think the customer won't be happy no matter what I do and is likely to leave a bad review no matter what).

- Authorizing a return even if the customer has washed their item or kept it longer than 14 days (my policy).

- Sending out a replacement for an item that was lost in the mail (not my fault, but I earn a happy customer).

Do I get taken advantage of now and then? Probably. But the number of customers who complain is low enough, and I'm committed to their happiness enough that it isn't a big deal in the scheme of things. Assuming good intentions and taking the loss instead of adopting an attitude of suspicion has been key to my success.

Replacements, Refunds, and Lost Packages

I see questions about these three issues on the Etsy forums all the time. "What should I do if the post office loses my customer's package? It's not my fault!" Or "This customer is asking for a replacement when it's against my shop policy. What should I do?"

Here's the thing: Etsy will stand behind you if you have clearly stated shop policies and decide to hold your ground. Etsy will also stand behind you refusing to refund or replace an order that got lost in the mail (as long as it was shipped with an Etsy label and tracking shows it's in the system). Does that mean you should hold your ground and be a hard-nose? As you can probably guess from my previous sections, I wouldn't recommend it in most cases.

In most cases, swallow your annoyance and keep the big picture in mind. Be generous, be flexible, and strive for great reviews. Unless this happens to you all the time (and if it does, there's likely a reason for it/some work you need to do on your product or descriptions), do the thing that will make your customer happy, even if your policies or Etsy's policies will support you in not doing so.

That's not an absolute rule. Sometimes (RARELY) your instincts tell you that a customer is just yanking your chain. They'll take the free product and give you a bad review to boot. Or they don't bother reaching out to you and hit you with a terrible review. What should you do in that case? Read on:

Dealing with Bad Reviews

So what happens when you've been as pleasant as a peach and still get some furious person who leaves you a steaming, stinking one- or two- or three-star review?

First things first: Deep breath. Bad reviews suck. They suck so much. It feels terrible to see your hard work disparaged, especially for silly reasons (and you WILL see some silly reasons. I once got a one-star review from a woman who "Loved her shirt, but did this ship by COVERED WAGON?" (The shirt shipped in five business days, as stated in my shipping timeframes and product descriptions since it is handmade).

There's a few important strategies for dealing with bad reviews. Start with number one, and proceed from there.

1. You took that deep breath, right? Remind yourself that bad reviews happen, all shops get them, and it doesn't mean you're a terrible person or artist. People are complicated. If I'm sure I'm doing my best, I imagine to myself that this person may have hemorrhoids flaring up.

2.   Reach out, kindly, through Etsy messaging. After you've taken that deep breath. Something along the lines of, "Hey Karen, I just saw your review. I wanted to let you know I'm so sorry you were disappointed in your shirt. It sounds like you were expecting it for a birthday and it didn't arrive in time. I'd feel disappointed if I were in your shoes too. I was wondering if I could offer you a partial discount on your order to make it up to you? I appreciate your order so much. I'm so proud of my work, and I want you to love it too. As a small business, I will never take my customers for granted."

Make this message your own. Don't justify yourself. Don't rationalize what happened (unless there is a HUGE piece of information they are missing), and don't ask them to change their review. Just empathize and offer your best way to fix it. You'd be shocked at how many people will respond with gratitude and change their review without being asked. For the ones that respond with gratitude (but haven't changed their review after a few days), try sending another message like this:
"Hey Karen, I just wanted to reach out to you to ask if there's anything you'd like to change in your public review before I reply to it. I know how frustrated you were when you wrote it (completely understandable). If you're set on the review, I respect that, but I try to follow up with my customers first to make sure they'd like to keep the review as is first before I reply to the review as a shop owner (since my response will lock the review and prevent future edits for both of us)! Hope you are doing well."

Most of the time, you'll get a bump in stars (the buyer can edit their review any time until you respond to the review publicly).

3.   If you don't hear back from the customer, they aren't willing to work with you, or your gut feeling tells you that this is one of those situations where someone is just mad and taking it out on you (this is rare but happens), go ahead and respond publicly. To respond publicly to a review, find the customer in your orders tab in the Etsy dashboard. You'll see the review attached to that customer's order. Click on the star rating, and then type your response in the dialogue box that appears. Stick to the facts, stay

professional, and take the high road. Other potential buyers will read your response for more information, and they may choose to purchase (or not) based on your reasonable response. Don't be afraid to add additional context or refute details that the (angry) person included in their review, but don't come across as spiteful or mean. Once you reply in this dialogue box, it locks the review. The customer can't respond or edit their original review (and you won't be able to edit your response, either so make sure you're happy with your response).

4.   Respond to bad reviews quickly and make it a practice of checking for them regularly. The sooner you reply, the more likely you are to get a positive resolution.

Encouraging Five-Star Reviews

Isn't that what we've been talking about this WHOLE time? Sort of. Being a relatable, awesome shop owner with great boundaries who avoids bad-review pitfalls will earn you some organic good reviews. But here's a surprisingly simple trick many Etsy shop owners overlook: To get the most good reviews, you have to ask for them. According to BrightLocal's article "Local Customer Review Survey," a whopping 70% of customers will leave you a review if you simply ASK. And since 97% of buyers look at reviews extensively before making a purchase, gathering all the positive reviews you can is really, really important.

Everybody's busy. And Etsy tries to help out with that fact by giving your buyers a notification when they log into their Etsy account, right at the top of their screen, that shows recent purchases and asks them to rate those purchases. Easy, peasy.

Unfortunately, many buyers will still ignore that notification. What encourages them to take the extra 10 seconds to give you a good review? You ask.

Send your ask in the text of your automated shipping notification and your order confirmation (more on automated emails in Chapter 10). In both places, thank your buyer for their purchase. Tell your buyer that as a small-business owner and handmade artist, you appreciate each and every one of your customers and that a five-star review would mean the world to you. You hope they love their purchase, and encourage them to reach out to you with any questions!

If you've successfully associated your shop and this purchase with a human, positive message that makes your customer feel like an important part of your shop (and I daresay life), that memory is likely to ping in their mind when they see the notification pop up on their Etsy dashboard, asking them to rate their purchase. It's such a simple way to encourage your buyers to take the extra ten seconds to review you.

Another way to encourage reviews is to run a monthly contest (which you'll want to advertise in your shop announcement. (We'll talk more about sales and promotions in Chapter 10!)

Setting Boundaries

The customer is always right. Which means you should strive to make customers happy even if it means setting yourself on fire, right?

No. Don't do that. You'll set yourself up for burnout and a bad experience. And you won't have better reviews or sales to show for it. Instead, you'll be spending a lot of time on one or two orders, while you could have been doing A, B, or C to make the majority of your customers happier.

What do boundaries look like? It'll vary depending on your shop, your personality, and your products. Here's what boundaries look like for me:

- I create clear shop policies that address the most common questions my customers may have or scenarios that tend to crop up (for example, lost packages, returns, exchanges, etc.) The stuff that's inevitably going to happen. Your customers may not read all of your policies, but most reasonable customers will recognize that they had the option to read those policies before making a purchase (and will be easier to deal with when you need to hold to your boundaries because of it).

- Keeping my shipping timeframes up to date, especially around the holidays. Again, your customers may not read them, but they are easily visible and help create boundaries for your shop.

- I don't offer rush shipping. For me, rush shipping means an extra drive to my studio, gambling whether the post office will get the package there on time (it often doesn't when you really need it to, Murphy's law), and lots of time with back-and-forth. If a customer asks me about rush shipping, I explain that "Due to the handmade

nature of my products, I'm not able to offer rush shipping."
Sometimes this is hard to do when someone is oh so sweet and has
a birthday the next day, or whatever. But remember: Someone's
poor planning is NOT your emergency. Be polite, and keep your
boundaries (which you've backed up with your shipping
timeframes and shop policies, right?)

- For any custom orders I offer, I lay out very specifically in the
listing description what IS and is NOT included. For example, I
offer custom family reunion t-shirts. If the customer provides an
image (EXACTLY as they want it, in 300 DPI, correctly sized)
there is no artwork fee. If I have to design something, I charge an
art prep fee and require specific details. This keeps me from doing
free work.

- I don't send free samples. Hardly ever, anyway. And I rarely send
out free stuff to influencers. Why? Because half the time it works
out, and half the time you never hear from them again. And those
aren't good odds. HOWEVER, I do often donate items to good
causes that align with my business. Silent auctions, gift baskets
that include my products, or even sponsorship of good causes with
high visibility can be a great feel-good opportunity that also puts
your business in front of new customers (make sure you attach
tags to your products that you send out into the world and include
business cards!)

- I encourage communication through Etsy. In the event that
something goes haywire, I have a record of all convos right in
Etsy's app.

   Bottom line: Be human in your customer service. But be a
confident, kind human with boundaries that keep you sane and your
customers happy.

A Few Thoughts About the Star Seller Program

In September of 2021, Etsy rolled out its Star Seller Program as "a
way to recognize and reward Etsy sellers who consistently provide
an excellent customer experience."

The Basics of the Star Seller Program

Here's the basics of what you need to know. Keep in mind that (in part because of a somewhat poor experience for many sellers), this program is still evolving. But for now:

- To even be in the running for the Star Seller badge:
    ○ Your shop has to be on Etsy for at least 90 days
    ○ Your shop must have 10 orders OR made at least $300 during that time.

- Each month, the Star Seller Program "grades" Etsy shops based on three metrics:
    ○ Message response times (95% of your messages got a reply in under 24 hours)
    ○ Five-star ratings (at least 95% of your reviews must be five-stars)
    ○ 95% on-time shipping WITH tracking (E.g., did your orders ship out within the timeframe you specified in your shipping settings for that particular product and did you include tracking?). Note: This is another good reason to use Etsy labels!

- The "grades" Etsy assigns are based on performance in these three areas over the previous 90 days, and shops that score 95% or above in all three metrics get the Star Seller badge.

Why Did Etsy Roll Out the Star Seller Program?

Etsy has become increasingly popular over the last few years. As of 2021, there were over 5 million sellers on the platform, and that number continues to grow.

Etsy obviously wants customers to have a good experience on its platform. The powers that be created the Star Seller Program both as a way to motivate good customer service and to let customers know when a product they're eyeing is being sold by an exceptionally high-performing shop.

Frequently Asked Questions About the Star Seller Program

The new program begs a lot of questions (we certainly scoured the resources available for these answers as soon as possible!). Here's the top questions and answers about the program:

Does the Star Seller Program Affect My Placement in Search?

This is a big question. And for now, the answer is no: Shops that qualify for the Star Seller badge *don't* currently get a boost in ranking. Conversely, shops that *don't* qualify won't have their listings demoted in ranking.

How Does Star Seller Benefit Me?

There are some benefits for sellers who achieve Star Seller status. Notably: All of the seller's listings will display a small purple star badge stating that that product is being sold by a Star Seller shop. And Etsy's system DOES give preference to Star Sellers when displaying suggested listings to buyers and when showing featured listings on the Etsy homepage.

How Attainable Is the Star Seller Badge?

The answer to this question depends a lot on your shop type. If you sell very straightforward items (e.g. coffee mugs) and have clockwork shipping and customer service, it may be possible to consistently earn the Star Seller badge.

However, for an Etsy shop like ours (that has a lot of variables at play with sizing and color), it can sometimes be more difficult to predict customers' responses. (For example, if the color of the shirt wasn't QUITE what someone expected because of their monitor display, or the size wasn't what they'd anticipated based on ordering from a different Etsy shop, they might choose to leave a 4-star review).

Basically, for many Etsy shops the Star Seller badge is a bit of a slippery thing: You can get it one month and it'll be gone the next. Because Etsy assesses each shop every month for how they performed over the previous 90 days, your Star Seller badge may not last very long.

How Is the Program Likely to Evolve?

There are some sticky points for the program, and it clearly still needs some honing. In other words, what Etsy thinks it's measuring isn't always exactly reflective of what's going on in reality. Here's what we mean:

Message Response Rate: Thankfully, Etsy has done some serious honing in this category since the Star Seller program launched. Etsy started out expecting sellers to answer EVERY message AND be the one to have the last word every time. They got some feedback about that from a lot of extremely frustrated sellers and made some changes. Now, sellers must respond within 24 hours to the *first message* in a conversation. None of your other responses count for or against you! Also, you don't have to respond to messages from Etsy itself. As for spam messages, you don't need to respond to them, but you DO need to mark them as spam.

Five-Star Ratings: This is exactly what it sounds like (unfortunately). Sellers basically get one point for each five-star rating they receive and zero points for ratings of four-stars and below. Etsy then divides the number of five-star ratings by the total number of ratings received and turns that into a percentage. This appears to be the metric that causes the most sellers to miss out on the Star Seller badge. And it's definitely the one that sellers have the least control over because a "good" rating can mean different things to different customers, and Etsy's decision to count a four-star rating with the same weight as a one-star rating is quite obviously not representative of which shops have good customer service and which don't.

Shipping: To meet the shipping requirement, sellers must include tracking information for 95% of their orders. For US sellers, this means 95% of ALL orders. You can mark orders that are picked up by the customer as finished without including shipping information, but this will count against your Star Selling shipping "grade." Hopefully, Etsy figures out some way to reconcile this in the future. For some countries that don't provide affordable tracking, Etsy only asks for tracking for items over a certain amount (equivalent to about $15 USD in whatever currency the seller uses).

Don't sweat the Star Seller Badge too much. If you don't qualify for the badge or are unlikely to be able to qualify, don't spend too much time and energy trying. Etsy has introduced a number of programs meant to incentivize sellers over the years, and this is just the latest iteration.

For now, the program isn't affecting ranking. This means that you're still better off honing your niche and keywords and doing some marketing and advertising to get eyeballs on your products than you are spending all your time trying to achieve Star Seller status. Do what you can: Respond to convos, provide the best customer service possible, and include tracking information for shipments as often as possible. But remember that the Star Seller program is far from perfect, and if you're doing the best you can and running an incredible shop, that will show in your performance.

Dealing with Claims against Your Shop

Claims are a different beast than bad reviews. Claims are private—between you and the buyer, and they happen if a buyer believes you have been dishonest in your descriptions or somehow cheated them out of their money. If the buyer contacts you with a problem, and you don't resolve it within 3 days, the buyer can escalate the issue to Etsy.

Etsy is NOT motivated to deal with squabbles. Even after someone has opened a case, Etsy requires the buyer and seller to try to figure it out for an additional three days before they intervene. (Unless the situation is super serious or there's harassment and potential scary stuff involved, then they may intervene earlier.) They'll give the buyer and seller every opportunity to deal with this issue among themselves and will really only step in if the buyer is quite persistent and insists the issue can't be resolved without help. For issues of package non-delivery, the claim will automatically be closed if you used an Etsy shipping label and the package is confirmed delivered via tracking.

Buyers have 100 days to open a claim from the time they receive their item. If you have a claim brought against your shop, and you're gridlocked with a customer, Etsy will step in and mediate. If you are in the wrong, Etsy can garnish your shop payment account to refund the customer. If you aren't willing to participate in mediation or are unhelpful, Etsy can even suspend your account. So be helpful and available if a claim is brought against you.

The good news? In the 10 years I've been an Etsy shop owner, I've had two claims brought against my shop. Both for packages that never showed up, and the buyers filed the claims without even reaching out to me. Claims are rare. You might deal with them, but if you're doing other stuff right in customer service, it should be very, very infrequently.

Stuff We Learned the Hard Way

I've learned a lot of things the hard way about customer service over the years. Every single piece of advice I've shared here represents something I've done wrong—and learned better from—at one point or another over the years. I've bent over backwards when I shouldn't have, stretched my boundaries until I felt used and undervalued, responded to customers in the heat of the moment and earned a bad review, and failed to ASK my customers for reviews for WAY, way too long.

Learn from my mistakes, and start earning those five-star reviews.

CHAPTER 7

Troubleshooting Your Etsy Account

At this point, I hope that you're up to your elbows in the business of creating a solid foundation for your Etsy shop. I hope you're creating a plan to hone the key components of your shop that will speak directly to Etsy's algorithm. I hope you're honing your listing titles and descriptions. I hope you're mining keywords like crazy and keeping track of your success (and then doing more of it). I hope you're experimenting with the easy-to-use tools in design and photography that will give you an edge over your competition.

And if you're doing those things, you may run into technical trouble. It happens to the best of us. Sometimes it's Etsy's fault, sometimes it's the internet's fault, and sometimes it's just a knowledge gap.

In this chapter, we wanted to give you a few tools for troubleshooting some of the most common questions and issues you might run across as you build your Etsy empire. We obviously can't imagine every single situation out there, but we can give you solid tools for solving these questions and issues as they arise. SO, let's get troubleshooting.

HELP! What to Do When Things Go Sideways

Sometimes, stuff goes wrong, especially when selling online (the internet is an ever changing beast). One of your Etsy listings may get wrongfully taken down. Something may go wrong during a payment or while you're trying to create and print shipping labels. An internet glitch or an Etsy bug may prevent you from uploading images or saving a listing you've worked really hard on (so frustrating!). And sometimes, you just want ideas for how to improve your shop. There are a number of routes you can take to find resolutions, and the first is always to check the Etsy Forums.

Finding Answers with the Etsy Community Forums

The Etsy community forums are located at community.etsy.com. This is where Etsy itself puts announcements about updates, opportunities, and new features for Etsy sellers. And it's also where sellers can post questions and contribute to discussions.

If something is wonky on the Etsy site, you can take comfort (and get actual solutions) from other Etsy sellers and Etsy's staff on these forums.

It's helpful to know that Etsy's staff monitors these discussions fairly closely and contributes when questions can't be answered by other sellers. It's also a good idea to contribute when you can to these forums, especially as you become a more experienced seller, because you'll want to keep them active in case you have a question in the future.

Help! There's a Bug or Tech Issue

One of the most frustrating situations is a bug or a glitch in Etsy's website. You try to upload a listing and get an "uh oh" message no matter what you do. That's the kind of side-quest nobody wants to spend time on. So, what can you do?

Figuring Out Where the Problem is Occurring

When trying to resolve a problem with your Etsy shop, figuring out whose fault the problem is more than half the battle. I realize that it sounds really petty when I put it like that, but placing blame in these situations is less about relieving yourself of responsibility than discovering who you need to contact (if anyone) to get the problem fixed.

Just like all online platforms, Etsy is constantly revising and updating its site, search algorithm, and features, and more often than is convenient, things go wrong. Are you suddenly having trouble uploading photos to a listing? Or updating your About Section when you've never had a problem with it before? Check the forums. If other sellers are having the same problems at the same time, it's probably Etsy's fault, and if the problem is big enough, they're probably working feverishly to fix it.

Another culprit for sudden and random technical issues may be your internet browser. Is your browser blocking pop-ups? Turn that blocker off for Etsy's domain. Etsy also doesn't really work for sellers using Firefox. Etsy's front-end site works there, so customers can browse Etsy and make purchases, but the backend, where sellers do their thing, isn't optimized for Firefox, which means getting a listing up is really painful. You're much better off using Google Chrome (best), Microsoft's Internet Explorer, or Apple's Safari when making changes within your Etsy's shop.

If you're using the Sell on Etsy app on your phone, it's good to know that the app is really buggy on Android phones (Google and Samsung) and works much better on iPhone. By all means, use the app on your Android phone, but recognize that some features won't work, and you'll need to perform certain actions on your computer instead.

Contacting Etsy about Bugs and Issues on Their Platform

Every once in a while, you'll encounter a problem with Etsy's platform that you can't resolve, and you'll need to contact Etsy's support team. To do this, go to help.etsy.com. You'll need to log in to your Etsy account if you're not already. This website puts you through your paces before allowing you to contact a real human. Etsy really wants you to make sure you can't resolve your issue by reading through the forums, Etsy's FAQ, or any of their other literature. If you're seeing what you think may be a bug, make sure to check Etsy's "Known Issues" at the very bottom of the help page under the section "Your Etsy Account." Etsy's staff lists here the problems sellers have brought to their attention that they're working on but haven't yet fixed.

If you still have questions or need to send feedback after scouring Etsy's help page, first click on the subject related to the type of problem you're having, scroll to the bottom of that page and click the black button that says "Contact Support." Just so you don't go looking for it, I want to emphasize that this button doesn't exist until you click the link related to your specific problem.

Even this button will take you to a list of issues, from which you need to further select the problem you're experiencing. Keep selecting stuff even if the options don't quite describe your problem. A few clicks deep, you'll finally be able to send a message through the browser to Etsy's customer service support desk, and they'll email you back within a day or so.

Help! Someone Copied My Work

Sometimes you'll find trouble when you run into a bug on the Etsy site or need help figuring out a technical question. And sometimes trouble comes knocking on your door when somebody yoinks your product and creates a copycat.

This can be one of the most upsetting situations to deal with, but unfortunately it's pretty common. But the good news is you have options, and Etsy has your back.

Here's the deal: Your original creations are considered under copyright the moment you publish them in your Etsy shop. You can indicate this by placing a little © (copyright sign) next to the name of your item in the listing description, but you don't have to—that © is more of a reminder to others that stealing your work is against the law. Copyright protection makes the most sense for designs, art, and handmade items that are unique and couldn't be created by someone else without the other seller having seen your item and deliberately copying it. Basically, the more unique your product is, the stronger the copyright protection.

Copyright law is complicated, and even if you have that little © next to the name of your product, it's not always easy to know what to do when someone copies your idea. So here's what you do:

Dealing with Copyright Infringement

What should you do if you think someone has copied your work? There are several actions you can take depending on where you find the copy and how receptive you believe the copycat will be.

One factor to consider in the discussion about copyrights is how obvious the copy actually is. Did another seller create a product similar to yours? Or is the product exactly the same? Is that person using your images, title, or listing description to sell the product in their store? I have the most trouble with this in Fourth Wave because people copy and sell my t-shirt designs as SVGs, which they then sell to other t-shirt makers. Sometimes my copyrighted designs turn up all over the internet, often sold by people who paid for the design and believed it was sold to them legally. It's important to note that even if someone purchased a copyrighted SVG in good faith, they still need to honor your copyright and take the image down, since the image was sold illegally.

If you can't get a hold of a seller or they refuse to honor your copyright, you can file an Intellectual Property Infringement Report within Etsy, and Etsy Legal will deactivate the offending listing after they have reviewed your claim. The other seller has the option to file a Counter Notice if they think your report is incorrect. Most true copycats won't do this though because they know exactly what they're doing in copying your work.

If you discover your product has been copied and is being sold by a seller on a platform outside Etsy, you should again begin by contacting the seller. If that doesn't work, you can go over a seller's head, to the platform (e.g. eBay, Amazon) or the web host (Shopify, Squarespace, Blogger) by sending a DMCA (Digital Millennium Copyright Act) takedown letter (for US-based platforms). The DMCA is an anti-piracy act protecting digital content and online items that legally requires a web hosting service to take down listings on their platform that violate copyright.

All of the large US-based platforms have a letter you can fill out, sign, and send, and there are generic "notices of infringement" you can modify and send to smaller platforms like the blog IPWatchdog.

Most other countries have similar copyright protection laws that you can point to for backup when demanding a take down if the copycat is selling on a non-US platform—"Notice and Notice" in Canada and the EUCD in Europe.

Help! I Have a Great Product, but I'm Not Getting Any Sales

I know that a lot of the last section was pretty technical with a pinch of legalese sprinkled in. Now, it's time to talk about some of the more common issues you may run into as an Etsy seller.

What happens when you've just launched your Etsy store or have had it up for a few months, but you're not getting many (or any) sales? Frustration and discouragement, and sometimes a feeling of personal betrayal. Are you doing something wrong? Doesn't anyone want the products you made with such love and care? What is *going on*?

Stage 1 Self Shop Audit: Product and Shop Quality

Before you throw the baby out with the bathwater, perform a quick audit of your Etsy shop by checking the following things.

Have you done your due diligence in making sure you have a healthy Etsy shop (e.g., the information in the previous six chapters)? Specifically your keywords and listings, the heart of your Etsy shop? If you rushed through setup and threw some listings together without doing much research or work on the backend, it's time to spend some serious hours getting your shop in shape.

Do you have a winning product? Are there other sellers on Etsy selling what you sell? Type the name of your product into the Etsy search bar and see how many shops come up. Click on one of these shops—does it have any sales? (The number of sales is listed under the Shop Name.) Scroll down—does the shop have any reviews? Are they good reviews? If other people are selling similar products to yours with good success, chances are that you have missed (or rushed through) some of the steps required to lay a solid foundation for your shop.

If there really aren't any other shops selling what you sell or the shops selling these items have very few sales and reviews, there may simply be no market (at least on Etsy) for what you're selling. Your product may sell better in person at a craft bazaar or in a boutique, or on another platform like Amazon or a quirky online shop with a very tight niche. Or, maybe, it's time to try selling something else entirely.

Again, if you find that similar products are indeed selling well in other Etsy shops, you'll need to take a hard look at your listings and your shop. You may even want to ask someone else (a friend or family member who can be honest with you) to take a look at your shop and give feedback. Consider these questions in particular: (1) Are your thumbnail images high quality and eye-catching? (2) Do your titles and descriptions describe what you're selling? (3) Is your shop professional looking and consistent in theme and tone? (4) Are you using all 13 tags?

If you find your shop lacking in some or all of these key elements, you've likely identified the reason for your lack of sales. Carefully read (and implement) Chapter 1 on Etsy shops and Chapter 2 on listings, and employ the tips and tricks there. Low-quality images, haphazard organization and design, and incomplete listings are some of the most common causes for low and non-existent sales on Etsy.

Stage 2 Self Shop Audit: Do You Need to Market More?

Okay, so you have a great product, beautiful images, well-written titles and descriptions, a cohesive and well-organized shop, and you're using all 13 tags, and you're still not seeing the sales roll in. It's probably time to take a look at your Etsy SEO (search engine optimization).

Take a look at your Etsy stats (right inside your Etsy dashboard). Are your listings being found and displayed by Etsy's search algorithm? For which keywords and phrases are they being found? Do these actually describe your item? If your listings aren't getting any views or are showing up for the wrong keywords, you may want to consider getting a monthly subscription with either eRank or Marmalead. These sites will help you identify keywords and phrases that both describe your product and get lots of queries from customers on Etsy. Even a month with one of these services can improve your sales drastically. If this sounds like an area you need to work on, check out Chapter 2 in the subsection about Titles for a lot more info on Etsy SEO.

If you've beefed up your Etsy SEO, have your listings and shop in order, and are still not getting the sales you want, it probably means you're just not getting enough eyeballs on your product. It might be time to invest some serious time, energy, and (perhaps) money into marketing and ads. There are also a few tricks you can employ to increase the number of eyes on your products, but none of these can make up for a half-baked or nonexistent marketing campaign. We'll talk all about marketing in Section 2 of this book (particularly Chapters 10-13).

You might be thinking, isn't marketing for big corporations with loads of cash? Not at all. And like I said, we're going to cover ALL the good stuff about ads and marketing opportunities very shortly. But for now, here's your first step: Join a few relevant Etsy Teams (Google that—it's pretty easy to find). Etsy Teams allow you to collaborate with and learn from other similar sellers on Etsy. These sellers can share tips and tricks about how to sell your specific product on Etsy as well as the best channels for marketing that they've found to increase sales. Once you've found the marketing channels that work best for sellers like you, try them out—there are a number of free advertising channels available like social platforms (Chapter 13) and email marketing (Chapter 11). Etsy also allows you to advertise within their platform (Chapter 12) and create sales and coupon codes to entice buyers (Chapter 10). Try things one chapter at a time, do what you can with the time and money you have, and watch your sales tick up. You've got this. Really.

Duplicate Listing Trick

If you want a quick way to increase your listing impressions (views), you can list a single product multiple times using different keywords. This helps your listings appear for several different search results. This obviously only works if you plan to sell more than one of that particular item (I don't recommend you duplicate a listing for an original piece of art unless you're going to watch all those listings like a hawk to ensure you don't sell two at once). But, assuming you have many of the same product or create products on demand, you can copy the listings for that item and use a new title and new keywords (or simply a rearranged title and different variations of your original keywords) to target different search terms and potentially different customers.

This trick is best used by new sellers since it can help you figure out which keywords perform best for different products. And it can give you some initial sales if you've been in a slump. Because duplicating at least a few listings sends a lot of positive signals to Etsy's algorithm that can help a new shop get off the ground.

However, be careful using this trick long term, when you're established as a seller. In fact, as your shop starts to grow I would avoid the practice entirely.

For one thing, if your shop is made up of a bunch of listings that are all virtually the same, anyone who actually visits your shop (instead of purchasing your listing straight from Etsy's search results page) is going to be pretty unimpressed by dozens of duplicated listings within each of your shop sections. And more and more these days, people click into Etsy shops to see what else the seller sells. You don't want to shoot your store in the foot by focusing too much on your individual listing's search result ranking.

A second downside to the duplicate listing trick is that there's a very real possibility that customers may see two of your identical listings side-by-side in the search results. Again, this looks tacky and can be confusing for buyers. This wasn't always the case. Etsy used to limit results from an individual shop to a single listing per results page. This is why older Etsy coaches often encourage the practice of duplicating listings as pretty much foolproof. But, nowadays, you need to be a little more careful.

Re-Listing Items

Again, if you're a new seller having trouble getting your listings to show up in search results, re-listing your items regularly can give you a slight edge. Re-listing is the practice of renewing a listing before it has expired (and paying another listing fee). This works because Etsy's search algorithm gives a nontrivial rank boost to new listings for the first few hours after they're listed.

If you think your listing is sending negative signals to Etsy's algorithms (e.g., you chose poor keywords to start out with), you can also do the following: duplicate your listing, then delete the original and start fresh with the new listing. That way, if your listing has inadvertently been sending negative signals to Etsy's algorithm that decrease its rank (e.g., if it's got a low conversion rate—which is pretty common for new listings in new shops), starting the item afresh with a new listing wipes out any "points" it has against it and gives it a new shot at ranking higher in search.

Ideally, you won't want to be re-listing items regularly forever. It can get expensive at $0.20 each time, and re-listing too often also prevents Etsy's algorithm from identifying what your item is and who best to display it to. As a new Etsy seller, you may feel that you would do a much better job than the algorithm at connecting your product with customers who want to buy it. After all, you know your product and your customers and Etsy clearly doesn't, at least at the beginning. But, part of selling through Etsy is trusting that the search algorithm will eventually figure it out and do a better job connecting you to customers than you could. And I promise it will—the algorithm can change much easier than our human minds can. It "learns" about your product over the life of a listing from an increasingly complicated web of signals that no person alone could navigate. And if you let Etsy's algorithm do its thing, you'll eventually find that it's connecting your product to customers you never would have found on your own (like people across the world!).

So, go ahead and use the re-listing trick, but be careful of overusing it. Etsy search is getting better and better, and your shop will succeed in the long-run not by tricking the algorithm, but by using it to its full potential.

Help! My Sales Just Dropped!

It's so frustrating to see some success in your Etsy shop, sure you're doing everything right, and then watch your sales suddenly plummet. If this happens, don't panic. It's normal for sales to go up and down week to week and season to season.

Here's some of the reasons you might see a drop (and what you can do about it).

Trends

One reason for dips in sales is "trends." Etsy's obsession with "trends" or "seasonality" means that its algorithm boosts listings based on when it believes the item will be most popular. Even for items that aren't seasonal, Etsy attaches a "season" (a number of weeks or months) to each listing, and when that season ends, the algorithm will suppress the listing in order to boost other products. The "season" can be a holiday like "Christmas," an event like "Wedding," or it can simply be the time period during which the item sold well the previous year. For example, certain rings and jewelry often get a boost in the late spring/early summer during what Etsy considers to be "wedding season." If you're interested in finding out what season your product most likely falls into, you can check out Etsy's yearly Trend Report (Google Etsy's Trend Report for the current year).

Etsy has Changed Something

Another reason for a drop in sales is that Etsy has updated their platform, which it does A LOT. Recently, Etsy changed the way sellers could advertise within Etsy, and the vast majority of sellers (I hesitate to say *all*, though I suspect it was all sellers) saw a drastic drop in how much money they were making through Etsy Ads (formerly Etsy Promoted Listings).

Etsy is also constantly updating its search algorithm to make the AI better. It's worth spending some time on the Etsy Forums and Etsy's blog watching for updates like these. For example, early in 2020, Etsy updated its search to recognize most pluralizations and many common misspellings. This meant that we could get rid of the "T-shirts" tag since we already had "T-shirt" and use that tag for another relevant keyword. Small changes like this may not impact your listings much in the moment, but if you miss a number of them in a row, you may find that your views and sales are dropping because your tags or titles are outdated.

It's wise to check regularly for algorithm changes. Someday, Etsy's algorithm might start looking at your descriptions for relevant keywords. Or it may stop rewarding keyword stuffing in titles. These would be BIG reforms that would rearrange the entire landscape of search results overnight. Etsy isn't doing this to make your life difficult. In fact, algorithm changes are supposed to make selling on Etsy easier for both sellers and buyers. The trick is to stay on top of the reforms and change with the times.

You're Not Engaging with Your Shop Often Enough

When your Etsy shop is doing well, you might be tempted to ignore it and let it chug along, bringing in sales for the products you already have listed. The problem is that Etsy's algorithm rewards shops with sellers who are highly engaged, and when it notices that it's been weeks since you added a new listing, made a change to your shop, or improved an old listing, it will punish your listings by not displaying them as often or as high up in search results.

This reality is extremely irritating, especially since Etsy is considered a platform for hobby crafters and creators who don't necessarily want their shop to be an everyday, full-time job. The trick, though, is that you don't need to make major changes everyday to look like an engaged seller to Etsy's algorithm. You simply need to change *something* every few days or so. This can be as simple as updating your shop announcement once a week and swapping out a few keywords on a listing twice during the same week. If you've created a bunch of new products, stagger your listing uploads—add one Monday and the next one on Wednesday, then Friday—instead of putting them all up at once.

The more often you make even a small change to your Etsy shop, the more positive signals get sent to Etsy about your shop, which means each listing will rank better in search results. And the better your products are ranking, the more people will see them and buy them.

Help! My Account Was Suspended or Limited

Unfortunately, Etsy account suspensions do happen. Etsy has a reputation to uphold, and it protects its marketplace by closing or limiting shops that are breaking the rules or treating customers poorly. You can read about the differences between limited and suspended accounts and reasons this can happen in Etsy's help section "My Account has Been Suspended."

Odds are, however, sellers whose shops get limited or suspended have known there was a problem for a while. A member of Etsy's Trust and Safety Team will have emailed them alerting them to the problem (or usually pattern of problems) and tried to work with them to correct it. Contrary to the internet rumors, Etsy doesn't use automation to actually suspend accounts—their automation helps them recognize red flags, but an actual human reviews the flags and decides what course to pursue (you can read Etsy's official statement on Etsy's site.)

The most common reasons for account suspension are policy violations (a seller is selling stuff prohibited by Etsy) and truly terrible customer service (not fulfilling orders on time or at all; sending low-quality, broken or the wrong items to customers; discriminating against or disparaging customers, that kind of thing).

Make sure you've read "Etsy's House Rules" for sellers. And make sure your shipping timeframes are accurate. You'd be surprised at how often shops become "at risk for suspension" because their shipping times are too short and their orders get flagged by Etsy as "overdue" one too many times. Etsy also has options for sellers going through periods of hardship and can't continue filling orders for some reason. Sellers always have the option to pause their shop by placing it in "Vacation Mode." I'll talk more about this below, but vacation mode often means that a seller will have to start all over building up their shop when they unpause, even if the vacation was only for a week or two. But using vacation mode when you're struggling is way better than not fulfilling orders and risking Etsy closing your shop entirely.

If, after everything, you do find yourself in a situation where your account has been suspended, you can appeal. Etsy generally treats its sellers quite well and will give most sellers a second chance if they show they can fix the problem and abide by Etsy's rules.

Potential Pitfall: Shop Vacation Mode

One question that more Etsy shop owners SHOULD be asking (but often don't, they just do it) is whether they should be using "vacation mode" for their shop. Most sellers think "Oh, yep. I need a break. Vacation mode, activate!" without much thought for the consequences.

So here's the skinny:

Vacation Mode seems like such a wonderful option for those of us who are burned out and need a break from our shops, but unfortunately, vacation mode seems to send negative signals to Etsy's algorithm. The vast majority of sellers who pause their shops see sharp drops in sales and often feel like they're starting over trying to get their products recognized by Etsy search.

I mention this not necessarily to deter you from ever taking a vacation. Please, take time off when you need it! No one wants to be tied to their Etsy shop 24/7, 365 days a year. But if you do decide to take an extended leave of absence from your shop, know that it may take some time to work back up to the sales you were getting before the pause.

One option I've used (successfully) to both take a vacation and keep my shop open is to temporarily lengthen my shipping times. Instead of 6-10 business days, I changed my shipping temporarily to 2-3 weeks. I explained the change in my shop announcement (and told my customers that I was going to Thailand for two weeks so they'd understand) and put a large note at the top of each listing description about the slower shipping times. It meant that I could go enjoy my vacation and come back to plenty of orders without needing to put my shop on pause.

Help! I Need More Variations Options

So far, this chapter has been kind of heavy. I've given you the low-down about the scary problems you might run into as an Etsy seller like copyright infringement and account suspension. But sometimes, you just need advice on how to work around the limits of Etsy's seller platform. And one of the most common questions I see in this category is how to navigate variations when you need more than the two Etsy gives you.

Combine two options into one custom variation

Say you're selling helix earring studs. You offer three colors—gold, silver, and rose gold—and two different closure options—ball and labret—as well as four options for bar length—4mm, 6mm, 8mm, and 10mm. Since the *front* of the earring is the same, it makes a lot of sense to have one listing with all three variations as options for customers. But, of course, Etsy only allows you two.

What you can do in this case is offer a "Color" variation and combine the other two options into one custom variation called "Bar style + Length." You'd list the options in the second variation as "Ball end 4mm, Ball end 6mm, Ball end 8mm, Ball end 10mm, Labret 4mm, Labret 6mm…." You get the idea.

This also works for matching sets where you want to offer color and size options for each item in the set—mother/daughter tees, his and hers rings, that kind of thing.

Check a Box to Offer Different Prices or Quantities for Your Options

Say you sell glicée posters and want to list each size at a different price. In this case, you'll only need one variation, "Size," with the box next to "prices vary with each size" checked. Once you save and exit the variations pop-up, Etsy will allow you to fill in a custom price for each option. This is true for quantity as well. Say, you've made six pink baby blankets but only five blue. Check the box that says, "quantities vary," and Etsy will give you the option to set quantities for each option in your variation.

You can take these boxes even further if you need to also. For example, say you sell posters and want to offer different sizes and different finishes (gloss, matte, etc.) at different prices. If you click "prices vary" for BOTH of your variations, "Size" and "Finish," you'll be able to set different prices for each combination of variations—in other words, you'd be able to offer your "8x10 in gloss" option for $15 and your "8x10 in matte" for $17 and so on for the other size/finish option combos.

I won't give a million more examples because I think you get the idea. Play around with your variations and those "price" and "quantity" checkboxes until you find the ideal options for whatever you sell.

Use the Personalization Box

If you find that you need one more variation or your variation needs a bit more explanation than just "size" or "color," you can use the *personalization box.* Technically, this box was created for monogrammed items and custom orders and stuff like that, but you can use it creatively—for example, to simplify variations that have become unwieldy. I've used it when selling face masks—in addition to choosing "size" and "color" options, my customers could "personalize" their masks by letting me know if they wanted ribbon or elastic and if they wanted nose wire or not.

TIP: Make sure you keep variations the same across all similar listings, especially as your shop grows. It can get really hard to buy materials for a lot of orders if your options aren't consistent. I learned this the hard way. When I was ordering supplies for 10 on-demand orders a week, it was pretty easy to remember that "charcoal" and "dark gray" were the same color shirt, but as I scaled up, the discrepancies made ordering a nightmare. So, either use Etsy's standard variation options or, if you create your own, keep them consistent as you create additional listings.

Using Etsy's variations creatively allows you to sell lots of product through a single listing. It makes your store cleaner and easier to navigate, and it saves you money! Every four months, when Etsy automatically renews your listing whether it's selling or not, that's $.20 saved for each variation you might have listed separately had you not known how to use variations.

99 Problems But Etsy Ain't One of Them

The good news is that most of the time, Etsy works really well. Bugs are usually manageable, and the more Etsy grows, the bigger its capacity will be for addressing issues quickly. Don't forget you have a whole army of other Etsy sellers on your side, who are going through the same things you are and thinking of creative solutions. So don't despair if you run into a roadblock. There's a solution to be found.

When it comes to troubleshooting as an Etsy seller, creative solutions are key. Instead of becoming daunted by the problems that arise, try to see them as an opportunity for growth. You got this.

SECTION 2: GROWING YOUR SHOP

How to Drive Growth: AKA, Marketing

Take a few minutes to celebrate. When you implement the strategies you've learned in the first section of this book you're laying a solid foundation for your shop that will pave the way for long-term success and sustainable growth.

In Section 2, we'll be revving up your shop with strategies for growth, more eyeballs, more shop visits, more positive signals to Etsy's algorithm, and more SALES. We'll start with a discussion on branding, then move into strategies you can use within (and beyond) Etsy to grow your shop.

CHAPTER 8

Branding

Branding encompasses a LOT. At it's very simplest definition, it's what sets YOU apart from THEM (your competition). Think about the concept of branding cattle: It creates a definitive mark of ownership and recognition. Branding helps your customers recognize you through visible signals (your name, logo, etc.) and associate your product with your company.

Branding is the culmination of your design, your writing style, your photos, the type of product you sell, the ads you run, and the way you position your business to buyers. For this chapter, we're going to focus on some specific, actionable elements of branding that layer on the foundation we've been building. Just know that we'll cover in depth additional key elements of branding (including design, copy, and advertising!) later in this section. So read up, and let's dig into some of the key aspects of branding your business!

Evaluating Your Business Name

I know we talked about your Shop Name right at the beginning of this book (because you need one to get started). But armed with a more global understanding of your shop's components, it's now time for a more in-depth discussion of how your Shop Name (and other components that we'll talk about in this chapter) speak to your customers and impact their buying choices.

Your business name is a highly visible piece of branding that sends signals to your customer (or fails to send signals) about what you make, who you are as a person, and what sort of shop you're running. Many Etsy owners rush through this process, and that's okay. What's important is taking the time to make sure you do it right sooner than later (like when you read this book).

A lot of people are surprised by how long it takes to come up with a good business name. Why? Because for one thing, in the internet era, it's not an easy feat to come up with a name that isn't A) Taken by another business in your state, B) has an available URL with a .com address, C) Sounds really good and coveys what you do, and D) Isn't spelled in a weird way.

Spend some time spitballing (anything goes!) business names with your friends and family. Create a Google doc or spreadsheet where you can workshop the sound of different names and verify that a .com URL is available (for your Pattern site, or simply to snag in case you decide to branch out onto a standalone site at any point). Here's some of the important things you should consider as you name your business.

By the way, if you gave your business a horrendous (or not particularly effective) name in the early days and want to change it, that's okay! It's better to print new business cards and buy a new domain than to have a confusing or strange-sounding business name.

Create the right feeling: Words are important. Some words evoke a feeling of prim and proper society, while others are humorous or potentially vulgar. Some words carry more weight than others. Make sure that the words you choose to combine for your business name create the right feeling FOR YOUR AUDIENCE (it doesn't matter what your Aunt Gayle thinks unless she's in your target audience). Do you have a bunch of hipster liberals who buy your stuff? Don't choose a name that sounds corporate or overly conservative. Don't try to get cutesy. Know your audience, and name your business accordingly.

- **Choose a name with an available URL** in case you want to create a Pattern shop or another ecommerce shop in the future (you may at some point be glad you gave yourself the option).

- **Identify the three most important verbs, nouns, and adjectives related to your business.** The actual product you produce, for instance. Where you're located. The key material or fabric you rely on. The generic name of the product you sell (e.g., t-shirts). Then consult a thesaurus for synonyms (don't get too weird). Use these core words as a starting point and a springboard for naming your business.

- **Keep it simple, schnookums.** People don't remember long names. Long names are a pain to fit on business cards and branding materials. Don't do it. You want people to remember you, and you don't want to cause yourself headaches down the line. Keep your name short and easy to spell. And make SURE you don't create an unfortunate acronym like Penny's Emu Eggs (PEE).

- **Don't limit yourself too much.** The goal is to choose a name that's specific enough that people aren't confused, while choosing one that allows you to expand and evolve without confusing people, e.g., if you name your business "Meg's Mug Emporium" and then expand into selling tote bags, you might regret your name choice.

- **Be unique, not weird.** Your name should be unique and recognizable (after all, you want to stand out from the crowd). If you use too many generic words, your customers might have a hard time telling you apart from the competition. But if you get too wacky, you're going to confuse people and run into spelling problems. Try not to use trendy language and phrases that may not be relevant (or smiled upon) in a year's time.

- **Use geographical names with caution:** People sometimes get turned off by geographical names when you run an online shop (like Etsy) and market to folks around the world. Some may think you primarily service a local demographic and scroll past you. Others may have a reaction or stereotype about your geographic area. I'd recommend you steer clear of including geography in your business name unless you are SURE you are selling to a local audience.

Taglines/Slogans

You should have a tagline for your business. An elevator pitch, if you will, to quickly relay information to your customer in a way that expands on your Shop Name and vibe you're trying to create.

A tagline or slogan is often included on a business card or "about" sections in social media, Etsy, and anywhere else your business is highlighted. It expounds on your business name and helps your buyers understand what you're all about. For example, Bounty's tagline is "The quicker picker-upper." One of my favorite taglines for my t-shirts (that helps convey the idea of activism, through wearable art) is "Put on your power."

Here are some tips for creating a killer tagline or slogan. This tagline or slogan can evolve or change over time (just think of the different commercials you hear or ads you see). Slogans and taglines should be re-evaluated as needed, or as the times change.

- Hone in on the most important benefit that sets you apart from the competition or adds value to your customers' lives. Your tagline should revolve around this benefit.

- Keep it short and snappy. Your tagline can be several words and doesn't have to be a full sentence. The shorter the tagline, the more memorable it's likely to be. Five to eight words is generally considered to be the sweet spot. If you can get it done in fewer, awesome! But try not to go much longer.

- Give it some rhythm or even rhyme when possible. Think of your slogan or tagline as a form of poetry. It should be a compact, memorable little package of meaning that communicates, "Oh THAT'S what this business is all about."

Like your business name, it's going to take some time to find that perfect tagline. Stay with it, and brainstorm away!

Labels, Tags, and Packaging

Tags (the paper kind), labels, and packaging not only provide a place for barcode or price information (if you're at a farmer's market or you're selling your items wholesale), but they give you an opportunity to help create an association with your brand.

We'll cover the logistical ins and outs of packaging and labeling (like where to source your materials so you don't cut into your profits too much while still delivering a delightful experience for your customer) in Chapters 17-18. For now, let's talk about branding opportunities that these elements offer to connect with your customer and create a strong and cohesive message and vibe.

- **Tags:** Don't waste the opportunity to connect with your customer, create a positive association with your brand, or add value with tags. Think of tags as a business card you're attaching to your items. The tag should visually match the style of your website and online presence, and should resonate with your customers in terms of font style, any graphics, and overall aesthetic. Make sure you include your website, logo, and business name so that if the item is purchased or given as a gift they'll know exactly where it came from.

- **Labels and packaging:** Labels and packaging are often a missed opportunity to make your customer smile and strengthen brand association as well. Instead of using solid colored packaging or simple gray and brown poly mailers, I use decorated mailers with donuts, unicorns, or flamingos. It makes my packages look different from everything else in the mail, and the fun, stand-out packaging is right in line with the brand image I want to project. Other options to dress up your packaging and labels might include stamps (You can purchase personalized stamps on Etsy or Amazon) that speak directly to your customers. E.g., "Hey, you beautiful human being! Have a great day!" Or a sticker (you can buy bulk, personalized stickers quite cheaply. Basically, give your customer a reason to think, "Wow, this was made just for me," while making a connection with your logo, brand name, and website.

Branding with a Good Logo

Your logo is an important mix of text and design that's meant to be totally unique from any other business. You should have several iterations of your logo that include your initials, your full business name, or both combined to use in different situations. For example, your full logo should be used as your profile picture on Etsy and social media channels to help customers immediately recognize your brand when someone searches for you online.

Here are the most important principles of a good logo:

- If you haven't read the chapter on design, go back to that first. A good logo is a well-designed logo. (Check out Chapter 4).

- Remember, a good business logo reflects your business well: It's an ambassador of your company that reflects your style, level of professionalism, and attunement to your audience.

- Use color carefully (again, read that chapter on design!). Use your colors to communicate strategically rather than haphazardly.

- Use fonts carefully. Don't choose a "cool font." Fonts communicate LOADS and can hurt your business or help it. Choose a font that embodies the personality qualities you want to communicate. Whether that's sleek and professional or earthy and casual. Choosing the wrong font will confuse and annoy people, even if it looks cool to you.

- Keep it SIMPLE. Too many fonts, too many colors, too much information does not a good logo make. Be prepared to pare down your first attempts. Simple, clean designs also help encourage brand recognition and associations. A complicated mess doesn't make much of an impression.

- Create a black-and-white or monochrome option. Sometimes you won't have the option for a full-color design on different platforms.

- Make sure your logo looks good, small or large. People will be looking at it teeny tiny on their phones, or blown up on a sign at a farmer's market. Give yourself room to be versatile.

- Don't try to go it alone, especially if you're new at design. Logos are very important and will stay with your company for a long time. Consider sticking very closely to a pre-designed Canva template or hiring someone on Fiverr.com (or Etsy!) to create the logo for you. It will only set you back between $50 to $100 for a decent logo.

Business Cards

Once you've got a solid name, tagline, and logo (in terms of colors, style, and the audience you're speaking to), creating a business card is simply a matter of combining those elements.

Keep your business card simple (are you sensing a theme here?). Include your logo, your contact info (at least your email and website, possibly your phone number and business address if you want to give it out). I tend NOT to include a physical address on my business cards because as a small shop, that address changes somewhat frequently, and I don't want to get new business cards when it does.

Many places that offer business cards for a good price in bulk (like Vista Print) have a variety of templates you can use to create some. Simply plop in your logo and information into the creation wizard. Just be sure to use templates that match your branding style.

TIP: You don't need to go full-foil design, with raised embossing on your business card. Those bells and whistles can be cool, but they aren't necessary. But DON'T choose a super thin paper weight. You want your business card to feel substantial, not flimsy. A flimsy business card is the number one way to communicate "amateur."

TIP: Keep a small pile of business cards in SEVERAL places. Your car, your studio, your house, your purse, your wallet, etc. Inevitably, people will ask for one in the most unexpected places!

Stuff We Learned the Hard Way

The thing about branding is that mistakes typically create missed opportunities instead of outright and obvious disasters. If you have bad branding (or some aspects of bad branding), you won't even realize that certain opportunities are passing you by.

You'll only know it later—when you take a hard look at your branding—and see those types of opportunities start to trickle in. How do I know this? Because that's exactly what happened to me! When you're new at owning a business, just starting out, and trying to wrangle Etsy and a side hustle, branding often falls through the cracks as a "nice but not necessary" afterthought. Unfortunately, it's the first impression your business delivers to the world. How cohesive and professional you appear is how professional and legit people will think you ARE. If I could go back in time, I would make the time to get my branding message and my appearance aligned.

The good news? You're one step ahead of where I was when I had just started out: You're reading this! Don't let branding be an afterthought. Spend the time to get it right and really nail it. You'll never regret that decision.

CHAPTER 9

Content and Copywriting

SQUEE As editors in our past lives, we LOVE talking about writing and how it can help you grow your shop and make more sales.

"Writing?" you ask skeptically. "I don't have a blog. I have an Etsy shop."

Yes you do! Most people who own Etsy shops are surprised when they hear that they are copywriters. Sounds fancy, right? They don't necessarily consider the work they're doing in writing listing descriptions or posting on Instagram to be "copy." By the way, you'll hear us use the words "copy" and "copywriting" throughout the book to refer to all kinds of writing—whether a tiny bit of text on a social media ad, or the description in your shop's About Section.

Taking your copy seriously is one way to boost your sales, your shop credibility, and better connect with your audience. In this chapter, we'll talk about why, and where content matters the most.

Why Good Content Matters

We've already talked about how much good visuals matter. The photos and images your customers and potential customers see are the visual hooks that bring customers into your shop. So, what about good content? Good content pulls it all together, answers your customers' questions BEFORE they have to contact you (most won't and will just go elsewhere), signals Etsy's search algorithm, and seals the deal on sales.

Customers Care What You Have to Say

More than once as a customer, I've clicked on a beautiful photo or listing in Etsy, only to then delve into the listing description and wrinkle my nose. There's not much information. The information feels hastily put together. The information is contradictory or obnoxious or very vague. The information isn't well-written or has lots of spelling or grammatical errors. I click out of that listing. I bounce. And your customers will do the same thing in many cases.

The way you present yourself in your shop is your chance to speak directly to your customers. To show that you've anticipated their questions, their needs, and their potential concerns. To show that you KNOW them. That this listing was MADE FOR THEM. Good copy does that. Bad copy does the opposite.

Search Engines Care What Your Customers Think— and Use Copy to Get to Know Your Shop

If your customers are bouncing because of bad copy, what kind of signals does that send to Etsy's algorithm? We all know the answer. Bad ones. So even if Etsy isn't cataloguing and combing through every single word you write in your listing descriptions, many customers ARE. And if they signal Etsy that they aren't really interested in what you have to sell (through leaving your shop to purchase another item, or quickly disengaging from your shop), Etsy's algorithm will take note.

And then there's the fact that Google and Etsy DO use your copy to categorize your shop in search results. Some sections are weighted more heavily than others (Etsy cares a LOT about your titles as you now know) but your descriptions, About Section, and shop updates matter too—especially to Google. And if you can start ranking in Etsy AND Google, that's extra traffic straight to your shop.

Remember, as an online shop, you are relying on Etsy and Google search (among others) to connect your products to the customers that want to buy them. Bad copy equals poor rankings in search results or your listings being displayed for the wrong searches (this is the WORST). And both will cause your sales to suffer.

So, how do you write descriptions and other copy that both Google and Etsy are going to be like, "Oh hey this shop is speaking my language"? The short answer is, you should write copy with your customers in mind first and the algorithm in mind second. Because while Etsy's algorithm doesn't weigh your descriptions very heavily in terms of KEYWORDS, they do care about how your customers react to your listings. And Google (which honestly has a more advanced algorithm than Etsy) is more finely attuned to keyword stuffing and highly values natural, easy-to-read descriptions that customers appreciate. So, your CUSTOMER is the person you need to speak to before anyone else. Here's what you should know about writing descriptions that speak to your potential customers (on Etsy and Google) and how to make sure you're being strategic about it:

- The first 150 characters of your Etsy description is where you want to strategically speak to Google's algorithm (and your Etsy customers). And the first 40 characters of that 150 characters are even more important. You don't need to keep your description this brief, but this is the part of your description that's going to send the strongest signals to Google.

- Now, contrary to what you're doing in your titles, keywords should NOT be your main focus in your description when you write it. Because for one thing, Etsy doesn't weigh it as very important (while google does). And for the next, it's hard to write a really compelling description when you're trying to retrofit in keywords. So don't think about keywords while you write. The first thing I want you to do is just write the best damn description you can. As concisely as possible. Telling your potential customer what your product is, why it's so amazing, and why it's just what they're looking for.

- AFTER you are certain that you have crafted a description that is purely beneficial for your customer and makes your product sound as compelling as possible (with the most critically compelling info first), then go through and look for keyword opportunities. CAREFULLY. Just because you can squeeze in a keyword to your copy doesn't mean you should. Use your best keywords, and massage your copy until it reads naturally.

Writing copy that's both precise enough for a search engine and interesting enough for a customer can sometimes feel like a tug-of-war. Is it even possible to speak to both audiences at once? It is, trust me (although it's not always easy). The key is really understanding your product and your target customer—not only what she's searching for but why she *needs* what you're selling. A keyword phrase like "heart-shaped bath bombs with rose hips" is perfect for a search engine, but if you add "for Mom" at the end, suddenly, you've connected with a customer looking for the perfect Mother's Day gift.

Where Copy Counts the Most (and Least)

So, where does your copy really need to shine? The short answer is "everywhere," but the realistic answer is these places. These are the places that customers care a lot about. And these are the places that Google and Etsy care about the most as well (not coincidentally):

- Your shop politics and FAQs
- Your listing descriptions
- Your social media captions
- Any copy you overlay on a photo or graphic on social or listings
- Any blog posts or guest articles you write that will be publicly seen
- Your shop announcements and bios
- Email copy

Where is it okay to loosen up and not obsessively check for grammatical errors and partial sentences?

- Listing titles (people expect these to be fragmented. You see it everywhere as a result of Etsy SEO)
- Private convos with customers or potential customers
- Comments on social media, responding to customers

Basically, most things that are public facing need to be scrutinized and carefully written. The more public, important, and visible something is, the more carefully you need to write it. The more people that are going to see something, the more carefully you need to write it. That especially applies to evergreen content as well (e.g., content that you're going to use over and over, ad finitum like parts of your listing descriptions).

Best Practices in Creating Content for Your Etsy Shop

The best practices for creating content in your Etsy shop aren't revolutionary. These rules apply to good content across the board, in a variety of different outlets and applications. But we could all use a refresher. If you're totally new to writing—or haven't written much of anything since high school—I'd recommend that you read a couple of books to drive home the principles of good content. These books aren't long, but they ARE really helpful if you feel out of your depth right now.

- Read these books:

    ○ *The Fortune Cookie Principle,* by Bernadette Jiwa.

    ○ *Start with Why,* by Simon Sinek (this book applies to SO much more than copy, but it's INCREDIBLY helpful in writing!)

    ○ *On Writing Well,* by William Zinsser

You might notice that the list I'm about to relay seems strangely similar to the "good principles of design" list we ticked off earlier. And that's not by accident. Whether visually or in writing, your goal is good communication with your buyers:

- Know your audience, and work to anticipate how different words and registers will affect them:

    ○ The register you use is a matter of how formally or informally you speak. If you're selling high-end items to a very posh audience, a high register might make sense and appeal to your audience. If you're selling fun kids' paraphernalia, it might backfire.

    ○ The words you use change the meaning of what you're communicating to your audience dramatically. We're all pretty good at picking up on subtle verbal cues (even written verbal cues) through syntax (the way we put sentences together) and vocabulary. Be yourself, but be wary of using words and phrases that carry a lot of weight or might unconsciously bother your audience.

- Keep it simple. Run-on sentences and overly wordy descriptions only serve to annoy and frustrate customers who have to sort through a lot of text and throwaway phrases to get the information they need. Break up information using bullet points, short sentences, and paragraphs. For reference, 23 words is about the max you should strive for per sentence. Otherwise, readability goes down!

- Be consistent. Don't go California Valley Girl in one social media post, and erudite back-east professor in another. We all have lots of aspects to our personality, and most of us can shape-shift to communicate in different ways when the situation arises. But you want to cultivate a dependable, consistent persona as a business. Which means using a consistent, dependable tone of voice when you write across different platforms.

- Be yourself. It's hard to consistently keep up a pretense. Embrace who you are, because chances are that your Etsy shop is an outgrowth of who you are. Identify which aspects of your voice and personality resonate most with your audience, and really lean into them.

- Stay focused. Identify the purpose of a given piece of content whether that's a listing or a blog post. What is it that you want to communicate? To whom? What do you want them to do or feel after reading this? And make sure your finished piece of content is an outgrowth of that focused goal.

- Practice! Writing can be intimidating for some people. Don't let that stop you. Practice makes perfect, and it will become easier over time. Lean on Etsy groups, colleagues, spouses, or friends for feedback when it comes to important pieces of copy.

- Be honest and transparent. It can be easy to try to make your product sound better or bigger or fancier or more WHATEVER than it is. Try to be clear and transparent about what you're selling, who you are, how it's made, etc.

- Don't be afraid to be real. This might sound like a contradiction after I just told you to make sure you're speaking to your audience in a way that resonates with THEM. But often the best way to do that is to speak from the heart, talk like a real person (instead of a robot or a corporation) and bring in emotion (humor, joy, excitement) whenever appropriate. Remember, your audience is on Etsy in large part because they want to buy from a real live person, not a bot on Amazon. Lean into your realness and uniqueness.

- Keep content current. Don't forget about it if you include information about Christmas, Halloween, or another major event in your listing descriptions. Customers reading that months later aren't going to be impressed.

Should You Have a Blog?

The decision of whether or not you should have a blog comes down to cost-benefit analysis. For some people, a blog can be a great tool to speak to customers. For others, it ends up being a drain on your time that can be better spent elsewhere. Let's look at pros and cons:

Pros of Maintaining a Blog

A blog can benefit your business in a couple of different ways. Here's the main benefits:

- **If you create good content, other people will link to and share your content**. Linking to your content gives Google good signals that you are a credible source of information (as long as the entity who is linking to your site is credible as well!). Each time someone links to your blog (especially if they're considered a higher-quality website, e.g., they have a higher "domain authority") your ranking score in Google goes up.

  HOWEVER, this is only true if your blog is part of your Pattern site, e.g., if you just create a Wordpress blog alongside a standard Etsy shop, it might get you eyeballs on your shop (if you link to it), but it won't increase your Google score/domain authority since it isn't directly attached to your domain.

  So, if you're trying to improve your domain authority through your content (which can help you rank higher in Google search results), create a Pattern site first and then a blog as part of that.

- **A blog can be a great way to humanize yourself to your audience** (always a good thing with Etsy!) and share longer-form content to your email list (via a link to your blog post) that adds lots of value to your emails. It can help balance overly "sales-y" emails with actual value.

- **A blog can help establish your name and authority on different subjects** (including being a business owner and a maker!) which can lead to different opportunities. It can make you more findable by journalists, other business owners, and people looking for quotes or articles from experts for their articles and workshops.

Cons of Maintaining a Blog

Okay, so those are the potential advantages of a blog. But there's also some drawbacks you should consider:

- For most people, **blogging takes a lot of time**. It's not particularly easy to come up with a fresh, shareable take on a subject lots of people care about. And then you've got to consider the time it takes to find images, format stuff on the blog itself, monitor comments, share, etc.

- **Blogs aren't likely to directly have an impact on your bottom line/take home profits**. It's a longer-game strategy, and it won't likely pay off quickly.

- **It's totally possible to succeed without blogging**. Blogging gets way more attention than most other aspects of running a small business. If you're hesitant, don't do it. Really.

Basically, I'd recommend having a blog if you have a lot to say, enjoy writing, and really want to work this angle to improve your domain authority. But if the writing on the wall shows that your blog isn't doing much to further your business, don't be afraid to cut it out of your strategy!

Should You Outsource Content?

This question comes up a lot. And it's not a straightforward answer (sorry). For most Etsy shop owners, outsourcing is going to be a significant headache. You'll need to be in constant communication with your writer, you're going to have to pay that writer a significant amount, and your needs for content won't go away anytime soon.

I'd recommend digging in and brushing up your writing skills, taking a big breath and jumping in, then relying on colleagues and Etsy groups of like minded owners to help you hone the important content. You'll get into a groove. Your writing will improve. You'll learn what works if you make sure that honing and improving your content is a priority.

As you grow, and have the budget to bring on some help, outsourcing some aspects of your content creation can make sense. Particularly when it comes to different platforms, e.g., updating listings or posting on different social media platforms.

Basically, if you have the bandwidth to develop an ongoing relationship with a freelancer or gig-economy-minded friend, outsourcing content selectively can be a great way to up your game. But don't just hand over the reins—make sure you're very involved with the content being created until everyone is on the same page and comfortable!

Stuff We Learned the Hard Way

I'm an editor and marketer by training. I'm comfortable with content (maybe you've guessed that, since I wrote a book). But even so, creating content for my OWN shop had its challenges. Here's the top hurdles we navigated:

Buttloads of blogging: We blogged a lot for a while. Which was fun, and we created some very cool content pieces that have probably contributed to positive associations our customers have about my business in the long-run. Which is AMAZING. But, like I mentioned earlier, it took a lot of time. Some of which was probably better spent elsewhere. We still blog once in a while when we want to talk to our audience in a long form way. But it's on an as-needed basis instead of twice a week.

Blogging outside our shop domain: Speaking of blogging…we used a Wordpress site for a long time before we switched our best blog posts over to our Pattern domain. This was my fault. I thought our blog posts would be shared more often if they weren't directly connected to my shop domain. Unfortunately, those shares didn't do much to benefit my business. Our current blog isn't as cool looking as the Wordpress one was (because Pattern has like five options for customization instead of the hundreds Wordpress offers) but when people link to our blog content now, it helps our domain.

Not updating content regularly or often enough: This one is tough. When you're running a barebones operation, just getting started, or scrambling like crazy to scale without the infrastructure (more on expanding up next!). It's hard to be super diligent and consistent about updating social media content, updating your listings all the time, and making sure your copy sparkles. But being more diligent does directly correlate to improved sales and conversions when done well.

Playing it too safe: In the beginning, I still had that corporate attitude in my marketing bones: Don't offend anyone! Play it safe! But that didn't resonate with my audience. The beauty of Etsy is being a free agent to talk to your audience in a real way. And if you offend the folks who are NOT in your target audience and don't care about your stuff? It's okay. It means you're honing in on your real audience.

CHAPTER 10

Marketing Within Etsy

Want an easy (and kind of fun) way to make more money from your Etsy shop? Of course you do. That's why you're reading this book.

It's time to talk about the FREE marketing tools right at your fingertips within Etsy. Etsy's native marketing tools are incredibly easy to use, very cost effective—and most sellers don't use them. Because they don't realize that they're marketing tools (even though you can find them inside the marketing tab of your seller dashboard).

Etsy allows you to run three different types of marketing campaigns within Etsy itself (**sales, coupons,** and **targeted campaigns**) to help you get eyes on your listings and inspire customers to make a purchase.

What I'm saying is, before you go crazy on Facebook ads or hire a virtual assistant to help you pump out social content, master these three marketing moves within the Etsy platform. Why? Not only are they *free*, but they take very little effort on your part for a significant boost in sales and rankings.

Sales vs. Coupons vs. Targeted Campaigns

First, let's get some definitions straight. Because if you're not a marketing person, all of this can sound like nonsense.

Etsy uses the phrases **Sale, Coupon,** and **Targeted Campaign** to describe distinct marketing options for your business.

It helps a lot to understand the nuances, tips, and pitfalls of each option right out of the gate so that you can use them most effectively to boost your sales and rankings.

Sales

In Etsy, a **sale** is a public promotion that's discoverable by anyone who happens across your shop. When you run a sale, any listing you include in the sale will display an appealing message beneath it that advertises the discount. You'll find sales in the Marketing > Sales and Coupons tab of your Shop Manager.

Running a sale is easy:

- Decide whether you'd like to offer free shipping or a percentage off purchase (and what amount). You can specify whether your buyer has to purchase a minimum quantity of items or reach a minimum order total to qualify for the sale.

- Decide how long the sale will last (sales can run up to 30 days).

- Choose a name for the sale (your buyers won't see this name, it'll just be for your records.)

- Decide which listings you'd like to include in the sale.

Most sellers don't know that sales boost your ranking in Etsy search results quite a bit. I see a lift in the number of organic purchases (zero advertising on my end) whenever I run a sale, which is why I almost ALWAYS choose to run a low-grade sale (think 10% off).

Etsy actually creates an automatic category within your shop called "On Sale" which can be very enticing to buyers—but overwhelming to sort through if you put hundreds of items on sale constantly. I usually rotate through putting different shop categories on sale to keep buyers excited instead of overwhelmed.

TIP: After initiating a search, buyers can sort displayed listings by "Items on sale." This can often bump your listings straight to the top of an otherwise packed crowd.

TIP: In your Sales and Coupons hub on Etsy, you can see how many times people used a given sale (and how much revenue you pulled in).

Warning! Because I run a low-grade sale almost constantly, I don't usually advertise it to my social media audience. Be careful of constantly promoting a low-grade sale, or your audience will tune you out quickly. Not to mention that since there's no need for a coupon code, your audience may unfollow you since they may not see a need to watch your account for coupon codes.

The bottom line: Use low-grade sales OFTEN as a way of quickly and reliably increasing the amount of eyes (and purchases) in your shop. Make it a habit of creating a new low-grade sale for at least part of your shop at the beginning of each month.

Coupons

So how is a coupon different from a sale?

Basically, a **coupon** is just a promotion that is NOT displayed in Etsy search results and requires the buyer to use a code for redemption. So, any old person can't find your shop and use a coupon code unless they're following you on social media.

Coupons are a great way to reward your social media followers for paying attention to your feed in Facebook, Instagram, or anywhere else. Coupons can also be a great tactic when collaborating with influencers (more on that later). Simply create a tailored coupon code for an influencer to share with their audience. This creates a stronger call to action for their audience (e.g., if you're selling rugs and being promoted by a sustainability influencer, you could create the code SUSTAIN20).

You'll find coupons in your Etsy seller dashboard. Go to the Marketing > Sales and Coupon tab of your Shop Manager. To create a coupon, follow these steps:

- Decide whether you'd like to offer free shipping, a fixed amount off a purchase, or a percentage off of a purchase (and what amount). You can specify whether your buyer has to purchase a minimum quantity of items or reach a minimum order total to qualify for the sale.

- Decide how long the coupon will be good for (you can choose a set period of time or opt for no expiration date).

- Choose a name for the coupon (your buyers WILL see this name and need to enter it when they order from your shop to get the discount).

- Decide which listings you'd like to be eligible for the coupon.

TIP: You have the option to set up a coupon as a "thank you" gift for customers who purchase from your shop. You can only mark one coupon at a time as a "thank you" offer (just check the box as you create your coupon). When anyone purchases from your shop, they will be sent an email with this coupon code, enticing them to make another purchase.

TIP: Etsy shows you how many buyers have used any given coupon code, which can help you gauge the success of a partnership with an influencer or advertiser.

TIP: I typically use deeper discounts with my coupon codes than I do with my sales. Why? Because coupons reward my social media followers/email subscribers for paying attention to my feeds/emails. I want them to have a compelling reason to watch out for those coupon codes they would miss otherwise.

Warning! Try not to make your coupon codes random. Correlate them with the holiday, influencer, or product you're promoting so it's easy to remember the context for each coupon and evaluate success.

The bottom line: Coupon codes are a fantastic way to reward your social media followers/email subscribers and collaborate with influencers. Use them sparingly, as needed, and offer deeper discounts.

Targeted Campaigns

Now, let's talk about targeted campaigns, which are basically Etsy's bare-bones version of automated email marketing.

Targeted campaigns are a way of "nudging" promising or interested buyers by giving them extra motivation to follow through with a purchase. You'll find targeted campaigns in the Marketing > Sales and Coupon tab of your Shop Manager.

Etsy sends these "nudges" to buyers in the form of an email with a coupon code any time a new buyer shows behavior that indicates they might be interested in buying from your shop. Targeted campaigns are heavily automated through Etsy.

Activating a targeted campaign is simple:

- Decide which (if any) triggers you'd like to activate.
- Decide whether you'd like to offer a percentage off purchase (and what amount), free shipping, or a fixed amount off (and what amount). This promotion will apply to your entire shop.

- Choose a name for your promotion (be aware that the promotion name/code name will be visible to your buyers in the email Etsy sends). Put a little thought into your coupon code.

Currently, Etsy offers two different triggers to nudge interested buyers:

1. An Etsy user "favorites" your item.

2. An Etsy user adds one of your items to their cart but doesn't complete checkout (abandoned cart).

Targeted campaigns never expire (unless you deactivate them) and don't cost you anything, other than your standard Etsy transaction and processing fees (these fees are outlined in Chapter 5) if the buyer completes the purchase.

TIP: A code that makes your buyer smile is more likely to get their attention. The code HOWYOUDOIN is going to get you a lot more clicks than SALE15.

TIP: Don't feel like you need to offer deep discounts on targeted campaigns. Remember, these buyers were interested enough to favorite your item or add it to their cart. They just need a little nudge.

Warning! If you deactivate a targeted campaign, buyers who received that code previously will no longer be able to use it.

The bottom line: USE. TARGETED. CAMPAIGNS. For real. Turn these babies on as soon as possible. It's essentially free, automated email marketing. A steady trickle of my total sales come from these targeted campaigns at any given time. The targeted campaign emails are also great places to invite customers to join your email list. More on this in Chapter 11.

How Often Should I Run Sales/Promotions/Targeted Campaigns?

There's really no right answer here (don't you hate it when people say that?). If you follow the best practices surrounding each type of promotion, you'll be able to hone what works best for your shop and product with minimal trial and error.

Run Low-grade Sales Often

Personally (like I mentioned in the section on Sales), I choose to run low-grade (10% off) sales for a portion of my shop nearly constantly to boost my rankings. Likewise, I keep my Targeted Campaigns on at all times to bring back customers who have left something in their cart without purchasing or favorited one of my items but haven't pulled the trigger yet.

Use Coupons Sparingly

As for coupons, I'd recommend using them sparingly for a couple of reasons:

1. If you promote coupon codes to your audience all the time (every week or every month), you train your audience to purchase only when you offer a deep discount, which means you might create an audience that waits to buy until they see a coupon code from you.

2. You'll get a lot of messages from buyers who purchased between sales—then looked at your social media feed and saw a ton of coupon codes—and ask you to apply one of those recent coupon codes. You don't have to do this of course, but if you refuse, you set up a negative experience for that customer before they've even received their product. Using coupons more sparingly helps you avoid this weirdly common situation for the most part.

3. There's already SO MUCH NOISE on social media. You are vying for your customers' precious attention. Don't burn them out with the same type of offer over and over again. It'll feel less urgent and special.

When to Use Coupons

This is when I personally use coupon codes:

- Any time I work with an influencer or advertising partners so I can gauge the success of the partnership by giving that influencer a unique code.

- Once or twice, randomly per year—at an unexpected or slower time of year, like post-Christmas or during the middle of summer, to reward my followers and email list.

- A couple weeks prior to Black Friday, extending through Cyber Monday. Make sure you also run a moderate sale during this key buying window, since Etsy will boost your listings accordingly, and buyers expect to see sales during this time.

And that's about it. Use sales and targeted campaigns smartly and often. Use coupons smartly and sparingly—and you're all set!

How Sales, Coupons and Targeted Campaigns Affect Listing Positions

Here's the short answer: Targeted campaigns don't affect your listing positions much; sales and coupons, however, can affect them a lot. Here's how:

Like we talked about earlier, sales boost your listing positions whenever a customer searches for keywords that match your listings. Why? First of all, because Etsy's algorithm rewards sales, and also, whenever a buyer types a search term into Etsy, they see a grid of results—and a sidebar of ways to filter those results. What's the first thing most buyers do? Check the boxes to sort by items that are ON SALE or offer FREE SHIPPING (You should do both, we'll talk more about why in Chapter 17.) This means that if your items are on sale or offer free shipping, they'll automatically blaze past other listings that AREN'T on sale. Pretty great, eh? There's plenty of other ways Etsy customers can narrow down their search, but it's no coincidence that these boxes are right at the TOP of the sidebar. Often, it's the only box customers check when narrowing their search.

How do coupon codes affect your listing rank? When you promote a coupon (or an influencer does) through social or email along with a clickable link, you get more views, favorites, and more cart-adds for that listing—which boosts its position in search results for other buyers. Even if the customers don't purchase, a cart-add sends positive signals to Etsy's algorithms and improves your ranking for that item in results. We've tested this ourselves.

Roadmap for a Successful Coupon Code

There's more to a coupon than creating a code and deciding whether you'll offer 10% or 15% off. Once you set the stage by creating a stellar coupon code, set yourself up for success in promoting your coupon code by doing all of the following:

1. **Timing.** We've already covered this, but it's worth repeating: Don't burn your buyers out or make them ignore you by throwing coupon codes at them all the time. Less is more.

Another aspect of timing is WHEN you (or an influencer) shares your coupon code. Get into your ideal customer's head. When are they relaxing and cruising social media? When are they likely to ignore vs. open an email?

    o   For the most part, Mondays are the worst time to send or share any kind of coupon through email and social.

    o   Sunday evening when everyone is combating the Sunday night blues before the work week begins by surfing their feeds is a good time.

    o   Thursday or Friday morning when folks are in a good mood as the work week wraps up (and all too happy to kill a little time with a fun purchase instead of working) is another good time to share.

    o   Your audience may differ—we'll talk about using stats to hone in on audience behavior in Chapter 14.

2. **Graphics**: We dug into graphics in Chapter 4, and I'll repeat myself here: Keep graphics simple, and make sure you include all relevant information. Your customers will scan right over something that looks messy, is complicated, or looks confusing. You want them to say, "Ahhhh, look at that!" instead of squinting at the screen. Be sure to include

    o   Dates the coupon code is good for,

    o   The percentage or amount off,

    o   A link to your site.

You can include some information in your caption if things get busy, just make sure you include all of it!

3. **Urgency**: While you'll have the option to make a coupon code last forever if you want to, I don't recommend it unless that coupon code is being sent out as part of an ongoing email campaign (or you've marked it as a "thank you" to be sent to repeat buyers.) Urgency encourages more people to buy right then while the offer is in front of them (instead of waiting and thinking they'll remember later—spoiler: they won't). I usually make my coupon codes last for three days to a week.

4. **Third Time's the Charm:** You'll want to promote your coupon on email and social several times—I recommend three: Once when you announce your coupon, a second time when you remind your audience that the offer is ending soon and a third time when you pull out the urgent "Last chance to take advantage of this awesome coupon!" post. Post these reminders on different days of the week at different times of day. That way you'll reach different personalities and schedules through each of these reminders.

Hot Tip: Using a "Last Chance Sale" to Jumpstart Less Popular Listings

You should always keep an eye on your Etsy stats and which items are selling and which aren't. This is important information. And it's important information that you can use to your advantage in a lemons-into-lemonade move where you use those less popular listings to boost your sales and shop stats. Here's how:

First of all, it's normal for some items that may have been popular at first became less so over time. Or, on the other side, some items become so popular that Etsy's market gets flooded with similar listings, and your original listing stops selling in the deluge of low-ball copycats.

Because Etsy boosts all of the listings in your shop if your conversion rate is high, it's a good idea to deactivate listings that aren't selling so they're not getting impressions and bringing down your conversion rate. BUT there's nothing that says you have to let listings go defunct quietly. Or that you can't use those lackluster listings to your advantage.

Just like in a physical store that's trying to clear out old merch, put the listings that aren't selling into their own section with a steep discount (30%-50%). This is the concept behind the **Last Chance Sale.**

I can't take any credit for coming up with this one. I learned this one from someone smarter than me (Joanna from EWD Marketing).

What I can offer is a great testimonial that the Last Chance Sale works! I created a section in my shop called "Last Chance," which I later changed to "Close Out," and put all the items that hadn't sold more than twice in the last year into that section at a 30% discount. Anything that started selling better after three months, I moved back into the general shop, but anything that still wasn't selling great, I deactivated. My conversion rate jumped, and I was able to sell some of my older designs that don't sell very often, which was a lot of fun. I think every shop should do a Last Chance Sale at some point, even if you end up selling some of the items for very narrow margins. I was surprised at how much it jump-started my sales.

Things We Learned the Hard Way

Coupons: I learned how to use coupons the hard way. I ran WAY too many when I first got started with my Etsy shop. It felt like such an easy way to get my audience excited! But pretty soon, I noticed sales dropping a lot when I wasn't dangling a coupon on social media. My audience had gotten wise to what I was doing, and nobody wanted to buy at full price.

Sales: I also didn't start taking advantage of sales for way too long. I didn't quite grasp the subtlety of sales vs. coupons and just sort of neglected sales. Once I realized how valuable they were to boosting me in searches and helping customers discover my shop, I kicked myself for all the time (and money!) I had lost.

Thankfully, you don't need to make my mistakes. You're ready to kill it with sales, coupons, and targeted promotions. Get going!

CHAPTER 11

Email Marketing

Etsy doesn't allow you to speak to your customers en-masse because Etsy wants to be the gatekeeper of all interactions within the Etsy universe. You can convo one-on-one. You can create a shop update. You can craft your automated "thank you" emails. But you can't send out a blast email directly to your customers about a sale, a promotion, or a new product.

But that doesn't mean you shouldn't be doing exactly that, just not through Etsy.

If you've done even the briefest of dips into what the interwebs have to say about email marketing, you've probably seen this sentence at least once: "Despite what some experts say, email marketing is *absolutely not dead.*"

I'm still not sure who these illusive "experts" are that keep insisting that email marketing is in fact dead, but the consensus on the internet (presumably, the non-experts? i.e., the regular sellers like us?) is that you should absolutely be gathering emails for a mailing list and sending out regular marketing emails. And I'm here to second that opinion. Email marketing really works.

Research blogs like DBS Data, Quick Sprout, and KISSmetrics (among others) have done studies on the effectiveness of email marketing. "40+ Email Marketing Statistics You Need to Know for 2021" from OptinMonster distills the important points from a number of significant studies on email marketing if you want more specifics. DBS Data found that ROIs (returns on investment) for email can be $38 in profit for every $1 spent! That's pretty incredible.

This chapter will walk you through how email marketing works for Etsy sellers. I'll explain the concept of opting in, give you some guidelines on creating exceptional emails, discuss the dos and don'ts of email marketing and several ways to measure the success of your email campaign. And finally, I'll introduce some email marketing tools that work well for Etsy sellers.

First Things First: Getting People to Opt-in to Your Email List

So, how do you start emailing people? Some shop owners decide they are going to mine data from their Etsy shop and pull emails from customers, then simply start sending out emails.

STOP. Do not do this. Not only is it against your Etsy seller agreement (if Etsy finds out, you could be facing repercussions for your shop), but it's also considered a really shady practice in the business world. If you want to be seen as a legitimate business, only EVER send emails to people who have chosen to opt in to receiving email from your company.

I get it. It's tempting when you're starting out in email marketing to add all your personal contacts into your business email list or (even worse!) to purchase a list of emails from another company. Don't do this. It's called cold emailing, and it's got a terrible reputation. It's spam of the worst variety. Build your email list ethically and smartly.

But how?

As an Etsy shop owner and reputable business person, you're going to want to get people to join your email list through incentivizing them with a first look at new products, sales, and coupon codes.

But how do you actually collect those email addresses from willing customers? You use Mailchimp or another email marketing program to create landing pages with pop-ups that ask your customers to join your mailing list. And then you plug those landing pages in your shipping notifications, your shop announcement, your listing descriptions, and anywhere else that makes sense and is highly visible on Etsy and your social media pages.

All About Email Opt-In Pages

As for the look of an opt-in page, keep it simple, and make sure it looks good on both desktop and mobile. Only ask customers for a first name and email, and never make customers scroll down to find the entry fields and subscribe/join button.

Once you've created your opt-in page(s)/pop-ups, you can be as brazen about asking people to subscribe as you like. We include this "Subscribe!" image as one of the ten in each of our Etsy listings. Our Etsy shop announcement asks people to join the mailing list. And all of the automated "Thank You for Your Purchase" emails sent out by Etsy to people who've purchased from our shop encourage them to sign up for our newsletter.

An uncomplicated opt-in process and a few (or more than a few) well-placed calls to action in your Etsy shop and customer communication can build up a good-sized mailing list in a relatively short time. Customers want free/discounted stuff, and they'll happily opt in to receiving emails to get it. After all, they can always unsubscribe after they've used the coupon code if they don't want to receive email anymore.

Unsubscribe Option

It's an unfortunate truth, but not everyone who you bride into signing up for your mailing list will stick around for the long term. Some people are only joining to get your freebie, and you have to let these people go if they want to go. It's actually illegal (worldwide) to not include an option to unsubscribe. It's even illegal to obscure the option to or make unsubscribing difficult.

Even companies that send mind-blowing emails are going to lose a few subscribers each time they send an email out. The rate is usually 0.2%-0.5% each time, but that's not too big a deal if you're steadily gaining new subscribers at the same time. If your unsubscribe rate is significantly higher than 0.5% per email, you're probably doing something wrong, and you'll need to up your email game.

Anatomy of a Killer Email

One of the main reasons behind high unsubscribe rates is unappealing or out-of-touch email content. Email marketing is one of the more personal ways to reach out to customers. It's targeted, one-on-one solicitation and is in the same category as snail mail ads, phone calls, and door-to-door sales. A killer email appeals to your customers in tone and content as well as visually. It has the following characteristics:

A Trusted Source

Open your email right now and take a look. Whether you're on computer or mobile, the very first information your eye takes in is who the email is from. This is something you'll be able to set in your email marketing tool for each campaign. You want your customers to know the email is coming from you, a person, and the owner of a shop that they love. For example, "Noelle at Fourth Wave."

A Catchy Subject Line

The subject line is the text that customers will see next to the "From" before they open the email. It's your email's first impression, so it needs to capture your customer's attention in a split second as they scan. You can use emojis in the email subject line, but don't use more than one, and don't rely on the emoji to convey information; it's there to catch your customer's eye. Too many emojis can take up space and distract from your message: "Don't scroll down until you've read this email!" Here are some ideas for subject lines that actually get people to open your emails.

- Call to action: Get it now! Grab Your [product] before it's too late! Show us your love. Last chance! Final Call!

- Teaser of the most interesting content from the email (be specific): Our newest designs, hottest tees, and more. Love your skin even more. 10 ways to get your dog to love bath time.

- Sale announcement: Everything 20% off today! Flash Sale— 25% off hats.

- Humor or poetry: Don't judge these peppers by their shape. Thank GOURD for Feminism (yes, we've actually used this one). Planting a garden is hoping for tomorrow.

- Question: How much will you save? Have you seen this? Are you interested in learning jewelry stamping?

Eye-catching Images and a "Shop Now" Button

Once you've inspired a potential customer to open your email, you want to show them some fireworks. In the marketing world, text-heavy, black and white emails are a thing of the past. Your emails need to pop with color and beautiful images. These images should be no longer than 600 pixels wide and, like the opt-in page, keep the important information "above the fold," so your customers don't need to scroll down to see what you're offering. Along with your image(s), include your logo in a top corner, and create an obvious "SHOP NOW" button with a link to your shop. This call to action in the form of a button adds a sense of urgency and encourages people to click through to your website and purchase something.

Concise, Creative Copy and the (Optional) Salutation

If you're using the email to sell products, you don't need much of an email body. Most of your content will be included below or even in your product images. Your content is basically going to be, "Here are a few awesome items I know you'll love."

If you're writing more of a newsletter or shop announcement, you're going to have more to contend with content-wise. Email is a very personal form of communication, so you want your newsletter to speak to the heart. One way to make an email feel more personal is to include a personalized salutation, "Dear Noelle..." —it can really make your customers feel like you're speaking directly to them. Mailchimp includes functionality in its toolkit to do this, but you will have to set up your landing pages to collect both a first name and an email or the salutation will read, "Dear [customeremail@email.com]" instead of the person's first name. Another potential problem with personal salutations occurs if someone signs up for your email list with a fake name. That personal touch will really backfire if all the emails you send to them start out "Dear Voldemort…."

Beyond the advice to err of the personal side, I won't go into how to write content for the body of an email. I'll point you to Chapter 9 for more on the subject.

A Text-only Version

You know those eye-catching images I told you to use in your marketing emails? Well, some of your customers (a small percentage these days) won't be able to see them, usually because their internet or phone connections are slow. You don't want to risk losing subscribers to this problem, so you'll want to make sure all the important text inside your images and buttons can be viewed in a text-only or plain-text version of the email.

This means accurately filling in all of the "alt-text" boxes for images in your email template creator (assuming you're using an email marketing platform like Mailchimp) and selecting the option to "send a plain-text version" for each campaign you create. Also, if you have important text you absolutely NEED all your customers to see, you'll need to put it in a text block rather than inside an image or other media. The plain-text version of your email will include any text you've typed into a text block as well as some of your image alt-text and your links written out as URLs. With this information, your customers with slow connections can still figure out what the email says and know where to go to see and hopefully purchase your products.

The Signature and Footer Text

Again, you want to make your email feel like a personal note to each customer, so you want to sign your name or your Shop Name at the bottom. Using a script text can make your signature feel handwritten like you "signed" each email yourself. It's a bit of a gimmick, especially for email, but it's still one of those things that helps your customers create a connection to you and to your shop.

Under the signature, your email marketing platform will include footer text like copyright info, your business address (if you choose to include it), an unsubscribe button, and the logo of the platform (usually, "Powered by Mailchimp/ConvertKit/[Other Email

Marketing Platform]). This is automatically tacked onto the end of each email you send, so just make sure on the very first email you send that the information is correct. Check the year of the copyright information and make sure your business name and address is spelled correctly.

There are paid versions on most platforms that will eliminate this footer text—specifically the "powered by" portion—which can boost your shop's professionalism and legitimacy. But you can cross that bridge later if you want when you're raking in those six-figures.

Takeaway: There's no magical formula for creating truly exceptional marketing emails, but if you focus on reaching your customers in a personal way and thoughtfully consider each of the elements listed in this section, your emails will stand out. You don't have to know everything about email marketing or create the perfect first email to get started using this powerful marketing tool.

Best Practices for Email Marketing

Writing a killer email isn't the only challenge when it comes to email marketing. You have to know when and how often to send emails. To succeed at email marketing, you'll want to follow these best practices.

- **Get that opt in!** Never send marketing emails to someone who hasn't opted into receiving them. I discussed this in the section on Opt-in, but I'll say it again here. Companies that send cold email or use harvested lists as well as companies that collect and use emails deceptively end up suffering the consequences. Basically, they end up getting flagged as spam and all of their emails are automatically archived or deleted by email providers before reaching customers. That "spam" label is a deathblow to an email campaign.

- **Don't offer one thing and send another.** When customers opt-in, they want to know exactly what you're going to be sending them. Is it a recipe a day? A 10-day challenge? Monthly newsletters? Product marketing emails several times a month? Again, if your customers signed up for a monthly newsletter and you start sending out marketing emails five times a week, your customers are going to unsubscribe or mark your emails as spam.

- **Don't overwhelm your customers' inboxes**. Sending three emails a day is another tactic that's going to get you in serious trouble with your customers and their email providers. There's no faster way to get labeled as spam then sending too many emails too close together. Basically, avoid sending emails for the sake of sending emails. Start by sending out an email once or twice a month and see how customers respond. Send emails about important sales and events. And keep a close eye on your unsubscribe rate as you increase email frequency.

- **Send emails at a time when the most customers are likely to read them.** This will depend on the timezone of the majority of your customers, so it will be different for each company. Studies show that people are most likely to check email during the work week rather than on weekends. 2pm in the middle of the week can be good because it's a somewhat tired time of the day when people are more likely to idly browse non-work related emails. 10am on Monday can be a good time for some because many people check email then and are rested and ready to dive in, so your email might be met with more enthusiasm than on a Friday afternoon. Studies aside, you're going to want to do some experimenting here to find out when your customers are most likely to open and click in your emails

- **Respect your customers' time.** Make sure you only send emails when you have something worth saying. Again, the better the emails you send, the more they'll get opened and the less they'll get marked as spam. Mailing lists can help you build loyalty with customers who are most likely to stick around and make repeat purchases over the years.

More Technical Practices That'll Put You Ahead of Your Competitors

- **Get an email with your domain after the @** (e.g., Noelle@craftranker.com). Email providers like Gmail see these types of emails as far more credible than a generic @mail.com or even (ironically) an @gmail.com account. Purchasing a domain and setting up private email based on that domain really shows that yours is a legitimate business with consistent branding, and you're much less likely to end up in the spam category automatically. You can get an email account with your domain from your domain registrar (more on this in Chapter 19).

- **Send out a mix of different style emails**—marketing emails, special offers, and some more informative, personal emails about your company. Customers can tell when you're using email to sell them something, and it's a fact that overt marketing emails get fewer opens and clicks. Customers sign up for your mailing list to hear about you, your business, and the causes you support because those causes matter to your customers too. Email marketing is a chance to build relationships with your customers and create loyalty to your brand, so try to mix it up from time to time and send out an email that's purely, "Hey, here's what we're up to."

- **Always test your emails before sending them out.** Send them to yourself or to a coworker or friend. This is something I learned the hard way. I'll tell you from experience, it's really embarrassing to shoot off an email to 200 subscribers and then realize one of your images or links is broken or that there's an obvious typo in the title. You lose credibility with your customers and they're more likely to ignore your future emails, label them as spam, or unsubscribe.

Measuring Success in Email Marketing

Each time you send out a marketing email to your list, you're going to want to check three stats that can give you a good idea for how successful your campaign was.

1. **Open Rate:** This is the percentage of people who opened your email. 15-25% is considered a good open rate, so congratulations if your open rate is higher than this! Don't worry too much if it starts to drop as your mailing list grows. As long as it stays above 15%, you're doing great.

2. **Click Rate:** This is the percentage of people who received the email, opened it, and clicked through to your site or on another link in your email. A good click rate is 2.5%, so again, if you're above that number, you're succeeding!

3. **Unsubscribes:** These are the people leaving your mailing list. A good goal is fewer than 0.5% for each email, or about 4-10 unsubscribes depending on your mailing list. Hopefully, you're doing a good job getting people to sign up, so your list is still growing despite a few people unsubscribing each campaign.

If you have a Pattern by Etsy site, you can also track purchases from email by connecting a Mailchimp account directly to your Pattern site. Unfortunately, this integration isn't available for Etsy shops without Pattern sites. Etsy Help has more information on how to make this work.

Email Platform Options

Neither Etsy nor Pattern gives you an option to send marketing emails to many customers at a time. And this feature isn't likely to be added in the future. Like we said earlier, Etsy gates all customer interactions WITHIN the Etsy platform on purpose. The best you can do is "Convo" individual buyers one at a time, and you definitely don't want to go that route as a substitute form an email marketing tool (Etsy will throttle you and start making you complete increasingly more difficult ReCaptcha puzzles. How do I know this? Because at one point a massive Christmas shipment was delayed by weather, and I tried to message 200 customers individually. And it was horrible).

You can, of course, simply send marketing emails to customers through your Gmail account, but I'd advise against this for several reasons:

* For one thing, you have no way to gather emails from customers. So where are you getting those emails from? In-person sellers can ask people to physically write their email down on a paper mailing list, but Etsy, of course, doesn't really offer sellers a good, ethical way to gather addresses.

- And second, regular emails from generic Gmail accounts, especially if your customer doesn't recognize your brand, often get tagged as spam, and going to the spam folder is an email marketer's nightmare.

Best practice for email marketing is to use a dedicated email marketing platform. We use MailChimp because it's free forever up to a list of 2,500 emails (WOW), which is more than enough for most small businesses. The free version of MailChimp does limit some functionality that you'll get if you pay for a plan at some point (at $30 a month for the basic plan), but it's still, in my opinion, the best platform for beginners. Mailchimp is also by far the most popular platform for email marketing and has been around long enough to have worked out any kinks. It's tried and tested even by some bigger-name companies like GrubHub and StackShare.

And an extra perk for Etsy sellers is that the only email marketing platform that Pattern integrates directly with is MailChimp, so if you're planning to use Pattern by Etsy, you definitely want to also use MailChimp.

There are dozens of other email marketing platforms you can check out, depending on your unique needs. And there are some great, in-depth side-by-side comparisons out there. If you have unique email needs, don't be afraid to dig around! In the next section, I'll talk about the basic functionality (the essentials) you'll get with any email marketing platform. All of the platforms listed in these articles offer the basics, and you get more cool (but not necessarily essential) functionality as you tier up in each one.

Key Tools inside Any Email Marketing Platform

No matter which email marketing platform you choose, it will have a base-level functionality that allows you to do the following things (we'll cover the fancier features you might want to consider in a second):

- **Tools for Collecting Emails:** Any email marketing platform is going to have tools that help you set up landing pages or pop-ups asking customers to subscribe to your email list. As you already know, emailing people without their permission (without asking them to first opt into receiving mail from you) is not allowed. I'll say it one last time: Spamming will destroy your marketing campaign and your company's reputation.

- **List Keeping and List Segmentation Tools**: Your email marketing platforms will keep track of your emails in a list, eliminate duplicates, and allow you to segment your subscribers into different groups using tags. This means you can send certain targeted emails to small subsets of your customers, targeting what they're interested in (for instance, you can send an email to all your customers who purchased a mug, versus customers who purchased a T-shirt).

- **Tools to Create an Email (Templates):** Each platform offers its own methods for creating an email and sending it out. MailChimp, for example, uses templates that you can fill in with your own images, text, and links so your emails include your company's branding and look professional.

- **The Ability to Send Email to Subscribers:** The sending of emails is, of course, the most important offering of any email marketing platform. It's also the reason the ROI for email marketing is so high: Sending emails is a free and direct way to communicate with customers en masse. Most platforms offer both HTML and plain-text display options to your customers, which is awesome when you're sending marketing emails to people with slow internet connections or settings that limit the amount of HTML their browser will display.

- **Tracking/Statistics:** All email marketing platforms offer you the ability to track the efficacy of your marketing campaigns. They'll show you how many people opened your emails and how many clicked on a link within the email as well as the number that unsubscribed from your mailing list. You'll also be able to see demographic and location data about your subscribers, which can be useful in deciding what to advertise and how to target emails.

Other Perks and Advanced Email Marketing Features to Consider

The basics are plenty to launch your email marketing campaign, but if you find that email is really working for you or that you want to spend some time really honing that marketing channel, there are other features that can be useful:

- **Integrations:** Some email marketing platforms allow users to integrate third-party tools into their campaigns. These integrations can add a powerful punch to an already established campaign by making opt-in smoother (for example, Optin Monster), gathering and sorting your lists of contacts, and automatically targeting emails to very specific groups by allowing the email platform access to your website's analytics and selling data, among other things.

- **Automation and scheduling:** There's power in being able to reach out to customers when they are most responsive, like right after they've abandoned a cart. But obviously, you can't monitor customer behavior 24/7. That's what automation and scheduling are for: your email marketing platform can work 100% of the time and target customers on their schedules. It's an incredibly powerful tool. Most email marketing platforms offer some degree of automation and scheduling, although this feature is usually not included in free or basic versions of the platform.

- **A/B Testing:** In email marketing, A/B testing means sending out two slightly different versions of the same email to similar groups to see which email your customers respond to more positively. This kind of testing can really hone your marketing approach. As with automation, the ability to gather this kind of data is usually not included in a free or basic version of the platform.

- **Purchase tracking:** Paid versions of email marketing platforms can be set up to track customer behavior *after* they click on a link in your email. Advanced tracking can show you how many customers purchase your products after click-through, how long they linger in your shop, and what causes them to leave (exit stats). These stats can show you how effective your email marketing campaigns are far beyond just opens, clicks, and unsubscribes.

Things We Learned the Hard Way

When I started out in email marketing, I knew next to nothing, so pretty much every piece of information in this chapter was hard won. Here are a few things that I wish someone had told me at the beginning of my journey.

Segmenting really works: One of the more powerful aspects of email marketing is also one of the more difficult to learn right off the bat—segmenting and targeting emails. I pretty much ignored the audience segmentation tools available in Mailchimp at first. It just felt so overwhelming. Not only would I have had to figure out how to divide up my audience, but I had to create multiple emails within a single campaign to target each group. Creating one good email felt overwhelming enough. I also honestly believed I didn't know enough about the people on my mailing list to divide them by any useful metrics.

Eventually, an opportunity for segmentation presented itself. We needed to get more five-star reviews. So, here's what I did—I pulled from our Etsy shop sales data all of the names and emails of our customers over the last year. Then, I sorted those names by customers that had purchased from us more than once during that time. I figured these customers represented our most interested and loyal contingent and the people most likely to give us good reviews.

Then, I cross-referenced this list to our MailChimp mailing list. Unsurprisingly, the majority of these customers were subscribed there. I then sent out a targeted email to only those customers, offering them a 20% storewide discount to purchase and review one of our products. I told these customers that they were among a small group of our most loyal fans and how much their support meant to us. I asked them if they'd like to help our shop grow with a positive review.

And guess what? Over 80% of the customers that received that email ended up giving us a five-star review (either on a new purchase or a previous one that they hadn't yet reviewed).

I couldn't believe it. Segmenting and targeting really work.

You don't have to be perfect from day one: One of the biggest revelations to me at the beginning of my email marketing journey was how *diverse* (read: conflicting) the guidelines were for how to do it well. There are 101 pieces of advice on the internet about every aspect of sending emails to customers, and they're all over the place.

This means that no matter how prepared you are to send perfect emails, there are going to be things you have to figure out the hard way about your customers and their email habits.

The nice thing, though, about email marketing is that you don't have to be perfect from day one to succeed. Remember that stat from the beginning of this chapter? The one about ROIs of $38 for every $1 spent? You probably won't start that strong. But that's your POTENTIAL right there. You'll get the hang of it with practice. Email marketing is one case where the rewards are much greater than the risks, so jump right in and start your mailing list today.

CHAPTER 12

Paying for Ads: Native Etsy Ads and Offsite Ads

As a general business principle, the expression, "You've got to spend money to make money" is true. Paying for advertising is a great way to grow your Etsy shop. But advertising can be a risky endeavor.

If you choose the wrong channels or put your advertising on autopilot, you're almost guaranteed to lose money instead of make it. Yikes! So how do you decide where to spend your advertising money to get the most bang for your buck?

This chapter is all about how to pay to advertise your Etsy shop and make sure your ads are working for you. I'll talk about the benefits of paid advertising, when it actually makes sense to use paid advertising in the life of your shop (because you don't need to pay for ads all the time), best practices for online advertising, some of the best channels available to Etsy sellers, and how to start small, experiment, and really dig into the data to evaluate which ad channels are working best for your shop.

Why Paid Ads Are Worth Your Time

Paid advertising helps businesses grow at a much faster pace than they would organically. By organically, I mean through unprompted customer searches, word-of-mouth, social media shares, that kind of thing.

Paid ads bypass these organic channels and basically hand out digital flyers to your potential customers—the people who don't know yet that they need what you sell. Which brings us to the next question: When should you pay for ads? The simple answer to the question is, *whenever you want to grow.* Now let's dig into the longer answer.

When to Pay for Ads

Like I said, the simplest rule of thumb is that you should pay for advertising when you want to grow. And when you're just starting out on Etsy, growth will be a primary focus. Going from selling nothing to selling something is the first step on the journey to success. And this is a great time to pay for ads. You need to get eyeballs on your products, and paid ads can really help you do that. Yes, it will be an extra cost (which can be intimidating when you're new) but remember that saying: You have to spend SOME money to make money. Carefully. And again, in the right channels.

Now, some good news about ad spend: After an initial period of ramping up and growth, you may not need to keep paying for ads forever. If you follow the advice we give throughout this book, your *organic growth* (without ads) will gradually trend upward. But there may be certain points where you want to grow and expand more rapidly (like when you start scaling or hiring and have the capacity to create more products in the same amount of (or less!) time. These are times when you'd want to turn those paid ads back on again.

Takeaway: Use paid advertising whenever you want your shop to grow faster than it would through organic channels.

When NOT to Pay for Ads

Okay, so before you pour a bunch of resources into paid advertising, we need to talk about when you should not use paid advertising.

If either of these two situations apply to you, you're not quite ready to leap into paid ads:

Before Your Shop Is in Tip-top Shape

You don't want to start paying for advertising before you've optimized your shop and listings for organic search. I know I just said you should pay for ads when you're starting out on Etsy, but I'm going to add a caveat to that: Get your shop in shape first using the principles in Section 1 of this book.

If your listings are showing up for the wrong keywords or your images are blurry or unappealing, you're going to be wasting your money on paid advertising. No amount of ad spend can make up for subpar listings or a disorganized, fragmented shop. Because you can lead your customers to your listings, but you can't make them add them to their carts.

It's fun to imagine just how big your shop *could* get, how much money you *could* make, but the reality is that (as a small business owner and perhaps sole employee of your shop) you only have so much time, energy, and even materials. It can really damage your shop and your reputation if you grow too fast that growth places a strain on your product quality and time.

In other words, if you're unable to fulfill orders in a timely manner while keeping a level head and keeping your product quality high, growth is not worth it and neither are paid ads.

The good news is that as CEO of your Etsy shop, you are in control of how much and when you want to grow. At some point, you may be comfortable with the level of growth you've reached. Maybe you're making as many crocheted baby blankets each week as you want to make and are happy with the amount of money coming in. Especially if your shop is also your creative passion and you don't really want to hire anyone. It's important to know when to be satisfied with where you're at and take time to enjoy that success. Maybe, a few months down the road, you can consider hiring an employee to help crochet more blankets. Then, you could start up your ads again, knowing you will be able to keep up with the increasing sales. Or maybe you don't want to do that. It's up to you.

Takeaway: Don't feel like you ought to be using paid advertising channels all the time. Be selective about when you use them and be prepared for an influx of sales. Don't be caught unprepared!

Best Advertising Opportunities for Etsy Sellers

Some advertising options are especially good fits for Etsy sellers, and others are less so. In this section, I'll give you a few options to consider. Of course, these aren't the only options. I guarantee that there are awesome advertising opportunities for your specific product and niche, and you'll have to seek these out. But this chapter will help get you started down the right path.

First up, we're going to talk about paid ads right WITHIN the Etsy marketplace. Etsy offers both Native and Offsite ad options for you to grow your business. Now, those might sound like an obvious fit for Etsy sellers, but proceed with caution. These relatively new ads options may not be worth your time and money (at least at present). So we're going to dig into the different factors you should consider related to both native and offsite ads. After we talk about Etsy, we'll also explore a couple more options beyond Etsy, so let's get to it! We've used all of these advertising platforms over the years with good results, and so have our clients.

Native Etsy Ads

Native Etsy Ads are Etsy's advertising program within its own platform. These are the ads that appear right at the top of the search results when customers type a keyword Etsy has identified for one of your products into the search bar.

Native ads can, for some sellers, be a good place to start advertising your Etsy shop. And it's completely optional, which means you can turn it on and off as needed throughout the life of your shop. Here's how it works:

- You pick your daily budget anywhere between $1 and $50.

- You pick the listings you want to advertise.

- Etsy will advertise those listings for relevant keywords (taken from your title and tags) within Etsy. The keywords your products are advertised for are chosen by Etsy's sales algorithm (which we're pretty sure is separate from their search algorithm —more on this below).

- You pay only when someone clicks on your ad, and the amount depends on the keyword you're being advertised for and how competitive that keyword is.

- Etsy will only advertise your listings until your daily budget has been spent.

That's your part. Now, here's what Etsy does once you start a native ad campaign:

- Etsy parses the keywords in your title and tags and decides when and to whom to advertise your listings.

- When someone clicks on your ad, Etsy follows them for a month with a "cookie," and anything they buy from you following that ad click counts as profit from that ad.

  TIP: This "cookie" can be good and bad. It's awesome when someone clicks on your ad and ends up buying that item plus a whole bunch of other stuff; you only spent a little bit on advertising for a lot of profit. But this can also go the other way. If a customer clicks on an item with competitive keywords and a high profit margin and then buys nothing or a different, low-profit-margin item, your ad spend can go way up for very little profit (boo!).

Best Practices for Native Etsy Ads

If you decide to use Native Etsy Ads, here's the formula I'd recommend:

- Pick a few (between 2-10) of your listings to advertise. Pick your newest listings or listings that are selling moderately well. Don't advertise your top sellers (more on this below).
- Start with a fairly low daily budget—I'm talking like $1-3 a day.
- Don't make any changes for 30 days minimum. This way, Etsy's advertising algorithm can get good data on when and to whom to advertise your items.
- Check the stats for each ad regularly throughout the month to see what keywords Etsy is advertising your product for and how much interest the ad is getting. (For more on Etsy Stats, see Chapter 14.)
- Keep an eye on the organic stats for each of the listings you've decided to advertise. If the organic views and sales start dropping, you may have to pull that item from Native Etsy Ads early.

So, Are Native Etsy Ads Worth Your Time?

The answer is a solid maybe. Let me give you a little background and then I'll dive into what types of shops might benefit most from Native Etsy Ads and which shops should steer clear.

A Few Glaring Downsides of Native Etsy Ads

I'll be very up front with you. The "new" Native Etsy Ads program (started in 2018) is, well, not my favorite thing. I liked the old program (Etsy Promoted Listings) A LOT. All of us sellers did. If you read over conversations on the Etsy Forums about Etsy Ads, you'll see that at least a quarter of the posts bemoan the death of Promoted Listings. With that program, sellers could pick the ad words for which they wanted their ads shown as well as how much they were willing to spend on *each word*. Sellers were seeing incredible ROIs of $20-$30 per $1 spent. Ah, the good old days when Etsy was small and sellers were the top priority.

Native Etsy Ads sets the price for ad words higher than sellers want to pay

Etsy ultimately decided (and was probably pressured into by shareholders) that it wanted a bigger piece of that advertising pie, and the new Native Etsy Ads was born. The advertising algorithm now decides how much certain ad words are worth, and it's a lot more than Etsy was charging sellers before for those same words. This amounts to higher ad spend and fewer sales for sellers across the platform.

Now, Native Etsy Ads isn't bad—on average, sellers still seem to be seeing ROIs of 3:1, which is considered pretty good in the online marketing world. For example, Google AdWords and other similar online ad channels only have average ROIs of 2:1.

The problem is that extremely small businesses like most Etsy shops require higher ROIs (they have narrower profit margins) than big box stores (which can run on extremely narrow margins because they churn out so much product) to make advertising worth it. Why? Well, the difference has to do with *fixed costs*: basically, chunks of money you have to pay regularly whether or not you actually made any money in sales. And if your revenues are small, fixed costs can take a much larger bite out of your revenue than the same fixed costs would for a store bringing in hundreds of thousands of dollars each month. The hard truth is that taking on too many fixed costs can sink a small business really fast.

One of the biggest strengths of Etsy's platform is that virtually all of the costs it imposes on sellers are *variable costs*, e.g., you're only charged when you make a sale. The listing fee is the only fixed cost, and it's only *60 cents* per year per listing—quite affordable. This model means that even the smallest Etsy shops can succeed. As sales increase, costs go up proportionately, but variable costs will never exceed your revenue.

This brings us to the crux of the issue: That daily budget you set in Native Etsy Ads? That's a FIXED cost. You still have to pay for clicks even if you get zero sales from those clicks. You may also have other fixed costs that are essential to your business such as studio space, utilities, subscriptions for any tools you use to make your products, etc. And the reality is that even if Native Etsy Ads makes you $90 for $30 ad spend one month, that $60 you made in profit from ads isn't going to go very far toward covering your essential expenses.

Now, if you start making $600 a month profit off of $300 ad spend ($900 revenue), now you're arriving at a place where Native Etsy Ads starts to become worth it despite the fixed costs. There are absolutely Etsy shops earning these kinds of profits from Native Etsy Ads. I'll talk about some characteristics of shops that make this more likely in the next section.

Etsy's advertising algorithm isn't great at picking ad words yet

A 3:1 ROI isn't guaranteed for every seller who pays for Native Etsy Ads: good ROIs depend a lot on product niche and even more, on the performance of Etsy's algorithm, which is still kind of in that awkward adolescent phase of development when it comes to natural language search. (To illustrate, the ad algorithm once advertised one of my political graphic tees for the term "koi fish" because one of my title keywords was the idiom, "fishing expedition." Not cool, Etsy.)

Etsy's algorithms—both search and advertising—are probably never going to be the powerful engines Google's are. This just means that you'll have to be a lot more careful relying on them to advertise your listings for the correct ad words. Watch your ad stats carefully, and if the ads aren't working, turn them off.

Organic sales seem to drop for advertised listings

This is a super frustrating and common problem seen by many Etsy sellers whose shops already have good sales from organic search. We saw it both times we tried Native Etsy Ads. About two weeks after beginning an ad campaign, our organic views and sales for the advertised listings dropped. The drop in sales was so drastic that the ad campaign turned out to be a net loss for our shop.

This is almost certainly a problem with (1) the current version of Etsy's ad algorithm and (2) with the way Etsy displays results. (1) If the algorithm is advertising your listings to the wrong customers for the wrong searches, it's not going to get any engagement, which, as I talked about in Chapter 2, brings down the listing's rating and prevents it from ranking well in organic search. A poor rank in search results means fewer sales. And (2) when Etsy's algorithm does get the ad words correct, Etsy often displays your listing twice on a page —once as an ad and again in organic search results. This means that someone who would have clicked on and bought your listing *without* the ad clicks the ad instead before buying the product. Native ads are supposed to broaden your customer base, not swindle you out of your profits from customers who already support you.

These last two downsides I've discussed are problems I'm hoping Etsy will fix. Maybe, by the time you're reading this, they already have. The takeaway, though, is to be cautious if you decide to use Native Etsy Ads and to keep a close eye on how your ads and your overall shop are performing during an ad campaign.

Shops That Will Benefit from Native Etsy Ads

Problems aside, I do believe that some sellers can have a lot of success with Native Etsy Ads. Also, the program is getting better all the time. Here are the types of shops that will get the most out of a stint with Native Etsy Ads. And even if your shop doesn't fit into one of the following categories, I'd still recommend you give the program a month trial when you can afford it. See for yourself if it works for you.

- **Native Etsy Ads may be good for new sellers.** Etsy has become such a competitive online marketplace that it's hard to compete in organic search right off the bat. A few ads can really jumpstart sales for new sellers.

- **Native Etsy Ads may benefit shops that sell all higher margin items**. An ROI of 3:1 is not enough for me to justify spending those advertising dollars. Many of my product margins are very low, and too many people would click on an ad for a higher-margin item and then buy a lower-margin product, driving my ad spend way up. Shops that sell mostly higher profit margin items may find they get higher ROIs or that 3:1 is enough to make a good-sized profit.

- **Native Etsy Ads may benefit shops that can move a lot of product quickly.** The nature of handmade items often means Etsy sellers want to sell fewer items at a higher margin. Realistically, you can only crochet so many baby blankets each month. But if scaling up your product production is possible (say, by outsourcing part of the creation or hiring people to help you), you may want to give Native Etsy Ads a lengthy try (90+ days) to see if you can work up to getting advertising profits in the "worth-it" range.

- **Native Etsy Ads may benefit very niche products or shops**. The cost-per-click (CPC) for certain broad-market/short-tail search terms has gone up dramatically in the last few years. This is probably because Etsy has grown so much. If your product is competing in a much smaller niche, a small daily ad budget of $1 will go a lot further because the ad words you're competing for aren't as expensive. This means more ads and subsequently more sales. **Warning**: If this is you, make sure you watch your ad stats like a hawk. Niche products are more likely to suffer from the lack of data collected by the advertising algorithm, which may begin to advertise your products for the wrong ad words.

Wrapping up, Native Etsy Ads has some downsides, but it can offer some compelling benefits as long as you proceed with caution. I'd recommend keeping an eye on Native Etsy Ads even if you decide not to use it right away. It's bound to get better and better as time goes on.

TIP: If you google the common question, "Is Etsy Ads worth it?" (most people refer to Native Etsy Ads as simply "Etsy Ads") make sure you only look at articles written AFTER about February 2020. Anything written about Native Etsy Ads before this will be discussing a different iteration of Etsy's Ad programs.

Now it's time to move on to Etsy's other paid ads option, which we highly recommend: Offsite Etsy Ads.

Etsy Offsite Ads

Etsy's Offsite Ads program is related to but separate from the Native Etsy Ads program. It's how Etsy has settled on handling advertising your products on other sites outside their own platform (e.g., Google, Bing, Facebook, Instagram, and Pinterest). It's also new, as in, it's only been around since April 2020. Here's how it works:

- If your shop earns more than $10,000/year, Etsy will automatically enroll you in Offsite Ads and will take a 12% of any revenue you earn from those ads. Shops earning under $10,000/year can choose to participate, but Etsy will take 15% of their ad revenue.

- Etsy pays the platforms listed above to show your top performing listings to interested customers. Etsy's ad algorithm takes care of purchasing appropriate ad words for your listings, and the offsite platforms figure out when and to whom to display your products.

- You can see how well these Offsite Ads are performing in Etsy's Stats section. Click the link "See more info on your Offsite Ads →" under the graph showing your organic sales. It looks like this:

See traffic and sales driven by Offsite Ads

We're promoting your items on high-traffic sites including Google, Instagram, Facebook, Pinterest, and Bing to drive new buyers straight to your shop. It's risk-free advertising—we pay the upfront costs to promote your items. You only pay when you make a sale.

See more info on your Offsite Ads →

The coolest thing about Etsy Offsite Ads is that you don't have to pay for ad words or clicks. Etsy buys Google and Bing ad words and Facebook/Instagram and Pinterest ad space on their own dime. You only pay that 12% or 15% fee to Etsy *when you actually make a sale*. The way Etsy is doing this takes away the risks of advertising on expensive channels like Google but passes the benefits on to you.

Why You Should Participate in Offsite Ads, AKA Why Etsy Offsite Ads is a Good Program (Even if You've Been Forced into It)

The first piece of good news about Etsy Offsite Ads is that the ROIs are usually higher than the average for Native Etsy Ads (as just one example, we're seeing an ROI of 7:1). And the listings advertised through Offsite Ads still maintain the same level of organic views and sales within Etsy. So, right off the bat, it's clear that this program doesn't have the main downsides Etsy's internal ad tool (Native Etsy Ads) suffers from. Additionally, Etsy has a lot more motivation to get offsite ad words for your products correct because they're taking on the cost of clicks on these offsite platforms. Sellers are only charged when they make a sale, so all the pressure is on Etsy to get us those sales.

That's a pretty sweet deal, but in my opinion, there's one even more important benefit that Offsite Ads offers sellers. The best thing about Offsite Ads (in my humble opinion) is that it brings you new customers from across the web and across the world. About 4-5% of our sales each month come from Offsite Ads, and most of these are people who are new to our shop and often even new to shopping on Etsy. They're people who might never have found our shop through Etsy search alone. A percentage of these people are going to come back, growing our customer base and leading to increasingly more sales over time.

As a platform, Etsy is growing significantly because of Offsite Ads (August 2020 Quarterly Report). This means Etsy itself is being seen as a more legitimate online marketplace. More shoppers than ever are choosing to shop on Etsy, and that increased traffic to the platform means more customers finding your shop and buying your products.

Takeaway: I believe Etsy Offsite Ads is well worth your time no matter how large or small, experienced or new your Etsy shop is. There's really no downside to trying it out since Etsy is taking on all the risk for you, and the opportunity to grow your customer base and increase brand visibility is too good to pass up.

As with Native ads, keep an eye on changes to Etsy's Offsite Ads program (changes will certainly happen as Etsy grows). What's working today doesn't always work tomorrow. Etsy (just like other ecommerce platforms) requires a certain amount of "continuing education" to make sure you're still on the same page with Etsy's behavior.

Ads Beyond Etsy: Going Rogue

You can do a LOT to grow your business with ads right inside Etsy via Native and Offsite Ads. But there are also good opportunities beyond Etsy that you may want to pursue. Before we dive in here, it's important for you to understand that while Etsy's ad options are totally automated (you just decide the amount you're willing to pay and whether you want to participate, basically) ads BEYOND Etsy allow more customization and give you more control. This can be a good thing, but it can also be a little intimidating. So first, let's talk through best practices for any kind of paid ads beyond Etsy.

Best Practices for Any Kind of Paid Advertising

Now that you have an idea for when to pay for advertising, I want to briefly touch on best practices for advertising online. Because the quality of your ads counts! We'll cover a lot of these basics in more detail in Chapters 4 (Graphic Design), 9 (Content and Copywriting), and 8 (Branding). But here's a few 'dos' and 'don'ts' to follow:

Dos:

* **Know your audience:** Before creating even a single ad, work up a profile of your ideal customer. You can find information about this customer (age, gender, likes and dislikes, etc.) from your followers on social media, pixels, or Google Analytics data.

- **Promote visually appealing content:** Ads must be eye-catching these days. It's no secret that online customers have very short attention spans, so if an ad doesn't first catch a customers eye and make them look twice, there's no chance she'll end up clicking or buying your product.

- **Be consistent in branding and tone:** Consistent branding helps customers recognize and remember your shop, and consistent tone will help them feel like they're engaging with a real person rather than a robot trying to sell them something.

- **Use a call-to-action:** All of the studies on online advertising show that customers are more likely to click an ad when it contains a call to action ("2021 Inbound Marketing Stats on the Power of Call-to-Action Buttons" from Protocol80.com). These phrases demand that a customer act and can be as simple as "Shop Now."

Don'ts:

- **Don't overwhelm your audience with ads:** Advertising fatigue is a real thing, so be careful not to create too many ads on a single platform. Advertising three times a week is a good goal with more than one ad per day being too much. Most of the time, your daily ad budget and the platform will keep ad overload in check, but it's good to keep an eye on your ad frequency, especially if you're in a very small niche or are advertising on a smaller platform.

- **Don't use too much text:** Again, online customers have short attention spans. You'll want to focus on eye-catching images and short but bold phrases that draw customers in. One example is an advertising phrase we've used with success —"Turn yourself into a walking political statement."

- **Don't try to advertise to a very broad demographic:** The data show that targeted advertising leads to more sales, so don't assume one ad will engage every customer in your demographic. This is where Google Analytics can come in handy (see Chapter 14). Segmenting your data helps you divide up your audience by characteristics and interests so you can target different ads for different groups.

- **Don't ignore data:** One of the mistakes new advertisers make is to assume you know what your audience will like, while ignoring the data about what they ACTUALLY like. Check the stats on your ad often and change the ad to reflect what your audience truly likes and clicks. Keep an open mind and go where the data takes you.

Paid Facebook and Instagram Ads

Facebook and Instagram ads are at the top of the list for the best bang for your buck opportunities outside of Etsy. They're pretty cheap, pretty effective once you hone in on an audience and tactic, and they're intuitive and easy to build (Facebook and Instagram definitely would love to spend your money!).

You should know that Etsy Offsite Ads will do some of your Facebook and Instagram advertising for you, so there's no pressing need to do your own advertising on these platforms if you're already participating in Offside Ads. But you can do a lot more if you take some of this marketing into your own hands.

I'm including Facebook and Instagram in the same section because they're owned by the same company and use the same ad program (Facebook for Business (FfB) to manage advertising on both platforms. Here are the main reasons we recommend advertising on FfB separately from what Offsite Ads is already doing for you:

- You know your product and customers better than anyone else, so you can create ads that reach customers in a way nobody else can.

- FfB ads are relatively affordable and user-friendly, especially compared to channels like Google AdWords.

- Advertising through FfB can help grow your social media following much more rapidly than it would grow organically.

How to Successfully Advertise on Facebook and Instagram

Your social media ads are going to be most successful if you already have a pool of followers you gained organically. If you don't already have a social following, we talk more about growing a social audience in Chapter 13. I strongly suggest you skip over there if you don't yet have business accounts on Facebook and Instagram before going down the FfB advertising route. Your ads will be a lot more effective if you start out with a decent social media presence and have a general idea of what your audience will like.

You don't actually NEED a ton of followers for Facebook and Instagram ads to reach their targets. Facebook and Instagram will advertise beyond the pool of followers you've gained. But, you won't really know how your audience reacts to different phrasing, content, types of images, etc., unless you've spent some time posting. And you need to have a good idea of how your audience reacts to things before you try to create an ad from scratch. Post regularly on your social channels, and keep records of which images and captions seem to get the most comments, positive reactions, and likes.

Create ads

Okay, so logistics: If you're ready to advertise through FfB, you'll need a business account on both Facebook and Instagram, which involves upgrading for free from your personal account and verifying your business. Creating an ad is pretty simple after that—you simply promote content you already know your audience likes or post your ads to your feeds and then promote them. Facebook and Instagram will display your content in your potential customers' feeds as "sponsored content." The basic elements you'll need to create an ad are a caption, an image, a clickable call to action, and a link.

Best rule of thumb for captions is, keep it pretty short and sweet. Don't make your customer read a bunch of text, because they'll often glaze over or keep scrolling. A few words is generally great. Keep it light, use the tone you've found that resonates with your audience, and move on! For images, a lifestyle image from your shop is often a really good choice. It's engaging, it's beautiful, and it doesn't look too "salesy" or corporate (big turn offs for people who might want to buy your handmade thing!). If you have a simple, gorgeous main image, that can work really well too. Make sure that you use A/B testing (with the only difference in the ad sets being your image) to see what resonates most with your audience.

Your link, of course, will typically direct potential customers to your product. BUT in some situations you may want to direct them to a specific shop section or your shop homepage. Specific is typically better, but don't be afraid to experiment a little with that good old A/B testing. For the clickable call to action, again keep it SHORT. "Shop Now" is usually a very safe bet. Don't get too weird here.

Choose your target audience and budget

Your last goal will be to choose an audience for your posts to be advertised to. Facebook or Instagram can do this for you by creating a lookalike audience (an audience that shares a lot of characteristics with your own Facebook following—another reason to gather a social following) or you can choose targeted characteristics, like "people who shop online often, people who are interested in environmental causes, people who like different TV shows," etc. This is where your customer profile will come in really handy, e.g., if you've got parents as your key customer audience, choose things that parents might love. This is a huge part of refining your ads—targeting them effectively. So don't rush this.

You'll also need to choose a timeframe for your ad to run and a budget. Let your ad run for a few days and start with just a few dollars. I recommend you always choose a very SMALL budget at first, especially while you're testing ads to see what resonates best. You can learn a lot from very small numbers, and the goal is to do more of what works. Launch a couple of A/B tests at a time, and choose the ad that's performing best. Once you feel pretty confident that you've got decent engagement and your targeting is pretty on track, increase your budget and monitor closely.

Check your stats

The business accounts on both Facebook and Instagram have awesome analytics tools. You can easily go in and see what kind of content really interests and engages your audience. Look for the posts with the most likes, comments, and shares/reposts. These are the types of posts you'll want to promote and the content you'll want to emulate when you create ads.

Advertising on social can take some experimenting, so be prepared to review and revise as needed. Never set your ads on autopilot, particularly when you're still in a learning phase or new to ads.

If you have the budget, it can be very helpful to find someone who can help you craft effective Facebook and Instagram ads. But be very careful here. "Gurus" are a dime a dozen. Don't take promises or impressive claims lightly. Ask for references before spending a lot of money, and make sure you're comfortable with the person you're working with.

Bonus: Pixels for Pattern by Etsy users

If you have a Pattern site through Etsy (Chapter 19), you can also add a Facebook Pixel to your page. (Unfortunately, as of June 2020, you can no longer add a pixel directly to your Etsy shop itself.) The pixel tracks people who visit and purchase from your site, giving you a detailed profile of who your customers are and their buying habits. This allows both you and Facebook/Instagram to target your ads directly to your customers or even to different segments of your customers. This kind of back-and-forth between your site and your advertising platform can make your ads more than twice as effective as they would be without.

Takeaway: If you have a Pattern by Etsy site and use Facebook for Business, add the Facebook pixel to your Pattern site in the settings tab. It will make your ads more effective and increase your sales and ad revenue.

Advertising with Social Media Influencers

Influencers are people who have a large number of followers on their social media account(s). That might be TikTok, Instagram, Facebook, Pinterest, etc. Good influencers are incredibly effective in swaying people's opinions about a product by promoting it to their audience. Getting an influencer to wear, use, or feature your product on their social media channels is considered one of the fastest ways to grow your audience and sell more products. If an influencer likes something, their audience will probably like it too, and then many of those people become part of your audience as well.

While some influencers will promote you in exchange for a free product, don't expect the really successful ones to be interested in this unless your product is quite expensive or very desirable to that particular influencer (if it is, that's wonderful for you!).

Identify the influencers who might share your values and interests, then send a message about pricing for product placement. Some influencers will want you to come up with the captions for their post, and others will want that creative control (after all, it's THEIR audience). Most will decline opportunities that aren't a great fit if your product won't really resonate with their audience.

Pricing for working with an influencer will vary a LOT depending on that influencer's number of followers. But don't be fooled into thinking that followers is the only number you should look at. Followers are important, but ENGAGEMENT is key. If someone has 100k followers but only 100 people are liking their posts and a couple people are commenting, it's very unlikely that your post will get much traction, and you shouldn't bother. If, however, an influencer has 20k followers and is getting thousands of likes and many comments, PAY ATTENTION. That influencer knows what's up and is very in tune with their audience. Expect to pay anywhere from $10 for a post to upwards of several hundred. You'll need to do your research for each influencer, weigh your options, and look at engagement and how well your product aligns with that influencer. Most influencers offer several "tiers" of post types, so you can decide how much you want to spend. If you find a lot of success working with an influencer, you may want to consider an ongoing partnership.

And as you grow, influencers may reach out to you. That's when you know you've leveled up.

Native Content Product Placement

Do you ever read blog posts that rave about a particular "find" or that include links for products? In the best ones, you'll never even realize you're reading an advertisement because the writer has so seamlessly and naturally woven in a reference to the "beautiful baby blanket" they found in reference to their DIY nursery blog post, or "my favorite sunglasses" in a post about summer fashion trends.

Blogging is not dead. And content influencers (often bloggers) are the long-form influencers who produce content that isn't overtly salesly but can still heavily affect their followers' buying behavior. Spend some time seeking out blogging and content influencers who align with your aesthetic, include links to similar products, and talk about stuff that aligns with your audience (e.g., fashion tips if you sell jewelry, or baby advice if you sell homemade bibs).

Don't be afraid to ask about views, engagement, and clicks when you reach out to these bloggers about costs for native advertising. You should also check the blogger's website domain authority through Moz.com or ahrefs.com. This will tell you how credible google considers the domain and how high that blog will show up in search for "baby advice" for example. If you find a solid content marketer or blogger with great engagement and domain authority, this can be well worth your money. Remember, start small and don't break the bank even if you feel really good about a collaboration. See how it works out. And if it goes well with a smaller promo, do more!

Where Not to Advertise as an Etsy Seller

There are two types of advertising—one ad channel and one practice —that you'll likely see recommended regularly as you delve into the world of marketing: Google AdWords and outsourcing your advertising to an ad company. There's nothing wrong with either one, but in my experience, neither is worth pursuing if you're an Etsy shop seller.

Here's why:

Google AdWords

For Etsy sellers, there's really no need to participate directly in Google AdWords because Etsy Offsite Ads does this for you at a huge discount. AdWords is a pay-per-click service, which means businesses often spend a lot of money up front figuring out which keywords they ought to be paying for. And then there's the "Google slap." Even if you find keywords to advertise for that don't cost too much per click, as soon as Google notices you are using those ads successfully and making money, the algorithm will raise the price of your clicks, often to more than you're making from those ads. It's an all too common phenomenon.

And as I discussed earlier in the chapter, Etsy shops are often on the small end of the small business spectrum and can't afford to take on large fixed costs like buying ad words on Google. It's just not worth it.

Summed up, probably don't bother with Google AdWords. It's really expensive. And you're covered if you're already using Etsy Offsite Ads.

Outsourced Advertising

There are a lot of companies and individuals out there who want to take on the advertising burden for you. The reality is that the ones most Etsy sellers can afford aren't going to be able to give your shop the time and attention necessary to run a successful ad campaign across multiple platforms.

If you're considering outsourcing your advertising, remember that you know your products and customers better than an outsider ever will. This means that you'll want to hire a person or company who is willing to listen to you and create an ad campaign based on your suggestions rather than simply putting in motion a cookie-cutter advertising approach.

This kind of personal attention and care is not cheap. In fact, I've found that anyone offering advertising "for a great price" is probably going to do more harm than good to your company image and reputation. Don't forget that bad advertising is worse than no advertising.

The combined risk of a large price tag plus the potential reputation damage that comes from poor advertising is why I don't recommend outsourcing your advertising as an Etsy seller.

Making Sure Your Ads are Working for You

As you explore the world of online advertising beyond Etsy, keep the following in mind:

- **Always start small:** Remember that any money you spend advertising means risking losing that money, so never commit more of your funds than you're able to lose without going under. This is especially important for small businesses like Etsy shops. Luckily, there are a number of ad channels available that allow you to start with a tiny investment and grow as you see the ads working for you.

- **Keep experimenting:** There's no foolproof method for success when it comes to advertising. Every shop is different, and customers are going to respond to some ads and not to others. Don't give up too quickly when first starting out in the world of paid advertising. If the first ad you try doesn't work, try something else. Trust that your passion and creativity will eventually come through and that you will reach the people who want what you sell.

- **Most important, check your stats:** All ad channels have analytics tools that tell you how well your ads are performing. Don't ignore the data—it may surprise you. Maybe your customers aren't using Facebook like you thought they were. Your stats will tell you this, and you can try a different social channel or ditch social media advertising altogether. If after 90 days, an ad channel is doing nothing for your business, it's probably time to try something different or to stop advertising there.

- **And lastly, never put your ads on autopilot:** When your money is on the line, you want to be tweaking your ads and budgets regularly to find what really works for your business. And even once you've found ad channels and ads that work, keep in mind that seasons change and customers' interests evolve. What's working this month won't work forever.

Free or Almost Free Advertising

This chapter wouldn't be complete without at least a mention of all the free advertising opportunities out there. It's absolutely possible to grow your Etsy shop without employing any paid advertising at all. It just takes some hard work, creativity, and sweat equity. You can learn more about all of these methods in other chapters, so I'll only give a brief overview of my favorite free advertising opportunities here.

- **Social media** is a great free advertising channel for online businesses. Social platforms give you the chance to connect with your audience and create a loyal customer base. And if your content is really good, these customers will expand your reach for you through shares, retweets, reposts, etc. It's like having a giant team of advertisers across the globe working for you for free simply because they like your shop (and you!) and value your product. And once you have a decent following on a social channel, advertising through that channel can really get a lot of eyeballs on your products. Facebook and Instagram are considered "pay-to-play" channels because they limit your organic growth on purpose at a certain point, but they're still excellent ways to get started with growing your shop and customer base. Chapter 13 talks more about how to use social media to promote your shop.

- **Email Marketing** is another free advertising channel that Etsy sellers should absolutely be using. It's a free way to connect directly with your most engaged and loyal customers. These are people who've signed up for your emails specifically, so they are especially interested in your company and your products. The how-tos of email marketing can be found in Chapter 11.

- **Content Marketing** (which largely refers to blogging) can get you a lot of free eyeballs. If you can write in a unique and interesting way about your product, shop, and causes you support, you can reach a lot of customers. For example, a blog post tutorial about how to make a leather bracelet will not only help you sell more jewelry but will help your customers remember your shop because you helped them solve a problem. Content marketing also includes guest blogging on blogs with larger followings than yours and writing articles/answering questions on online sites like LinkedIn, Medium, Quora, Etsy forums, and the Etsy Subreddits. You can read more about the pros and cons of content marketing in Chapter 9.

- **SEO**, or search engine optimization, refers to finding the right keywords that connect your customers with your product through a search engine. Optimizing your Etsy listings for Etsy's search algorithm is a powerful way to increase your sales for free. You can find out more about the ins and outs of Etsy SEO in Chapter 2.

- **Influencers:** While we focused on influencers as a paid strategy, some collaborations can be free or almost free. You can offer some influencers free stuff or run a giveaway that they post to their site. It may also help to offer a coupon code for an influencer's followers to use that will give them a discount in your shop. This often helps encourage good engagement for a post (which benefits both you and the influencer).

- **Donations:** Giving donations is a wonderful way to support organizations you believe in, and it can get your Shop Name on the websites, newsletters, and event programs of these organizations.

- **Personal connections:** Last but not least, I'd encourage you to embrace the fact that you are the face of your business. Sign your emails with your name followed by "Owner, Your Shop Name." Change your voicemail so people calling you know they're calling the owner of a business. And introduce yourself online and in person as a business owner in as many other contexts as possible. Print up business cards if you can afford it and give them out. I know. It'll feel strange at first. Imposter syndrome is a very real thing—I've felt it too. Don't let it hold you back though. You are absolutely the best person for the job.

Things We Learned the Hard Way

Advertising has been a journey for us, and we've made our fair share of mistakes. One was trying to outsource our advertising "cheaply." We ended up hiring a small company that promised they had some secret sauce for creating the perfect Facebook ads. It turned out they not only didn't have any secret sauce, but they didn't know our niche at all—certainly not well enough to create useful content, much less to advertise it to the right demographic. Unfortunately, we'd already signed a contract and ended up paying them a large sum even though they didn't help bring in new business or make us more sales. Even cheap ad companies still cost a bundle.

We also learned all of the stuff about Etsy Ads the hard way and have concluded that, in its current form, Etsy Ads isn't a great advertising platform for us. I hope you have better luck if you decide to try it out.

Overall, though, we've learned a lot on our advertising journey. It's easy to be afraid to jump into paid advertising, but hopefully, this chapter has shown you that it's possible to start small and iterate until you figure out what works for your business.

CHAPTER 13

Social Media

Social media, we love it, we hate it. But from a business perspective, it's an absolutely essential part of marketing, branding, and building a good reputation and following for your Etsy shop. Why? Because social media is a free way to get eyes on your product. It also gives you the opportunity to connect to your customers in a more intimate way.

If you approach social media the right way, it allows you to build a customer base that is loyal and genuinely wants you to succeed. It's the fun part—customers who stumble across your shop for the first time via a single listing become repeat customers and start to feel like friends.

There are also many different opportunities to pay for ads on social media that can increase your visibility and grow your business (we just covered a few of those opportunities in Chapter 12!).

But ... WHICH social channels should you use? What should you post? Where should you start? The world of social media is HUGE and can feel like a major drain on your time and energy. Which it absolutely can be, especially if you try to stretch yourself too thin. So let's talk about where you should be spending that time and energy:

Which Social Channels Should You Use?

There are SO many social platforms—Instagram, Facebook, Tumblr, TikTok, YouTube, Twitter, Pinterest, Reddit among others—and large companies usually try to have a presence on all or at least most of them.

But as the owner of a small, often one-person Etsy shop, I strongly recommend you pick TWO platforms that showcase your products and cause (if you have one) and excel at those. Don't get sucked into the trap of trying to be everywhere at once. Because you don't need to be. You'll spread yourself thin, and your content and following on social will suffer.

You need to be where the majority of your audience spends the majority of its time. Which, for most people, is still Facebook and Instagram. (At least that's where the people who spend money on Etsy hang out, anyway. Despite what you might hear, the stats don't lie—"Most popular social networks" from Statista.com.) In other words, if you decide not to use one of those two platforms as your bread-and-butter, make sure you're doing so intentionally rather than haphazardly.

Regardless of the platforms you choose to adopt as your social bread and butter, focus on quality content and building an audience. The likes, engagement, and rapport will follow. Treat your audience like your friends, and deliver quality. Then follow these best practices for your best shot at success:

Overall Best Practices on Social Media

Regardless of which platform you use (we'll delve into the details of how to use each individual platform to grow your Etsy shop momentarily), you'll want to follow some best practices around what to post, when to post, etc. Here's a breakdown of overall best practices for social media.

What to Post

We follow the 80-20 rule with content—80% of your content on social media should be about your cause, things that resonate deeply with your audience or add value to their lives. Non-promotional stuff. And 20% should be images of your products, shop info, and obvious advertising material. The audiences you build on social want to see stuff they love on their feed. That might be a screenshot of a tweet, a funny or beautiful image, or a quote (that's related to the brand image you're trying to project). If your social media accounts are purely promotional material, your audience will stop engaging with your content, and high engagement is the primary measure of success on social media.

TIP: Be sure to post different content on each social platform you maintain—you want your audience regularly checking all of your social channels because they're excited to hear from you and they don't want to risk missing a sale or special event.

Example of our 20% content—a t-shirt design we're advertising

Example of our 80% content—relatable and funny content our audience can engage with

How Often to Post

How often you post during the week or month will depend on the platform(s) you choose, but a good rule of thumb is the more text you include your posts, the less often you ought to post. Your audience has limited time, and if you're posting paragraphs on social media multiple times a day, they'll start to feel overwhelmed and stop reading your posts. Image-centric content, on the other hand, can handle a lot higher posting frequency.

You can spend all day posting on social if that's your jam, but for those of you that would rather create social content all at once, try a scheduling tool. Later.com will allow you to schedule posts, add links, and see which of your posts are getting the best engagement. It does cost $20 a month but is well worth it in time savings. Later can also help you research hashtags to expose your content to new potential followers and customers.

When to Post

When you're just starting out on a platform, Google what times during the day the most people are using that particular platform and post during those times. Generally, 3–4 pm and evenings on weekdays and the mid-morning on weekends for your timezone are good times to shoot for—think of when people often take mental breaks by browsing social media. As your audience grows, however, you can look at your platform's analytics to see when your audience is on social media, and you can start posting more during those times.

Using Hashtags

Hashtags are social media's way of sorting content and making it searchable, and people actually do use hashtags to find content related to their interests. This means you should include several different relevant hashtags on each post, especially on image-heavy platforms like Instagram, Pinterest, and Tumblr.

Tools like Later.com can help you find the best hashtags with the most engagement, but simply typing a hashtag and a keyword describing your post into the content section of your social media post can be almost as effective. Instagram, for example, shows you the number of other posts using this hashtag, which can give you an idea of how popular it is.

It's also worth noting that hashtags have become a way of expressing sarcasm or amusement, so you can go ahead and create your own hashtags whenever the situation calls for it. For example, taking a segment of your post caption and turning it into a hashtag can emphasize the funny or sarcastic part of your post that you think others will be most likely to relate to—#neildoyouwearshoes or #yougetwhatyoupayfor. These hashtags aren't really searchable, but they're pretending to be in a fun, self-aware way. This is also true for hashtags like #soexcited #icantwaitforNovember, which add an extra note of relatable excitement and anticipation to a post and can increase engagement.

#neildoyouwearshoes?

Building an Audience

Each platform has its own tips and tricks for growing your audience, but in general, the best way to build an audience is to post high-quality, interesting, unique content. Your goal is to get people to engage with your content and share it with friends by tagging them in comments or posting the content on their own pages as well—essential, free advertising for your social media platform (and later, when you share your trickle of promotional posts, your shop!).

Finding the right balance in tone, content type, and conversational style is really important. Think about how your audience might react to each post: will they feel like they can relate? Will they feel positive feelings when viewing it? Each time your posts make the people in your audience feel happy, excited, less alone, or righteously indignant (with you, not AT you), you forge a lasting connection between that person and yourself/your shop. People who feel included in your circle are more likely to become repeat customers and to share your shop with friends.

Of course, there are ways you can manipulate each platform to help grow an audience, but I'll talk more about building audiences on individual platforms in a later section.

Should You Ever Pay for Followers?

The short answer is no. Some of the social platforms do give special privileges to accounts with a lot of followers (e.g., Instagram rewards accounts with over 10,000 followers with their "swipe up" feature, which allows you to link your stories and posts directly to your website, whereas accounts with fewer than 10,000 followers are only allowed one link in their bio). But special privileges aimed at increasing your reach and your sales are worth almost nothing if your audience has zero interest in *engaging* with your content. And a lack of engagement is inevitable if you purchase followers rather than acquiring them organically. You want followers who are actually interested in you and what you sell—100 random Joes are not even close to as valuable as one loyal customer who purchases from you many times over the life of your shop.

Influencers

Influencers are people who have a large number of followers and can sway people's opinions about a product by promoting it to their audience. Getting an influencer to wear, use, or feature your product on their social media channels is considered one of the fastest ways to grow your audience and sell more product. If an influencer likes something, their audience will probably like it too, and then many of those people become part of your audience as well.

It's worth reaching out through direct messaging to influencers who might share your values and interests if your social media presence is fairly small. And as you grow, influencers may reach out to you (oh, yeah!).

Responding to Comments

You should respond to or at least "like" comments on your social media posts as often as possible without losing your sanity. And in general, comments should reflect the amount of effort the commenter put into their comment. If someone comments with an emoji, a "like" is sufficient, but if someone took the time to write out their thoughts in a sentence or paragraph, a validating or understanding response can really help someone connect with and remember you and your shop. (It also is just a decent, caring thing to do, especially since the internet has the tendency to descend into a faceless cesspool of anonymity and name-calling.)

Most social platforms allow you to restrict who comments on your posts and who sees those comments. Please use these options! You may think it's more noble or fair minded to keep the comments section open to anyone and everyone who has something to say, but I'm telling you, it's a recipe for insanity. No matter how innocent your post, there will be someone who absolutely hates it and wants you banned from the internet for posting it, which brings us nicely into the next section: How to deal with trolls and haters.

Trolls and Haters

By definition, trolls are people who are *not* part of your target audience or current followers. They're on the hunt for a fight with someone who represents everything (or at least something) they hate in the world, and their goal is to be contrary, and to get a rise out of you or your actual audience. The rule of thumb with trolls is to not engage with them—either ignore or delete their comments, and they'll leave you alone.

That said, there may be times when you will want to engage with a troll. One example is when it would be cathartic or healing for your audience to see you deliver a take down. Social platforms make it pretty easy to keep control of this kind of situation. In other words, you only need to engage as long as the conversation remains productive—just delete any comments the troll writes after that point, and restrict the troll from being able to comment further. You get the last word (and your sanity remains intact), and your audience goes away feeling validated and empowered.

Another time you'll want to respond to a mean or angry comment is when the "troll" is not really a troll but a disgruntled member of your audience. It's important to take dissenting comments from your own audience seriously. Maybe your post was out of touch or hurtful to a certain group within your demographic. Maybe it was misunderstood. Maybe the commenter is having a bad day and needs your support and understanding. Whatever the reason for the unkind comment, you need to respond, even if you simply say, "Let's agree to disagree on this point." Or "I see your perspective, I hadn't thought about it that way. Thanks for taking the time to comment." These kinds of emotionally mature responses more than anything show that there's a real person behind the company profile, a person that wants to give everyone in her audience a voice even if some of those voices disagree with one another.

A Short Guide to the Heavy-Hitters: Instagram and Facebook

Like I mentioned earlier, Instagram and Facebook are still the heaviest hitters in the world of social media. That doesn't mean they're the coolest or that they're necessarily the absolute best use of your time (you should decide that based on your product and audience), but they are statistically the place where the most people spend most of their time.

So, in that light here's a breakdown of the strengths of Instagram and Facebook (the two platforms we choose to spend most of our time) and a brief summary of best practices for posting and growing an audience on each.

Instagram

I'll admit up front that Instagram is my favorite platform. Its image-heavy focus showcases my t-shirts beautifully and the image-text-hashtag format is perfect for engaging my audience in causes I support. I think all Etsy shop owners should be on Instagram. It's a natural outgrowth of your listing photos (one of your biggest tools for sales and success!)

Here's the basics of Instagram:

- **When to post:** Post at least once a day and up to three times a day. With Instagram, a daily post is a good goal to start with, and it's okay to gather a week's worth of content at a time and schedule your posts on Later.

- **What to post:** I follow the content rule of 80/20: 80% of my content is not product related or branded and 20% is marketing material. The 80% largely consists of engaging content about the causes I support, funny memes my audience might like, or tweets that intersect with my brand values and my audience's interests. Use high-quality images that you take yourself or own legally and screenshots of text-heavy content. If you repost something from another person's account, give credit through tagging and text captions.

- **Growing your audience:** Each Instagram post has space for text below the image, and this text area can include up to 30 hashtags. I use several hashtags but not usually the full 30 (that can come across as overly aggressive in trying to win followers). Hashtags can help you grow your audience by making you finable by topic.

Facebook

Facebook is a more text-focused platform than Instagram. Of course, you can still showcase your products visually on a Facebook account. After all, the original purpose of Facebook was to put your everyday life online for friends and relatives you don't see in person. But Facebook business accounts tend to perform better if they post more controversial or thought-provoking text-based content. As with Instagram, engagement here is everything.

Facebook Best Practices:

- **When to post:** Post a few times a week. As with any text-heavy content, be careful not to overwhelm your audience.

- **What to post:** Interesting or controversial opinion posts with high-quality prose and links to well-written articles (your own or someone else's) do well on Facebook.

- **Growing your audience:** In Facebook, this means getting shares and engagement in the form of comments. Facebook pushes posts with a lot of comments to the top of people's feeds, which means the more engagement you get, the more of your audience will be viewing your post. Then, these people can share your content on their own feeds, and their audiences will see your account listed as the original source.

- **Remember, don't just duplicate your Facebook content to Instagram, or vice versa:** You don't want to signal your audience that they can go ahead and ignore you on one platform.

Other Platforms to Consider

TikTok and YouTube

If your product lends itself well to video demonstrations or if you have a talent for creating engaging videos, TikTok and YouTube might be great platforms to try out. TikTok videos are generally quite short and focused on a single interesting or funny event while YouTube caters to tutorials, interviews, and even full-length films. Video platforms (especially TikTok) are especially popular with younger users, and if you can master the art of short, funny videos you may gain a significant following quickly.

Pinterest

Although Pinterest isn't one of the two TOP platforms I've chosen to focus on in this chapter, I do have a Pinterest business account and know that it can be an excellent platform for Etsy sellers since it's so image-centric. Pinterest is all about images, and with its "Pin it" button, it makes sharing images incredibly easy. As with Instagram, Pinterest sorts images by hashtag, so you'll definitely want to include a few hashtags in the caption of each post. One downside to Pinterest is that this platform can take a lot of time—sellers who use Pinterest successfully need to post 5-30 times *a day*. So, if you're really drawn to Pinterest and enjoy using it, do it! It can be a great way to grow your business. Just don't force it if you aren't feeling the vibe.

Twitter

Although images are allowed on Twitter, it has a reputation as a pithy text platform, and who doesn't love a clever tweet that really captures your feelings on a subject? Because of its fast pace and volatility, I've found Twitter to be a difficult social platform and not particularly worth my time. It's also an extremely political platform. If you post the wrong thing, you might have an angry mob on your tail within an hour. That being said, certain products that make people's lives better day-to-day—tools, apps, courses—often appeal to a Twitter audience. If you try Twitter and find it's going well, definitely build up your audience there and try out Twitter ads when you have some cash to spare.

Stuff We Learned the Hard Way

Engaging with everyone: One of the biggest mistakes I made with social media at first was feeling like I had to engage with everyone, including the trolls who were just there to stir up trouble. Restricting who could comment on my Instagram hasn't decreased my followers or hurt my account—and it's been amazing for my mental health! Managing my social accounts also became less onerous when I started simply liking comments (clicking that heart next to each) instead of trying to come up with a snappy comeback to every one. People want to feel recognized when they comment, but most don't expect more than that. Doing these two things has freed me up to thoughtfully engage with comments I want to respond to, and it's improved the quality and tone of my social accounts a lot.

Too many accounts: Some of the other mistakes I made at first were trying to maintain accounts on too many different social platforms and duplicating content across all of them. I was wasting so much time trying to keep up on social media that I was stressed out all the time, and the extra effort wasn't even resulting in any sales. The reality is that most people only follow a business on one or two social channels anyway. They want to see unique content regularly and will unfollow you if you copy-paste across channels.

The takeaway here is to use the time you spend on social media efficiently and get the most out of your efforts. It's easy to get mired down in all the options. Don't be tempted to try to do it all. Choose two channels that work for your shop, post unique content on each, and make sure only your followers can comment on posts (and if you acquire a troll follower, don't hesitate to ban them—trolls just aren't worth the mental energy).

CHAPTER 14

Using Data and Analytics to Increase Your Sales

As an Etsy seller, you have access to a ton of "inside information" about your shop provided by FREE analytics tools. In this chapter, I'm going to take you on a tour through Etsy Stats followed by a brief visit to Google Analytics and a few social media analytics tools. We'll also talk about A/B testing and how to perform experiments on your listings and watch for results so you know without a doubt exactly what gets you sales and works for your shop.

Once you recognize the significance and applications of all the information right at your fingertips in Etsy, you'll wonder how you got by without using it before. Because I find time and time again that most Etsy sellers AREN'T diving into their data. They think, "data is boring." But I'm here to disabuse you of that notion.

Stats are FUN. Actually, checking the data (sales, trends, conversions) about your shop is addicting. I'm not kidding. Once you start, you won't be able to stop. You'll be clicking on Etsy stats every day just to get high off that sweet sweet conversion rate, those ever increasing impressions, and that upward trend in sales.

Etsy Stats: In-house Metrics

Thanks in large part to Google offering free and open access to Google Analytics, all the major ecommerce platforms include tools for capturing and analyzing data about your shop, and Etsy is no exception. Etsy stats can help you find out precisely how to improve your shop and increase your sales. It can maximize your efforts and time. Here's how it works and why you should monitor your stats regularly.

Key Metrics at Your Fingertips within Etsy

So, what are the main data points you should be looking at? Where can you find them? And what do they mean?

In your Shop Manager, click "Stats," and you'll arrive at the main page of Etsy Stats where you'll see an overview of how your shop is performing. You can set the timeframe you want to look at (the default is 30 days) along the x-axis and see how many visits and orders your shop is getting (y-axis) as well as changes in your conversion rate (the ratio of sales to views as a percent) and your revenue day-by-day. That's a lot of useful info right there.

The option to set the timeframe alone can tell you a lot. You can see how your shop performed yesterday, how it performed over the last month, or year, or even set a custom window to peek through. Etsy has said that looking at a 30 day stretch is the best way to get an accurate idea of your shop's conversion rate and top selling items. But looking at your sales over a full year can show you seasonal trends and give you an idea of when your shop will be busy and when sales will slow down. If you've been on Etsy for a bit, play with this. Try out different windows of time, and see if you can learn some new or interesting things about your shop.

Etsy will also overlay your shop's performance from the previous year on top of this graph. You can see the year-to-year changes written above the as percentages, e.g., "Sales are up/down X%." If sales are up, the percentage is in green and if sales are down, it's in red. The same goes for the metrics—visits, conversion rate, and revenue. It can be so validating to see that green "visits/sales are up" percent, but remember that a red "visits/sales are down" message can be even more helpful because now you know you need to make a change, and stats can help you solve the mystery of exactly what that change should be.

Using Data to Learn Where People Are Finding Your Stuff

Under the overview graph on your main page, you can see where your traffic is coming from. Website "traffic" means how your customers are finding you. Etsy shows you a breakdown of where your traffic is coming from in a handy little chart. This chart is CLICKABLE. That means if you click on a traffic source, say "Etsy Search," you'll also be able to see a more detailed graph of your visits over time and a list of the listings that get the most visits through this traffic source.

Let's say most of your customers are finding you through social platforms. Nice job! You should keep doing whatever you're doing on social and maybe even a little extra. Or conversely, you may find very little of your traffic is coming from social media even though you've been spending a LOT of time on your Facebook posts and ads. Irritating. But maybe Facebook just isn't where your customers are hanging out. It's probably time to transfer your time and energy to whatever traffic source is serving you best and give it your all there.

Using Data to Determine Effectiveness of Offsite Ads

Remember our friend, Offsite Ads? Well, underneath your traffic data, you can see how well those ads are working out for you. No guesswork needed. Just click the link "See more info about your offsite ads."

Warning! The stats on Offsite Ads are not included on the main page, likely because Etsy doesn't give sellers a lot of control over this platform. It's also worth noting that the Offsite Ads numbers you'll see when opening this section are pretty deceptive. Etsy wants you to have a good impression of the platform, so they only show the *revenue* your shop has earned from Offsite Ads without revealing the sizable chunk Etsy takes for itself. (We still think Offsite Ads are worth it as we said in Chapter 12. Just know the big bold numbers at the top aren't *profits*.)

Using Data to Determine Most Viewed Listings/Most Purchased Listings

That was a slight diversion, but let's return to the main Stats page. At the bottom, Etsy shows you your listings in order from the most viewed to the least viewed. I admit, I spend most of my time in Stats in this data. A dropdown list in the upper right corner of the listings section allows you to view "All Listings" or just your "Active Listings" among a few other options I haven't found particularly useful. I use this area to see

- Best sellers,
- Which listings are doing poorly,
- The conversion rate of individual listings. (Is a listing getting a lot of views but not many sales? That might mean you need to use more-specific keywords.)

Use this information when you're spitballing new products or deciding whether to make more of a particular product. Don't guess.

Don't do something that sounds like a good idea but you have no real evidence to support. Look to the data, and see what's growing and selling and what isn't. Then do more of what's working, and less of what isn't (or tweak what's not doing well). As artists, so many of us want to follow our intuition and make decisions based on our gut. And there's a place for that. But when it comes to making sales and growing, data is your best friend in determining what your best sellers will be!

Using Data to Evaluate Individual Listings

You now know how to identify listings that are doing poorly or have a low conversion rate, and you can click on these listings one by one to see data about each listing. (You can also access the data by going into the "Listings" section in your Shop Manager, clicking this symbol in the bottom right corner of the listing you want to learn about, and selecting "View Stats" in the dropdown.)

This is the deep dive part of Etsy Stats. It can take a lot of time to go through each of your listings, especially if you have 100 or 500 or 1,000. I'd recommend starting by taking a look at the stats on your top five best sellers and your bottom five performing listings. What you learn can usually be applied to the rest of your shop without scouring each listing individually.

The listing stats pages are set up the same as the main stats page, except, instead of showing information about your shop, it gives you details about how an individual listing is performing. You'll see the number of visits and sales for that listing, how customers are finding the listing, and best of all, a *list of search terms* that have resulted in views. This list of keywords can help you hone your title and tags to reflect how customers find your product and end up purchasing it. And you can also use these words to craft more compelling descriptions for your items and create ads in social media.

And that concludes our tour of Etsy Stats. Remember, when dealing with data, it's important to look for PATTERNS. Pull up your five top performing listings and your five lowest performing listings. And then look at what you're doing differently. Make notes. Become a data detective. And form hypotheses that you put to the test. Over time, you'll figure out how to use Etsy Stats to know with confidence WHY certain listings are doing better than others and how to improve.

Pulling Raw Data from Your Shop and Analyzing

Etsy Stats provides a LOT of data you can work with, and it attempts to analyze some of that data for you in the form of conversion rates and year-to-year comparisons among other things. But there's MORE. There's always more data to be had and more ways to use it.

Etsy keeps track of ALL the information about every sale you've ever made. And that raw data can be downloaded by time period (e.g., by year or by month) to help reveal global patterns in your shop. For instance, what color shirt do people purchase the most? Where are most of your buyers located? What time of year do you see the most sales and for which products?

Looking at your data in bulk is invaluable and can give you a bird's eye view of patterns that you won't be able to parse out in a day to day glance at your stats (largely because Etsy Stats limits what you can see so as not to overwhelm sellers). Here's how you access that RAW data:

In the Shop Manager, under Settings → Options, there is a tab titled "Download Data." Here, you can get a CSV file of data about your listings and your orders over any period of time. A CSV file can be pulled directly into Excel or into Google Sheets where you can sort however you want (e.g., by variation, color, shipping state, even customer name). There are so many possibilities (Mwahahaha!). All of that data, just sitting there, waiting to be sorted and interpreted. Really, who could ask for anything more exciting than that?

Using Data from Google Analytics

Most sellers don't know that in addition to Etsy Stats, you can set up a Google Analytics account for your Etsy shop to provide you with FREE additional data that informs your business decisions. You can find instructions on how to do this from Etsy Help.

You should absolutely set up a Google Analytics account. Why? For one, Etsy Stats gives you detailed data about how customers are finding your shop from INSIDE Etsy's platform, but Google Analytics can tell you where your customers are coming from BEFORE they arrive on Etsy.com. This kind of data from Google Analytics can tell you which platforms outside Etsy would be best to spend your precious advertising dollars to attract the most customers. Also, Etsy stats shows you sales and revenue data that you can't get from Google Analytics, but Google Analytics will tell you way more about your customer behavior (e.g., engagement, bounce rate, exits) than Etsy Stats.The two analytics tools actually complement each other very well.

Let me give a few more examples of this synergy. Etsy Stats shows you the number of "views" your listing received, while Google Analytics allows you to separate out those visits by where your customers live, age, gender, and where they came from outside of Etsy (like if you ran an ad somewhere). Google Analytics can show you when your customers leave your store (is there a particular listing that turns people off?), as well as the lengths of time they linger on a specific listing. And while Etsy Stats shows you which Etsy search queries brought customers to your listings, it doesn't show how engaged the customer was with your listing after visiting. Analytics can show you which keywords are actually working for you (from an engagement perspective) rather than just the ones that got you views on Etsy.

I'm not going to go into detail about how exactly to set up Google Analytics and interpret the data—there are plenty of tutorials on YouTube about how to do this. If you want a tutor on how to use Google Analytics specifically for your Etsy shop, I highly recommend the blog "Artisan Analytics." Lesley is my analytics guru. She really knows her stuff when it comes to both Etsy selling and using Google Analytics as a tracking tool. You can start with her blog articles, take her Analytics course, or purchase her book. Do it. You won't regret it.

Instagram, Facebook, and Pinterest for Businesses Stats

Each of the social platforms has its own stats to show you how well your account is doing—data like followers gained and lost (so you can see which of your posts are landing with your audience) and engagement (people commenting or "liking" your posts). You'll see demographic stats like age, gender, and where your followers live.

If you decide to run ads on these social channels, the statistics tools for Instagram, Facebook, and Pinterest can show you how well those ads are performing—stuff like click throughs and conversions (purchases).

I know that learning how to use statistics tools for your social media platforms in addition to trying to figure out Google Analytics and take advantage of Etsy Stats is A LOT. Statistics tools aren't always the easiest to learn, and jumping into data and analysis can be a mind-bending experience. But it's so worth your time and effort. Stats are the signposts on the road to success. Understanding and using data about your shop and customers can save you money in the long run and help your shop grow in ways you may never have imagined.

A/B Testing and Other Forms of Experimentation

We've mentioned A/B testing several times already in this book, but I want to give it its own formal section here. A/B testing is when you create two versions of a listing, ad, email, etc., with a few differences to see which one your audience prefers. The differences between A and B can be minor or drastic depending on what you're trying to test. For example, you may want to duplicate a listing and only change the price to find out whether your item sells better at $25 or $28. In this case, the sales results will tell you a very specific piece of information about how to price your product. For ads, the differences between A and B are usually more distinct and varied. You want to create two visually pleasing, complete and informative ads so you can see which version of your ad your customers respond to better. A/B testing can help you hone in on what prompts your demographic to look twice and buy your products.

There are other types of experiments you can run in your shop as well. Try segmenting your listings and using one type of main image on one segment and a different type on another. Or try nixing your shop categories and creating an entirely new product organization strategy (Costco does this in the real world ALL the time to get customers to buy stuff they wouldn't have otherwise stumbled upon).

Or, and this is my favorite one, find a high-volume (frequently searched) niche keyword with very little competition on eRank, and create a product based on that word. There are all kinds of oddly specific products that get hundreds of searches each month on Etsy but that almost nobody sells (or at least nobody is using those keyword phrases in their titles and tags)— "new mom gifts baskets," "blush pink throw pillow sets," "oncologist team gifts" (who would have thought that last one would have 784 searches a month?). Experiment with these niche, low-competition keywords in your products, and see what happens.

You can have a lot of fun experimenting (smartly) with your listings and shop components. And since you now know how to use analytics tools, you'll be able to see pretty quickly what's working and what's not. So get out there! Analyze some data—STAT.

Things We Learned the Hard Way

Once the initial feelings of being in over my head with stats subsided, I became a bit obsessed with checking them, so much so that I was peeking at my stats several times a day and overreacting to every little dip in views and sales. Don't be like me. Remember that changes often take a little while to percolate through to your shop, and stats don't reflect those changes right away.

Trends over 30 or 90 or even 365 days are much more valuable than the day-to-day numbers. (Even if it's fun, occasionally, when your shop sales are up, to change your timeframe to "Yesterday," and see a conversion rate of 18% or something AMAZING like that). Just don't let those one-day highs (or lows) guide your overall decisions. And don't do what I did at first and make constant sweeping changes based on your day-to-day shop performance. I mean, if one of those changes does make a difference, whether for good or bad, you won't be able to tell which one it was. Data is all about trends, so try to keep the big picture in mind as you check your stats and make decisions about how to run your business.

SECTION 3: GOING BIG

Taking Your Shop from Hobby to Business

You're taking the plunge. You're turning your hobby into a business. In the early days, when this moment was just a pipe dream, you probably imagined it with excitement and anticipation and maybe a little disbelief. After all, sometimes that imposter syndrome kicks in and it's difficult to believe that YOUR shop, your product could become a full-fledged business.

And when the sales start rolling in, when you find yourself busier and busier, it IS exciting. Don't get me wrong. And you should take a moment to CELEBRATE. Because behind that success is a lot of hard work. But sometimes (if you're anything like us), that excitement about growth comes with some anxieties, fear, and "what do I do about ____." Because finding yourself CEO of a snowballing business brings with it some new logistical challenges and uncharted territory.

But take a deep breath. Because everything is going to be fine. More than fine, in fact. All of your questions have answers, and all of this uncharted territory will soon be a well-mapped reality of your thriving Etsy shop.

So, let's talk about the ins and outs of setting up your business for scale, accounting, best practices for growth on Etsy, hiring (gasp!) and all the other good stuff that once sounded sort of boring but is now very, very important.

CHAPTER 15

The Boring Stuff: Setting Up Your Business

Consider this chapter a sort of quick-reference for the different challenges and logistical questions you're going to run into as you grow beyond making just a few sales per month. First up, we're going to talk about business structure. This is really important, because it directly affects your bottom line profits (a.k.a., how much you have to pay in taxes). It also makes sure you're covering your bases so that you don't get audited (or if you do, you've got all your ducks in a row).

Business Designation: LLC vs. S-corp vs. Self-employed?

The biggest question most Etsy-shop owners have when they're starting out—and the decision that will affect your business and growth potential the most—is your business designation.

You might think, "But I'm super small, do I need a business designation? It's just me." And the answer is probably yes (although you don't have to be a registered business to sell on Etsy). Create an LLC as early as possible once you've started selling on Etsy, especially if this is your dream to eventually grow your shop into a sustainable business.

Start an LLC

Even if you're just doing Etsy as a part-time gig right now, you'll have access to more opportunities, better supply prices and wholesale rates if you register formally as an LLC (Limited Liability Company) and get an EIN (Employer Identification Number). Registering as an LLC can also protect you from loss in certain situations.

We'll talk about another business designation you should (strongly) consider in a moment, but the long and short of it is this: 99% of Etsy shop owners (large and small) should form an LLC. Here's why:

- It's incredibly simple and pretty inexpensive. You'll choose a name for your LLC. If your LLC name is different from your business name, you'll also need to fill out a DBA form (Doing Business As) for your business name. E.g., my LLC name is Dynamite Gal, LLC. My DBA is Fourth Wave for my Etsy shop and CraftRanker for the coaching business that Jeanne and I run together. I did this because I wanted a more generic-sounding business name for my freelance writing and design work. Costs to officially file as an LLC vary by state, but expect to pay around $100.

- After you legally form your LLC with the Secretary of State (in your state), you'll need to apply for your EIN (Employee ID number, also called a Tax ID Number). You can apply for that EIN online, and you'll use this number to identify yourself as an officially formed business.

- When you create an LLC, you'll be required to create simple "articles of incorporation" to list your address and a registered "point of contact" person. You'll also need to create an "Operating agreement" which basically states who owns what. If you have multiple shop owners, this will require you to designate ownership (e.g., 50/50 or 60/40. This influences how much claim each of you will have on the business should you part ways.

- Creating an EIN will allow you to fill out a Sales Tax Resale or Exemption form, which gives you a backstage pass to the best wholesale prices for your product components—no sales tax required. Basically, you'll be able to buy wholesale supplies for your business tax-free, since you'll be creating items with those supplies to sell (and you'll be charging sales tax on those items you sell).

- "Limited Liability" means that you personally (as the owner) can't be sued/your personal assets won't be put at risk if you accrue debts or get into other entanglements. We all like to hope that won't happen (I've never had any such issues) but you never know! And if you do run up against a problem, you'll want to know that your liability is limited to the assets of your business —not your personal assets.

- Filing your tax return for an LLC business is really simple. An LLC doesn't actually require a return. You simply report your income and profit/loss from the business on your personal tax return as Schedule C income.

Summed up: Creating an LLC is easy, makes you look way more official, and protects your assets from potential legal situations. It also gives you the opportunity to get the best wholesale prices. DO it!

Whether or not you have an LLC, you're going to be paying both income tax (usually around 15%) PLUS self-employment taxes (usually around 15%) for a grand total of 30% in taxes. That's a frustratingly high rate. But as a self-employed person, the government requires you to pay that self-employment tax on TOP of your income taxes to account for medicare and social security (usually paid by an employer). Which brings us to our next section and arguably the most important reason to form an LLC as soon as possible in your Etsy journey.

What about S-Corps?

If your business takes off and you start thinking to yourself, "Maybe I could do this thing full time," you may want to apply to file your business taxes as an S-corp. You'll still be an LLC. But you'll file as an S-corp. I know that's confusing. But a lot of things about taxes and business entity stuff is. Just roll with it. I'll keep explaining.

S-corps are considered a "Pass-through" entity, which means that you'll be able to classify some of your earnings as "salary" (subject to employment taxes like medicare, medicaid, social security, federal withholding tax, etc.) and some as "distributions" (ONLY subject to income tax). You'll basically become a W2 employee of your own company, and you'll ONLY be required to pay employment taxes on the amounts you pay yourself as a salary. Put simply, as a self-employed person with an LLC, you'll pay around 30% in taxes on everything you make. If you file as an S-corp, you'll pay 30% in taxes ONLY on your "salary" and then just 15% in taxes on your "distributions."

Be aware that the IRS will scrutinize your business a little more carefully if you choose this designation, so most of the time you'll want an accountant's help in filing your yearly business taxes to make sure you're crossing your t's and dotting your i's.

The process of setting your business up as an S-corp is a matter of jumping through a bunch of bureaucratic hoops and red tape. It's a pain. And it's a learning curve to figure out which payroll tax forms you need to file yearly and quarterly (you must run payroll at least quarterly as an LLC filing as an S-corp), but I'm here to tell you that it's worth it when your business starts growing. Because it will save you a LOT in taxes. So find an accountant you trust, do the paperwork, and file as an S-corp once your business begins to grow and you're seeing regular income from your Etsy shop.

Setting Your Salary as an S-Corp

One of the biggest questions many people have about filing as an S-corp is how to determine the "salary" they'll pay themselves each quarter in payroll. The trick is to set a salary for yourself that is reasonable *for your business.* And when it comes to Etsy shops owners, that salary can be quite low. As in, your "salary" might only be a couple thousand dollars per year (or $500 per quarter) depending on the success of your shop.

I'm not an accountant. So, I'm going to remind you to get an ACTUAL accountant to help you navigate the process of filing as an S-corp. But I can tell you from personal experience that filing as an S-corp has saved me a lot of money in taxes and was absolutely worth the initial minefield of paperwork to get myself set up.

So, here's what filing as an S-corp functionally looks like for me each quarter during every three month period of the year (so Jan-March is Quarter 1, April-June is Quarter 2, July-September is Quarter 3, and October-December is Quarter 4):

- In month one and two, I pay myself a "distribution" or "draw." This draw isn't subject to any self-employment taxes. Just a straight 15% income tax. In March I run payroll for myself (because remember, I'm a W-2 employee of my company). I pay myself a quarter of my yearly salary, then pay a set percentage of that amount in taxes to medicare, social security, and tax withholding on EFTPS. (EFTPS is the government's online tax collection website, and you need to apply for an online account once you've been approved to file as an S-corp).

- Each quarter after running payroll for myself, I fill out a physical 941 form and send it to the IRS. I also pay a set amount in State withholding tax (to the state of Idaho in my case) and fill out form 910 online (you'll need to determine how much you pay in state withholding each quarter with your accountant).

- At the end of each year, I file 1099s for any contractors to whom I paid more than $500 over the course of the year, issue a W2 tax form for myself, mail in a FUTA form with payment (Annual Federal Unemployment Tax, so really it should be AFUT but I guess that sounded stupider than FUTA), file form 967 with my state to report my W2 and 1099 filings, and turn everything over to my accountant for taxes. Sounds like a lot, right? It WILL take you some time. It's a yearly task I don't relish any more than I relish my annual OB-GYN appointment. But it's a huge improvement over paying a straight 30% in taxes. And all things considered, it's not really that bad.

BUT (and this is important, because remember, I'm NOT an accountant) you will probably need some ongoing support from an accountant who can answer questions about all the tiny, badly phrased, and cryptic boxes on all those tax forms, and so on. Which brings us to our next section: Accounting!

Let's Talk Accounting

Deep breath: Accounting. No matter what business designation you choose, or how little/much money your Etsy shop brings in, you are going to have some expenses and some income (e.g., the price of your product components, the price of equipment, and the earnings you bring in from Etsy and other venues).

The VERY first thing I want you to do is to open a business bank account. Even if your business is not very big yet. Mixing business and personal funds is a recipe for confusion and potential disaster if you get audited by the IRS. Just open a business account (it should be free to open a basic business checking account). Your business checking account will come with a corresponding debit card, and I recommend you apply for a business credit card (that you pay off every month and gives you some fun perks like travel rewards). Again, the business account is free, and it'll help you a lot. Even if your account balance is 50 bucks, just do it.

If you're just getting started (and electing to be an LLC instead of an LLC that files as an S-corp) you don't need to get an accountant yet, necessarily. I'd recommend it if you can afford it, but it's not strictly necessary. But here's the thing I didn't realize when I very first got started: whether you have an accountant or not, you DO need to do accounting. Here's the big to-dos if you're doing your own accounting:

Expense Tracking

Expense tracking is pretty much covering your butt come tax time. You're assigning categories to the business expenses you make (whether by check, cash, credit card, etc.) to indicate why those expenses were necessary for your business to operate, e.g., you're classifying the wooden dowels you purchased as "cost of goods sold" because you used those dowels to create arms and legs for the handmade dolls you sell on Etsy. Or the paper you bought as "office supplies" because you used it to print out fliers for an art show. You're telling the IRS, in general terms, what different expenses are for (because it's not always obvious).

You'll need to use an expense-tracking or general accounting app for this (I mean, you can do it with pen and paper or an Excel spreadsheet but it's going to be the end of your sanity).

The beauty of an expense-tracking program is that it directly connects to your business bank account, debit and credit cards to pull in every transaction. Then all you have to do is open the program and categorize each expense (e.g., "Office Supplies" or "Rent" or "Cost of Goods Sold" or "Payroll Taxes." The different categories available to you are the same categories that your accountant will use to determine how much you're liable for in taxes at the end of the year (e.g., some expenses are totally tax deductible, some are partially, and some aren't at all).

You'll have lots of options to choose from for expense tracking. The big names include Xero and Quickbooks. You'll have to pay a monthly fee for them, which is a bummer, but I personally like using Xero because my accountant is familiar with it and can jump in/see all my work easily. You'll also find free (generally simpler) apps. Make sure you look into pricing BEFORE you choose an expense tracking/ accounting app. Because sometimes a "free" app may have hidden costs, e.g, it will only let you track a certain number of expenses per month before forcing you to upgrade.

Invoicing and Time Tracking

These are two separate logistical pieces of the business puzzle. But I'm grouping them together here because they dovetail well, and it'll make your life a lot easier.

You'll need invoicing for two reasons: To get paid by clients you complete work for, and to pay freelancers or employees you hire either on a regular basis or periodically for gigs. Using a time tracking/ invoicing app helps everyone keep things straight. Because it's easy to think, "Oh yeah I'll remember I paid Jenny for that artwork…," but then in 3 months both of you are like, "Wait, did I pay her? How much?" Invoicing and time tracking provide a one-two punch of good record keeping for everyone's sanity. Time tracking will also help you gauge how long certain tasks take and will give you a better idea of whether it's worth your time to outsource different tasks or do them yourself as you grow.

Choose an invoicing program that also allows you to track time against different projects. Harvest and Time Tracking by Intuit are my favorites (they both offer a free "Self-Employed" option). Both apps have the option to track time against tasks and projects—either by pressing a "Start/Stop" button while working, or entering time manually. It's so, so easy to over/under estimate time—especially after the fact, when you've done 80 other things in between. Tracking hours with a simple app helps make sure you're staying accurate, keeping organized, and giving yourself the option to look at patterns and historical trends over time.

And the best part about time tracking software? When you're ready to create an invoice (either for payment or to pay a freelancer), you just select a project or client, click a button, and voila. An invoice is generated. It's great. No need to add up hours with a calculator or spreadsheet.

TIP: When you're invoicing for physical items instead of time (e.g., if you sell your mugs at wholesale prices to a retailer), I recommend using PayPal invoices. They have a simple-to-use invoice template for items (rather than hours). I don't typically send the invoices through PayPal, however (otherwise they'll charge you a percentage of your earnings). I tend to create draft invoices, print them as PDFs, and send them to my clients via email or in person.

Let's Talk Business Plans

You might not think you need a business plan. Especially if you're still growing. It sounds very official and intimidating and way too lofty of a project for little old you, who makes felted hats for American Girl Dolls in your kitchen by night. But I'm telling you, make a business plan. It can be really simple. And informal. But it will give you direction and help you hone in on your niche of the market on Etsy and zero in on the goals you have for your business and income.

All you have to do is open a Google doc and do the following (update this regularly, say once every six months to a year):

- **Write your business's elevator pitch:** Two sentences MAX that describe what you do and who you do it for. Why this is useful? This will allow you to clarify for yourself exactly who you are as a business, and to make sure you're occupying a niche of the market that is specific enough to be unique and compelling enough to draw buyers. It will also give you a ready answer when potential networking opportunities come your way, asking, "So what do you do?" I fumbled my way through enough replies before I wrote out an answer that I PROMISE you this is worth it. You sound confident, polished, and professional. And that's a really good thing. For example, your elevator pitch could be, "I hand-knit vintage-style clothing for American girl dolls." Or "I own an ecommerce shop that sells pop-culture mugs and hats."

- **Write a longer business summary:** This one can be a few paragraphs. Tell us the WHO, WHAT, WHERE, WHEN, and WHY of your business. Who is behind this business? What is it exactly that you're doing? Where does the magic happen? What makes you unique? How long have you been doing this? And most importantly of all, WHY are you doing this? This information can be pulled when you're inevitably asked for a bio along the way (whether in a farmer's market ad or in an article someone contacts you for. It happens more often that you'd think.)

- **Pin down your market and average customer:** It's okay if this is a guess at first. Write down who you think you're selling to in terms of age, lifestyle, gender, location, interests, etc. Anything that you think makes your buyers unique. This will help you in crafting ads, creating sponsored and targeted social media posts, and in honing the voice you use to speak to these customers.

- **Create a detailed outline of profit/loss and expenses:** You need to know how much you're making on a given item you sell before you can start running sales, offer wholesale prices, or even gage whether you can turn this side-gig of an Etsy shop into a full-time job. Get as granular as you can, and update this often as you add new expenses. (See Chapter 5 for more info on how to price your items.)

- **Marketing and sales approach:** How will people find out about your items? Here's where you brainstorm, create hypotheses, and come back to evaluate what's working well (so you can do more of it and expand on it). This could include items like "Etsy Organic Search" or "Etsy Reviews shared on social media" or "Paid Facebook ads." (We cover Marketing and Sales in Section 2 of this book.)

- **Plans for growth:** This is always the part of the plan that intimidates me the most, and I'm sure I'm not alone. But this is where you dream big. How big or small would you ultimately like to get? It's okay if you want to stay small. And it's okay if you have huge aspirations. Define what you want, and write out what the smaller steps in between might look like to get there.

Business Licenses and Permits

While you will need to register your business with your state as an LLC or an LLC that files as an S-corp, you won't necessarily need a **business license.** Check your state's requirements. Most have a "regulatory wizard" you can use to determine which hoops you have to jump through so that you won't get in trouble legally. Most of the different types of business licenses required are related to products in a certain field (e.g., agriculture). Many Etsy shop owners won't need a business license at all.

You will, however, need a **sales tax permit.** If you sell products (you almost certainly do if you sell on Etsy), you'll need to register your business as an entity that is legally allowed to withhold sales tax. You'll need to pay that sales tax to your state either monthly or yearly (make sure you plan on this expense and don't consider the sales tax you collect on Etsy as part of your "income.") And don't worry, Etsy automatically collects sales tax from your customers based on your state and requirements.

Deciding on a Business Location

Okay, enough logistics related to taxes and payroll. Let's talk about WHERE you are going to do your work, make your products, and operate your empire. This one can be stressful to figure out especially if you're in a growth phase. And Etsy shop owners often have unique needs for a location because of the unique products they make.

Still, there's some helpful rules of thumb you can follow to find a good fit. Start by addressing these topics:

- Whether you're selling online or primarily in person.
- Whether you're selling direct to customers (e.g., at a farmer's market) or wholesale (e.g., to other stores who markup and sell your products to their customers).
- How much revenue your business in consistently bringing in.
- How messy your production process is.
- How much space and equipment your production process requires.
- Your mental health and sanity (sometimes it's stressful to have messy, in-process stuff lying around in your personal space that might get knocked over or disrupted).
- The volume you're producing.
- Your goals for expansion.

The best location for your business will likely change as your business grows and develops. When I first started out, I was in the experimental phase and was making shirts for myself and a few friends. So I purchased minimal equipment and worked out of my basement closet.

When I grew a little more and built out my Etsy presence/started seeing more sales, I moved my operation into a whole room in the house. Then a garage. And finally a 700-sq ft. studio that I share with three other artists who don't need much space. I've grown a lot, but I've found that I can save a LOT on overhead by staying compact and making good use of my space.

Here's a few of the top places you might consider running your Etsy business, depending again on the factors above (like size and income) along with pros and cons.

- **A room (or part of a room) in your house/apartment:**

Pros: No additional overhead. You can deduct some of your utilities and home internet and phone from your taxes since those are business expenses too. Very accessible. You'll generally be home to arrange any customer drop-offs or pickups. Good temperature control.

Cons: Unless you have extra room, you might be edging in on your living space. Potential for projects and crafts to get disrupted. Your spouse or SO may object. Customers may need to pick up or drop off, which can sometimes be uncomfortable or awkward. Not a ton of space for bigger equipment. Depending on your production process, this can get messy or loud and may damage your carpet, sinks, or counters. May not be ideal ventilation if you use paint or products that produce VOCs.

- **Your garage (or an extra bay in your garage):**

Pros: No additional overhead. You can deduct some of your utilities and home internet and phone from your taxes. Very accessible. You'll generally be home to arrange any customer drop-offs or pickups. More space. Less concerns about mess or noise. Better ventilation if you use paint or products that produce VOCs.

Cons: You may be edging out a car or other storage. Potential for projects and crafts to get disrupted (or run over, or eaten by your dog). Your spouse or SO may object. Customers may need to pick up or drop off, which can sometimes be uncomfortable. Cold in the winter, and very hot in the summer. Insects like spiders and flies. Not always the most professional appearance to customers or others you want to impress.

- **A Co-op (an artist's co-op, or a shared maker space in your city):**

Pros: Less cost than renting an entire studio or warehouse. More space. No worries about making a mess in your own home. Ability to leave work for the day and keep your home a sanctuary. Good temperature control. Networking and social opportunities with other artists. Low risk, depending on your lease terms. Access to shared equipment like easels, sinks, break room and microwave, etc.

Cons: More monthly overhead. Not as accessible some of the time (may have restricted entry hours). Some restrictions on how you may use the space. Potential for projects and crafts to get disrupted or "borrowed" by other artists around your space who have access to your materials. Not a ton of space for bigger equipment. You might not be welcome if you use paint or products that produce VOCs. You may be responsible for some kinds of studio damage.

- **Your own leased studio or warehouse**

Pros: You can choose the amount of space you need. More possibilities for larger equipment and assembly areas. You determine hours and work environment. No worries about making a mess in your own home. Ability to leave work for the day and keep your home a sanctuary. Typically decent temperature control. Ability to sublease with other artists if you have more space than you need (this is what I do, to cut down on rent costs and enjoy some socializing and good vibes in the studio). Very accessible whenever you need it. Crafts and projects won't get disrupted. Better ventilation. You have the ability to create the environment and working space you desire.

Cons: Significant responsibility signing a long-term lease. More cost than a shared co-op. More monthly overhead. May still be some restrictions on how you may use the space. You may be responsible for some kinds of studio damage that would come out of your deposit.

Creating a Business Presence on LinkedIn, Google, Social Media, Etc.

When it comes to your business, the web can feel like an ever-expanding black hole that requires all of your attention and time. That's not entirely untrue. But just because you CAN spend all your time trying to keep track of and create a business presence in every corner of the web, but should you? Probably not. Like we said in Chapter 13 when we dug into different social media platforms, your time is valuable, and you should spend your time and effort where it's actually going to make a difference to your business.

As you look at where to establish a business presence, ask yourself, "Where do most people spend time networking, finding business help, and exploring?" And most people don't fly all over the web. They use the same handful of large, established platforms, which means you need to be present on those platforms—not everywhere. Here's where I recommend you create a business presence. It doesn't have to be fancy, just make sure you update it somewhat regularly.

LinkedIn

Everyone uses LinkedIn. It's the Facebook of business. It lends legitimacy and potential networking opportunities to your business. Create a business profile and update your personal profile to show that you are the owner of said business. Then spend an hour adding some beautiful photos and written descriptions to tell everyone what you do and where you're located (even if that's online). Not having a LinkedIn presence can make folks suspicious that you're fly-by-night or not very well established.

Google

Claim your business and create a profile for it on google. Not only will this allow people to review your business, but it will help you with visibility and may very well be the first thing that comes up in search (because, let's face it, everyone uses Google as their search engine). Keep your business hours and location accurate. If you work out of your home, there's no need to put your address, just list a website.

Facebook and Instagram

We already talked about tapping social media for paid ads and promotions in Chapter 12. But if that wasn't reason enough to put your business out there on social media (namely Facebook and Instagram, the heavy hitters), consider this: Facebook is the top social media platform that connects people (and businesses and ideas and events). You absolutely need a business Facebook page even if you think Facebook is dumb and you don't spend much time there personally. It helps people find you, it allows you to launch ads, it gives you the power to create events or quickly communicate information to your base of followers, and it allows people to discover you online in a way that highlights your personality and offerings (because you can share away!). Facebook helps legitimize your business as real and thriving. And there's no need to post to Facebook all the time, just enough to add value to your customers' lives, make them smile, and communicate important information (we talk more about this in Chapter 13.)

Instagram can likewise generate a LOT of social capital for your business and even connect you to new opportunities locally for your business. In-person business opportunities, potential partners, potential workspaces, potential clients, and potential contractors will often peruse your social media accounts prior to deciding whether they want to work with you. So make sure you are reflecting your business well (and that you are findable!)

Things We Learned the Hard Way

Basically everything in this chapter was at one point hard for me. I thrive on creativity, and the nuts and bolts of starting a business made me feel dead inside.

That means I willfully ignored some aspects—like creating a business plan, taking the time to put my business on different important platforms, and finding the right fit for invoicing and time tracking. Don't be like me. It meant backtracking and frustration and missed opportunities that I later recognized. Do the boring, soul-killing stuff. Just do it. Most of this only has to be done once, and the earlier the better!

CHAPTER 16

Expanding and Scaling

CONGRATULATIONS AGAIN! YOU ARE GROWING! (Or you're reading this chapter in case you need to scale in the future, in which case, great job for being prepared and having the foresight and confidence that you CAN grow and succeed!)

My biggest advice on scaling is to spend 80% of your energy focused on the terrain coming up ahead—and 20% on the horizon: The place you're eventually headed. Big dreams are the result of little dreams falling into place through dedicated work and planning. And trying to force growth, or scale before you're ready, is going to result in wasted resources and misguided attention that needs to be spent elsewhere.

Basically, don't FORCE scaling. And don't get so focused on the horizon that you go off-road. But vice-versa, don't get so caught up on the rocky road that you forget where you're headed and why. What I mean is, work hard to facilitate growth and sales and achieve the smaller goals that will get you to your bigger goals (e.g., instead of focusing on 100% year over year growth, a great big-picture goal, focus on setting a goal to create a solid keyword strategy for five new listings each week). The biggest mistake I see from over-eager Etsy sellers is trying to artificially force growth before doing the work to reach those goals (e.g., by buying a larger studio space WAY earlier than needed or shelling out a lot of money for Kim Kardashian to promote your product when you have 53 Instagram followers). Take it easy. Celebrate the signs that you are growing (we'll talk about those next), and adjust your business as needed to grow.

Are You Ready to Scale? Evaluating Your Growth

Most of the time, you'll grow and scale little by little without even realizing it (that's a good thing, because scaling overnight is hard and stressful). Here's some positive signs that your business is growing:

- Your stats dashboard tells you so! Check it often. Look at your conversion rate, number of sales, and weekly/monthly visits. All of these things should be improving on a monthly and yearly level. Sometimes if you get too granular, it can look like something is wrong (e.g., day by day). But remember, the day of the week, the economic atmosphere, and the season all play key roles in whether or not people are shopping. Some fluctuation is normal, and growth isn't a straight line. But your overall trend should be upward.

- You find yourself buying in larger bulk amounts for supplies as you see consistent sales and positive trends.

- You're paying a LOT in taxes and it sucks (but hey, that means you're earning a lot)!

- You're spending more time on your Etsy shop (and seeing corresponding sales).

- You're bursting at the seams in your original space.

- You find yourself trying to streamline your processes to make them increasingly efficient and productive .

- You find yourself daydreaming of doing this job full time—and feeling like that might be a possibility based on your sales and traffic .

All of these are good indications that you're growing. In general, you don't need to worry that your sales are suddenly going to disappear overnight. Etsy rewards good sellers and good products with increased traffic and visibility. Just like it penalizes poor sellers and poor products with lower visibility. When you make money, Etsy makes money. That's a symbiotic relationship, my friend. So keep doing what you're doing, keep doing more of the things that seem to correlate with good reviews and more sales, and you can be pretty confident that you'll continue to grow.

Don't be afraid of growth, especially in areas where that growth creeps up on you. It can be easy to go on autopilot, for instance, and keep buying that 10-pack of envelopes when you should really be springing for the 100-pack (even though it's a more expensive upfront investment). Look at your growth trends and stats regularly, and use those trends to inform you of the risk level it's acceptable (and desirable) to take in improving your profit margins by purchasing in bulk, spending money on ads, etc. Always make sure your risk and expenses fall in line with your growth level. Being too conservative or too aggressive is not going to serve you in the end.

How to Scale: The Big Three

Again, if you're incorporating the advice in this book and spending consistent time on your shop and your product offering, I'm willing to bet that you are already scaling. Most of scaling is intuitive, and most growth you'll take in stride as you adapt and adjust to your business's changing needs. But there are a few key aspects of scaling that stump all of us: Primarily, moving into a dedicated workspace, changing your business structure, and hiring employees or freelancers.

We've already talked about the logistics of different workspaces and business types (in Chapter 15), but how do you know you're ready to take the leap? It's one thing to order a REALLY BIG package of stamps. It's another to sign a year-long studio lease or make a foray into running payroll for the first time!

Let's talk about those three big aspects of scaling.

Making the Leap to a Dedicated Workspace

First of all, there is no rule that says you're only a "real" business if you have a brick and mortar presence, or a super cool decorated studio. Those things might be ideal, but it all depends on your business and how you make your products. Some people will NEVER need a dedicated studio space no matter how much they grow because the supplies and space they need to create their product are minimal, and they don't really interact with customers much outside of virtual spaces. If so, that's great. You are legit. Don't add extra expenses to your plate if you don't need them.

However, many Etsy shop owners may grow to the point where a shop, studio, or dedicated workspace is beneficial and will facilitate future growth (instead of stalling you out because of your space limitations).

Here's the top three signs that you should make the leap to a dedicated workspace:

- You consistently make enough sales that you can afford rent for a dedicated workspace. (This doesn't have to be a ton of money. Like we talked about in Chapter 15, a shared studio space can be surprisingly affordable.)

- Having more space would allow you to streamline and increase production, to bring in more sales (e.g., you purchase equipment that speeds up your process but doesn't fit in your current workspace).

- Your current workspace consistently creates logistical barriers to creating your products or interacting with customers.

Hiring Employees, Contractors, Consultants, and Virtual Assistants

Hiring ANY kind of contractor or employee can be very intimidating. I was so intimidated that I allowed myself to burn the midnight oil far longer than I should have because hiring and managing sounded so scary. I honestly should have hired someone part time much earlier.

But how will you know if you're ready to hire in any capacity? Part-time employees, consultants, and full-time employees are different options with benefits and drawbacks for each. For any hire you make, you should consider your needs, the type of commitment you can offer, and your budget.

When to Hire Consultants

You should consider hiring a consultant if you have a knowledge gap that's keeping you from doing something you want to do. In other words, when you need someone with more knowledge than you have to reveal some trade secrets—for a price—whether that's advertising, supply chain issues, design analysis, branding, etc. Hiring a consultant is basically hiring a very knowledgeable freelancer to step in and say, "Do this, stop doing that, here's why." Most consultants step in to impart knowledge, then step out of your business. They teach you to fish. The actual work of fishing is still up to you.

Be very careful who you hire as a consultant. The web is full of flashy gurus who claim that they can deliver the sun and moon. Ask for lots of recommendations before you commit to a consultant (especially for a high price tag), and set clear expectations of the type of interaction you'd like to have.

When to Hire Contractors or Virtual Assistants

A contractor or freelancer is someone who will help you with your business on an ongoing basis (this might be several hours per week, or once a month). You can find contractors available for hire on sites like freelancer.com, through networking on Etsy forums, or simply in your circles of friendship by asking for recommendations. When you feel yourself getting stretched thin as your business grows, or you identify a gap in ability or interest that you have (e.g., you want someone who can help you write copy or do design work because those just aren't skills you want to hone), a freelancer or contractor can help you take your shop to the next level and free up your time to focus on the big picture.

Choose someone you can trust who has the ability to work independently and think on their feet. Trust your instincts, and make sure you do a short Zoom interview (or an in-person interview if you're in the same city), and don't be afraid to walk away if it's not a good fit. It can be a good idea to do a "trial period" to make sure that you jive in terms of work and personality. Set clear expectations about what exactly you need, what your budget for contracting is, and how that contracting help will free up your time to run your business. Getting clear on these points yourself will help ensure a good relationship with freelancers. Answering these questions will also help you prioritize the type of work your contractor does in your Etsy shop.

Put your requests for work, prioritization, and any other tasks for your freelancers in writing, through email or google docs. Not only will this force you to nail down what you want your freelancer to do, but it will be a useful point of reference as you adjust workflows and tasks and can be very useful for a freelancer to reference.

You'll need to issue a 1099 form to any contractor who completes work in excess of $500 total throughout the year, come tax time. And make sure you order a PAPER form from the IRS well in advance of the tax deadline. Because the government has decided that's a hoop you'll need to jump through.

Basically, don't be afraid to hire freelancers, virtual assistants, or contractors in some capacity when you have the bandwidth to do so. Trying to do everything yourself might feel like the frugal or the easiest option, but if you're mired down in the details and trying to wear too many hats, it can make it very difficult to move forward in your business and grow. Give yourself some breathing room and bring on some help, in whatever capacity you need, as you are able.

Changing Your Business Structure

For most Etsy shop owners, the big question is whether or not to file as an S-corp. We've talked about structuring your business a bit in Chapter 15, but how will you know when to make a change?

The short answer is, talk to your accountant. And if you don't have an accountant, find an accountant. Every situation is slightly different, but in general if your Etsy shop grows to the point where you're thinking of it as a very substantial part-time or full-time job, it's going to be important to look at your business structure and how to minimize your tax burden. I file as an S-corp, and honestly I wish I'd made that move sooner. It was a pain to make the switch but 100% worth it. TALK TO YOUR ACCOUNTANT.

Making the Leap to Full-Time Etsy Shop Owner

Deep breath. This is the dream that so many of us have. It's the dream I had when I started out on Etsy. And I still feel so happy that I've been able to achieve that goal.

So, I know this probably isn't what you want to hear: But I can't tell you when or if it's the right time to make the leap to full-time status.

I left a full-time, traditional corporate job to pursue my Etsy shop full time. And it was exciting, but it was also SCARY. I was giving up insurance benefits, a salary, and an office. But my Etsy shop was bursting at the seams (because of the very same strategies we've shared with you so far in this book!), and I had to make a choice. Either I was going to back away from my shop to keep it as a manageable side gig, or I was going to go full steam at it and quit my day job. I chose to quit my day job—after spending a lot of time with spreadsheets and budgets and worst-case scenarios.

Like many Etsy shop owners, I often take on work outside of my Etsy shop when the opportunity arises and it's a good fit. I also work as a freelance writer and consultant. This keeps me VERY busy, but it also gives me a bit more job security. If something happens on Etsy (like a market crash, a lull, whatever), I still have other sources of income. Making the leap to full-time Etsy can be significantly less scary if you do the same. Use your skill sets (I know you have MANY!) to branch out and freelance in other ways, whenever possible, to create multiple smaller streams of income as a safety net.

It's worth nothing that there's also nothing wrong with deciding to keep your Etsy habit small or as a permanent side gig. But if you want to pursue it as your career and your day job, it's absolutely possible and doable. If you have a good idea, are able to scale, and are seeing consistent sales by implementing the strategies in this book, the chances you'll succeed are quite high.

Thinking Like a CEO

So, is there something beyond a full-time job doing what you love? That all depends on your dreams, personality, and production process. Some Etsy shop owners who grow enough to make their hobby or passion as creators a full-time job find that they get burned out by running a full-time business. If that's you, it's time to start thinking like a CEO. Because, well, you are!

Which parts of your (thriving! Look at you go!) business do you love the most: Creating things? Social media? Which parts do you get burned out on: Marketing? Customer service? Now is your chance to redefine your role in your own company and business, and bring on others to help with growing pains, new needs, and skill-set gaps.

Some Etsy shop owners get discouraged when they finally realize their dream of running their Etsy shop full time and think, "Man, I hate some parts of this." Don't despair. And don't give up.

YOU are in charge of your destiny here. It's your business. Make it work for you!

Things We Learned the Hard Way

There's no way around it: Scaling is hard and very individual work. It requires creativity and the ability to read signals from a lot of aspects of your business. Scaling also requires you to take an honest look at weak points in your business and to take some calculated risks as you grow.

Basically, it's kind of hard. And that's okay. Everyone does this the hard way. So don't be afraid to ask for help, pace yourself, and get creative. You don't have to grow in the same way everyone else does. In fact, I'd call *that* the biggest lesson in scaling that I learned the hard way: Trying to grow like everyone else. Every time I've gotten too caught up in some arbitrary benchmark of growth (like Instagram followers, for instance) it throws me off my game. Grow in the ways that make sense to you, at the pace that works for you. Don't be afraid to set goals or take calculated risks as you grow, but do so in a way that serves your business and you as a person. Because when you own an Etsy shop, you are your business.

CHAPTER 17

Shipping and Fulfillment

When my Etsy shop was really small, shipping was no problem. But as we've grown and this has become my full-time job, shipping is a little more complex. Which is why we've included this section here, after we've talked about growing and scaling your business.

Making a slew of sales is the shiny, fun side of the coin. Shipping and fulfillment is the "oh crap" on the flip side.

I understand. I was So. Bad. At shipping and fulfillment when I was in the awkward growth phase of my business. It was the bane of my existence when I really started to get the Etsy snowball rolling, bringing in enough sales to sustain me as a day job. Shipping and fulfillment was easy when I had two or three or ten or even twenty sales each week. But my exhilaration at seeing the sales numbers go up was dampened by the mess of shipping and fulfillment.

This wasn't all my fault. Back then, Etsy's tools weren't exactly made to accommodate larger shops or high-volume sales. They've come a long way, and so have I. In this chapter, we'll make sure you're all set to deliver on your promise of sending your products to your waiting customers efficiently and cost-effectively (and at SCALE!).

Shipping Timelines

Good shipping and fulfillment starts with good communication in setting realistic timelines. You have the option to choose one of Etsy's timeline options when you create your shipping profile (e.g., 1-day, 3-5 days, 1-2 weeks, etc.).

Faster is always better—as long as it's realistic. Especially since Etsy's algorithms reward you for faster shipping by allowing customers to sort listings by shipping speed! So, make sure you are shipping out your items regularly and as quickly as you can (while taking your capability, schedule, and production process into account. You'll only have upset customers and bad reviews if you over-promise and under-deliver).

You probably already know that once your buyer makes a purchase, the shipping countdown automatically begins for both you and them. You and your buyer can easily see the status of their order and whether or not it falls into the shipping timeframe you specified. A couple things to know:

- Again, your buyers can search for products based on shipping speed. And (unsurprisingly) they often choose to narrow their search based on short shipping timeframes. But like I said: Stay realistic. If your buyer expects a shipment within a day, there's typically a reason. A birthday, a Christmas present, a vacation, etc. If you don't make good on your end of the bargain, you're going to get bad reviews and frustrated convos.

- Holidays and weekends don't factor into your countdown. So, if you ship once a week on Mondays, you can choose 3-5 days as your shipping time frame, and even if a customer ordered over the weekend and their order doesn't come until the next Friday, that still counts as 3-5 *business* days.

- Update your timelines regularly. If you're sending out products more quickly (because you innovated or because you hired someone or whatever), don't forget to update your shipping time frames.

- Shipping in batches means fewer post office trips and the ability to "assembly line" your packaging process. I ship either once or twice per week, because it saves me a LOT of time by packaging everything up at once and hitting the post office just once.

Calculated Shipping

Take the time to weigh and measure your products, then input that information into Etsy. I know it's a pain. Do it anyway. Even if you sell a number of different variations of a product that weigh different amounts. I avoided doing this for a long time because it sounded like a huge pain. I sell t-shirts, and each size (I list sizes as multiple variations within a listing) weighs a different amount. An extra-small shirt weighs about 4 ounces, while a 3XL weighs about 9. But Etsy only allowed me to list one shipping weight for all the variations in the listing. So here's what I finally worked out:

1.	The hours I was spending in the post office having each item weighed weren't worth the 50 cents I thought was saving per item by doing my own shipping. I should have made my life simple and estimated generously on my weights in Etsy.

2.	In the end, the amount I saved by purchasing through Etsy (instead of retail at the post office) more than made up for any overly generous estimations.

To set up calculated shipping, I broke my listings down into categories by product type—with weight and size being the most significant factor. And then I weighed the heaviest and largest item in each category, e.g., my largest sweatshirts weighed 13 ounces. My largest t-shirts weighed 9 ounces. And my largest baby outfits weighed 3 ounces. I used the same packaging for all of them, so that was constant.

Then it was just a matter of inputting the maximum weight into each listing (depending on its product type) as well as the size of the product once it was ready to be packaged (make sure all dimensions are slightly smaller than your package preference sizes, or else Etsy will think your item won't fit in the package.

You'll need to make sure your packaging preferences correspond with your calculated listing dimensions and weights that you just input into each listing (e.g., if your item will fit in a 15-inch flat-rate envelope, make sure you list its length as less than 15 inches). Etsy automatically lists common package sizes, along with all of the flat rate packaging options offered by UPS and FedEx. You can also create custom package preferences that allow you to input the dimensions of the specific packaging you use along with any handling fees you want to tack on.

Carefully read through the different options in your Shipping Settings (within your Etsy Dashboard, go to Settings > Shipping Settings). These settings have the ability to save you lots of time. For instance, if you allow Etsy to fill out your customs forms, you won't have to spend time at the post office with those obnoxious forms. And if you allow Etsy to pre-fill your label information, all you'll have to do when printing labels is review them to make sure all the information looks correct.

Why I Recommend Using Etsy Shipping over Third-Party Apps

There are a number of integrations designed to make your shipping experience "seamless," like ShipStation. Some Etsy shop owners love these apps. I find it adds more hassle to my process than keeping everything in one place (Etsy), especially since Etsy and the post office have added more features recently that streamline the shipping and tracking process. Keeping everything within Etsy is simply less hassle and less back-and-forth. Not to mention, Etsy affords you many of the organizational features you'd get with apps like ShipStation for free (like discounts, tracking on every purchase, and the ability to refund a label right within the dashboard).

Purchasing labels through Etsy and USPS (or your country's national postal service) also mitigates any loss you might incur by overestimating on weight. For US customers, the post office now actually REFUNDS you if you overestimate on your package weight. That's right. Each week I now see an email stating that the post office has adjusted a number of my labels—refunding the difference to my Etsy account. So, don't worry too much about overestimating when you buy your labels in Etsy for USPS.

Using Etsy's Labels and Packing Slips

Again, I wholeheartedly recommend that you use Etsy's labels and packing slips.

Not only do you get around 15-30% off retail prices on shipping labels, but it saves you endless time at the post office and allows you to track every single package you send right from within Etsy.

Even better, as soon as you create a label within Etsy, it sends a notification to your buyer with their tracking number (saving you time answering questions about tracking).

As for physical labeling supplies, I get my physical labels from Amazon in bulk. (I buy half-sheet self-adhesive shipping labels.) You can also purchase labels in bulk from Uline.com and other paper wholesalers.

I don't include packing slips when I send orders to customers. (That information is so readily available in a customer's inbox), and so many people purchase their item as a gift that most don't want the packing slip included anyway. But I DO use a PDF print of these packing slips to tell me exactly what I should be putting in each customer's order.

Warning! If you frequently ship outside the country your shop is located, you may want to consider including packing slips AND invoices in your packages so that if customs opens your packages, they can see exactly what's in there and how much it's worth. This very rarely happens with Etsy parcels, but some sellers have had problems, so it's worth noting here.

Step-By-Step Instructions for Creating Labels and Packing Slips

Here's my process for printing **labels** (the thing you stick on your package) and **packing slips** (the list that shows what's in a customer's order and tells you what to put in their package) when I ship.

1. First things first: Review your orders for any buyer notes or private notes you've added to remind yourself to update an address or name on any of the labels (more often than is convenient, you'll get messages from buyers who forgot to give you the correct shipping address). You'll also want to make a note for yourself of any orders that need two labels/need to be sent using two packages (e.g., if you're sending a greeting card and a T-shirt in separate packages so the card won't get bent).

2. In your Etsy Dashboard, select all the orders you'd like to print labels for. Then hit the "Get Labels" button at the top of your orders.

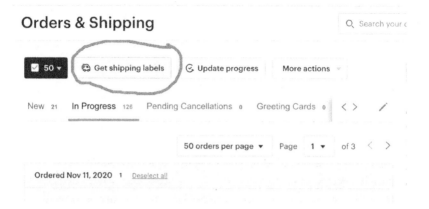

3. Now, review for any problems/change any addresses you noted. Look for any red warning signals that an address isn't formatted correctly. (Sometimes people put in REALLY long names, and Etsy only allows a certain number of characters, so you'll need to shorten the names. I just do this as best I can.)

4. Here's what the interface looks like when you're purchasing labels. Notice that Karen is first, followed by Amanda. When you are satisfied that all the addresses look good and are all correct, simply click "purchase."

5. Once you hit "purchase," a dialogue box will pop up that gives you a few different options including "Print shipping labels," "Print packing slips," and "Create a USPS SCAN form." DON'T CLOSE IT. First, choose "Print labels." Then print your physical labels using your printer.

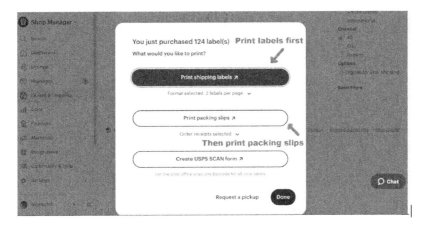

6. Here's the PDF etsy generated for my package labels. Again, notice that Karen is first, followed by Amanda.

7. Now go back to that dialogue box and choose the option "Print Packing Slips." This will produce a PDF (complete with pictures!) of the order items that should go in each package. (You can print this to include in each package if you want!)

8. Here's what the first page of my packing slips look like. Again, notice that Karen is first. These packing slips (that tell me what to put in each package) correspond with the order of the shipping labels I just printed to place on each package. Now I can stuff packages in order.

Basically, if you have 124 open orders (like I do here) you'll now have 124-pages of packing slips that show you exactly what to put in each package. The order of your shipping labels will correspond with the order of your packing slips. As you affix each label to your mailers or packages, simply refer to your handy packing sheet. This process makes packing up products a breeze. You'd be surprised how easy it is to mix up packages and customer names (e.g., put Karen's order into Amanda's package) when you're packing everything up. Keeping your packing list and labels in the same order makes for one less headache. This becomes more and more important the more orders you have coming in.

TIP: A USPS SCAN form allows the USPS to scan all your packages in one push of the button. It's a very handy feature, but you will need to print out a form for the post office—and you won't be able to do so if you're printing your labels to ship at a future date (Etsy allows you to print labels up to two days in advance of your mailing date). So usually I save time printing and just let USPS scan my packages. Sorry USPS.

Supplies for Packaging

Let's talk about the packaging you'll use to send your items. There's a few ways you can make sure your packaging logistics support your scaling efforts. Start by asking yourself the following questions:

1.   Will this packaging keep my product safe enough to withstand the journey through the postal system?

2. Is this packaging the most cost-effective way to send my items? For US shops, usually USPS is your cheapest bet. I use them almost exclusively. They're fast, inexpensive, and reliable. Wherever you sell, your national postal service is also likely (but not guaranteed) to be your cheapest, most reliable option.

3. What types of packaging do I need to ship my products? Purchase this packaging in bulk (as long as you have a proven product). If you're still testing a new product's viability, it's probably worth it to pay more per piece for a small amount of packaging so you aren't left with a pile of boxes that go nowhere. For small and mid-sized shops, Amazon has quite a bit of well-priced bulk packaging supplies. If you get really big, wholesale shipping suppliers like Uline have even deeper discounts.

4. Within parameters 1-3, choose something fun that will make your buyer smile. Most of the time, there's no need to choose brown paper. Opt for something with donuts or unicorns or choose fuchsia pink instead of manila. This typically won't cost you much more, but it will make an impression on your buyer (we talk more about aligning your labels and packaging with your branding in Chapter 8).

Using Progress Steps to Stay Organized

Etsy allows you to create "progress" categories to keep yourself organized. USE THEM. Here's my process. (You should feel free to create your own categories depending on your unique creation process. You can create several different categories and name them whatever you'd like!):

- All your incoming orders will automatically go into your "New" category. While you can create as many "progress" steps as you want, I prefer to keep things simple and divide my orders up into "New" "In Progress" "Pending Cancellations" (there's a delay between when you cancel an order and when Etsy removes it from your "New" orders, so I don't want to get mixed up and fulfill a canceled order) and "Greeting Cards" (since I treat this type of packaging differently).

- You should choose names that mirror your process of creation and fulfillment. Here's my process and how I use progress steps:

  o As soon as I start working on a group of orders (ordering the supplies I need to create them, actively working on fulfilling them, etc.) I move them into the "In Progress" step. Later, when I'm ready to ship these orders I simply select everything in my "In Progress" tab and print those labels/packing sheets.

  o It takes a while for Etsy to process cancellations. So I created a step especially for pending cancellations so that I don't accidentally start making those orders/they're out of sight, out of mind until they disappear/are fully canceled.

  o Sometimes, when I'm testing a new product or just don't have the capacity to make it on my own, I drop ship (we'll talk about that more in Chapter 18). I group these orders together so I don't worry about them. I check my drop shipping account once per week to verify that they've been sent out by my drop shipper, then mark them as shipped in Etsy.

  o For products that I ship more frequently (like Greeting Cards) I create a "Misc" step so that I can select all the orders I'd like to send out that day, plop them into the Misc category so I can easily see them all, and then send them out. The way you use steps will depend on your product and how often you ship, which brings us to our next section.

Shipping Frequency

I know we already covered shipping timelines—that's what you communicate to your buyer. Now let's talk about frequency—that's how often you *actually send out products*. I know some sellers that are packaging and shipping every single day. That works for some people, especially when you have a product you can package up and prep for shipping ahead of time or in bulk. Then it might make sense for you to ship every day.

However, for most sellers, the process of packaging and shipping is a bit onerous and takes a while. In that case, consider the assembly line philosophy. Onerous tasks with lots of moving parts are usually more efficient when you can group tasks together. Sending out five orders each day over five days is usually less efficient than sending out twenty-five orders in one day when you consider the time it takes to gather supplies, set everything out, go to the post office, arrange for a pickup, mark things shipped in Etsy and purchase labels, etc. That's why I ship once per week. I find it saves me the most time without allowing orders to build up too much. You'll want to find your own frequency, but be sure to consider efficiency and your sanity when doing so—not just your sales.

Using Order Notes to Stay Organized

Sometimes being an Etsy shop owner feels like one big game of concentration: There's a lot of moving parts, a lot of convos coming your way, and a lot to remember.

I stay organized (and sane) by using **Etsy's private notes** to remind me of anything important that comes my way in a convo. When you click on an order, Etsy opens a pop-up with details about that order and gives you the option to "add a private note" that only you can see. If someone needs an address change, I make an order note. If someone is anxious about arrival time and I decide to bump their shipping up to priority as a courtesy, I make an order note. If someone has been a huge arsehole and I want to include an extra goodie to make them feel warm and fuzzy inside when they open their package, I include an order note. Your buyer can't see these order notes, but they're easily scannable as you're looking through your orders.

I scan for order notes before I print labels (to look for address changes), before I purchase components for my products (in case someone changed a size or color on me), and while I package my products. It takes five minutes to scan even several pages of orders, and it allows me to stay supremely organized without a ton of effort on my part.

Basically, order notes are there for YOU (your customers can't see them), so use them to remind yourself of anything that will improve your workflow or customer service when fulfilling your orders. And scan often!

Warning: Private order notes DO show up on your packing slips when you print them, so if you include these in your packages, you'll probably want to delete "notes to yourself" so customers don't see them.

Stuff We Learned the Hard Way

I've done so many things wrong when it comes to packaging and shipping. And the stuff I do now seems like a "duh" when I look at my process and how well it works, but in the beginning I made a lot of mistakes. Here's the biggest ones:

Overly elaborate packaging: When I first got started selling on Etsy, I got intimidated looking at other sellers' packaging. I once ordered a shirt that was carefully wrapped in tissue paper, included five different free decals, was tied together with a sweet little twine bow, and included a heartfelt note. While this was beautiful and lovely, it didn't encourage me to make a repeat purchase, because the shirt didn't really fit me very well. Still, for a while I tried to make my packages very fancy and heartwarming. And then I got tired and overcorrected to very boring basic packaging. And guess what? My sales didn't suffer. I didn't get as many awesome reviews specifically praising my packaging—but I didn't get negative reviews about my packaging either. I finally found that a balance of EASY fun packaging was just as effective (and MUCH more efficient) than the super special packaging with cutesy wrapping. Value your time, and focus on what matters.

Hand-writing addresses and waiting in line at the post office: While I was still getting started—and even when I started to really grow—I hand wrote addresses on packaging. Finding the right labels sounded difficult, inputting the right information for calculated shipping sounded difficult, and the unknown was off-putting. So I wrote out my labels by hand and dutifully carried everything to the post office each week. Not only did I overpay by doing this, but I wasted WAY too much time. Do you know how long it takes to write out a bunch of addresses without making mistakes? A LOT OF TIME. And nobody got automatic tracking emails. Learn from my wasted time and inefficiency. Take the time to figure out calculated shipping and labeling. You will thank me, especially when the holidays hit.

Not keeping a strict order: Before I learned the trick of printing labels and packing slips at the SAME time (and in the SAME order), I wasted lots of time Control+F searching for names on my Etsy orders to match up labels with packing items. Don't do this. Not only was it more time consuming, but it resulted in regular errors as my eyes glazed over and I put Susan's shirt into Marianne's package because my brain got tired of doing the extra busy work.

The Bottom Line: Shipping and fulfillment doesn't have to be a nightmare or the dark side of making sales. If you're willing to put in a bit of time on the front end by using calculated shipping and Etsy's labels, you're going to find that packaging and fulfillment gets to be very streamlined and even easy. Don't go crazy with the packaging, but make it your own in easy and creative ways. Keep it simple, keep it accurate, and keep it organized.

CHAPTER 18

Supply Chain and Product Quality

Just like shipping and packaging, your supply chain (where you get the stuff to make and ship your products) and product quality (how well your product is made), are often put at risk by growth and scaling.

And we don't want that. We want to make sure that you can scale efficiently and cost-effectively—and that your products don't suffer.

By this point in the book it should be very clear, but it's worth repeating that WHERE you get the materials to hand-make your Etsy products is really important. Those beautiful, handmade products you create and send out into the world are only as good as your supplies. And the profits you bring in depend on the cost of those supplies. Basically, your income and your customer satisfaction depend heavily on your ability to source quality supplies at a great price. And at scale.

Whether you're just getting started or ESPECIALLY if you're expanding, it's important to understand a few important aspects of the supply chain (where you get your supplies). Because where you get the raw materials to make your products—and how good that final product actually is compared to what your customer expects and your competition's offerings—will have a direct impact on your reviews, sales potential, and profit margins. And ensuring that you continue to focus on your supply chain and quality as you scale will position you for sustainable growth instead of popping at the seams!

Supply Chain: Where to Source Your Stuff

For most people who create handmade goods, there are basically five places you can source your stuff. I use all five, depending on my needs and as I've grown. Now that I run my shop full-time, I rely more on wholesalers and bulk Amazon purchases, but I still use the other places on this list when I need a small quantity of something or am in a pinch.

- **Craft or office supply stores:** This is a great place to get small amounts of an item you use very infrequently or to create and test new products without investing a lot of money in bulk supplies. Craft shops tend to be reasonably priced, and you can usually find coupons. They're also useful in a pinch (e.g., you suddenly run out of adhesive or buttons and don't have time to reorder in bulk). Like we'll talk about in just a bit, it's not a great idea to buy stuff in bulk when you have an untested product or aren't really sure how much volume you'll be selling. Even if you're sure you have a great idea, iterate small until you prove yourself right. Craft and office supply stores are a great place to get the supplies to test ideas and find resources in a pinch.

- **Other Etsy shops:** Whether you're looking for bulk supplies, just a few supplies, or a particular kind of supply or material that you're having a difficult time sourcing, turn to Etsy. It's surprising how often this is a last resort for Etsy sellers. Turning to your fellow Etsypreneurs for your supplies can often help you find exactly what you need, at a great price, in either bulk or small quantities. If you find something close to what you're searching for but not exactly, there's also a good chance that you can request a custom product or component (a huge perk not available in most stores!). Rely on other artists to help you shine in an area they specialize without having to learn all the ropes yourself. For instance, I tried creating my own photo templates of apparel photos (photographing a blank t-shirt so I could photoshop my designs onto it later) with middling success for some time. But then I realized there were already people on Etsy doing the work for me—at a fraction of the cost (when I considered my time and subpar results). So now I purchase many of my blank apparel mockups from Etsy sellers who specialize in just that.

- **Amazon.com:** Amazon has a huge array of office products and some craft components that can be purchased in either smaller or bulk quantities. You'll typically find prices that are more competitive than Staples or other office supply stores, and it's easy to compare prices. I tend to use Amazon for my paper, office supplies, and other relatively boring things that I need to keep my business running.

- **Wholesale print shops:** For sourcing tags, business cards, and other marketing materials you may want to print, there's a good variety of wholesale printing presses online. Printrunner.com is my personal favorite. It's not as flashy as VistaPrint, and it won't hold your hand through the process, but it's straightforward and fabulously priced when you buy in bulk. I get my stickers and tags there. If you sell printed products like greeting cards or wall prints, you'll likely find that when you factor in the cost of good ink, a good printer, and good paper, it's actually cheaper to have someone else print your stuff in bulk.

- **Specialized wholesalers:** Since I print t-shirts, blank tees are the bread and butter of my business. Whatever the bread and butter of your business might be, find a wholesaler that offers exactly what you need and has the ability to sell it to you inexpensively and ship it to you in a timely manner. There's likely several options, so do your due diligence and price out wholesale options. Let them know you're shopping around, and ask about even deeper discounts as you establish yourself as a repeat customer with volume. As a general rule of thumb, if a wholesaler offers its prices to the public without requiring you to input your EIN (Employer ID Number) and business information to verify that you are indeed a business looking to buy wholesale (instead of a direct customer trying to score a few cheap items), you aren't going to get the best prices.

How to Know if You're Getting a Good Deal on Your Supplies

There are a few indications that you're getting a good deal on the supplies to create your product. As you grow and are able to scale, your margins should generally increase in a healthy way because you can justify buying more bulk supplies at a lower per-item cost. However, you may choose to narrow your margins to outpace your competitors and sell more items instead. The strategy is up to you, but what should be trending down at all times is your *cost per item* as you grow. If your costs are staying flat or increasing, take a careful look at your process, your supplies, and your fixed costs.

Here's a few questions to ask yourself when you evaluate your supply costs:

1. When you consider the cost of your time (e.g., if you can make 4 products in one hour, and feel good about making $20 per hour, mark that as $5 per product time cost) plus the cost of your supplies (including packaging, labels, and materials), how comfortable are your margins? Are you able to replace or resend a product (e.g., if it's damaged in shipping or not quite up to snuff) and still come out ahead? If not, it's time to take a hard look at your process for creating your goods, the cost of your supplies, or your retail price. We talked about how to price items in Chapter 5.

2. Have you done your homework and compared different wholesaler prices, asked about discounts for repeat and proven customers, and consistently find that you're getting the best deal for your needs?

3. Are you buying in bulk where it makes sense to save money when you have consistent needs and proven sales potential? You can always expect deeper discounts for larger bulk orders, but sometimes spending a lot upfront to score a better price per item is going to put a strain on your business or doesn't make sense because you have a new product or idea that has yet to be evaluated in terms of sales potential. You'll need to evaluate the health of your business and establish sales potential (while accepting smaller margins) before you spring for those bigger bulk purchases. Because here's the thing: If you get 800 popsicle sticks for five cents a piece (instead of buying a conservative 80 popsicle sticks for ten cents a piece) and then don't use the majority of those popsicle sticks, it doesn't really matter that they cost five cents apiece because you won't be able to recoup your costs without *sales*. So you'll just be out $40 instead of $8.

4. Are you able to offer similar pricing or undercut competitors' pricing because you've been savvy about how you purchase

your materials and spend your time, without sacrificing product quality?

How to Verify the Quality of Your Components and Products

Maybe this is super obvious to some of you, but in case it isn't, let's talk about how you measure quality. It's not a completely objective process. Some people hate what other people love. But if you know your audience and your market, you should have a very strong sense of what MOST of your audience prefers. You won't be able to please everyone. But your goal should be to earn an A+ approval rating in impressing the vast majority (of your target audience, that is). Here's how you do that:

- **You enjoy using your own product:** If you don't find yourself using it or feel hesitation about wearing it/putting it into your kids' hands, displaying it in your house, those are huge warning signs. If it breaks quickly or starts to look shabby after washing, you have a problem (unless that's what it's supposed to do).

- **Handmade tends to be synonymous with one of two things:** Superior quality and workmanship, or deeply inferior quality and workmanship. I'm sure you can guess which one you'd like to be associated with your brand. Etsy is all about the high-quality handmade. Which means that your shop will be held to a higher standard in many ways than products that appear to be mass-produced and sold on Amazon. That might seem a little unfair, but for better or worse that's the general consensus.

- **If your product wasn't designed for you (e.g., if you're a man, and women use your products primarily or vice versa) do NOT neglect market research:** You'd be surprised by how much reliable information you can gain from even a small audience (as long as it's the right audience). Don't guess. Don't assume. Don't ask a friend or your spouse. Give your product to strangers who don't have a stake in pleasing you with their answer, and find out what they hate about it and what they love about it.

- **Shop around, and don't settle:** You'll usually have a number of options for product components. Don't purchase until you find one you really, really like. You'll thank yourself later when you get those sweet reviews.

- **Listen to your negative reviews:** Yeah, negative reviews are painful. But do you want to know what's even more painful? Numerous studies have shown that for every person that takes the time to leave you a negative review, there's about 10 other people who stay silent but think the same thing. They just won't buy from you again, and studies show they'll probably steer their friends and acquaintances away from you without your knowledge ("The Secret Ratio That Proves Why Customer Reviews Are So Important," Inc.com).

Iterating Small with New Product Launches, (e.g., Testing the Market BEFORE Buying Bulk Supplies)

I've mentioned this in other chapters, but we're going to sit down and have a solid chat right now about testing the market and iterating small when you create new products to sell. Because too many Etsy sellers, once they taste a little success, will go nuts creating new products and listings in an attempt to snowball and grow faster.

But that's not usually a good plan of action. If you create a new or different product, it's better to start off slow, wait for the good signals from the market, and THEN proceed by buying supplies in bulk and going wild with advertising. Just remember: One success does not guarantee another success. And one successful product does not guarantee another successful product. It's a good start and a good launch point, but you should ALWAYS create a "minimum viable product" to launch new items in your shop. This is the most basic version of the product with the most minimal cost to you, to test the market's response. If you get good signals, then you're off to the races! If you don't, you've avoided spending a lot on sunk costs.

The following are some best practices to determine viability of new products. Now, if you're just getting started on Etsy, some of the information in this chapter might sound a little overwhelming. That's okay. Start where you're at, and use the ideas that make sense for your shop and situation; however, even if you're just getting started, you can test the market in easy ways to avoid the work of putting a bunch of dud products out there on Etsy.

The most important thing that new or established Etsy shop owners can do is to use data, not hunches, to decide which products you'll put in your shop or create. That's very important with any aspect of your shop, but especially costly new product launches.

Use Data, Not Hunches

Both new and established Etsy shop owners can make the mistake of putting a lot of work into "hunches" for good ideas about new products. If you're a new shop owner, you don't necessarily know what will sell yet. As a more established shop owner, you might not be aware of all the factors that go into whether a product is selling or not. Even if a product seems very similar to one you've released successfully, the small factors that make it different can tip the scales in a way you don't expect.

I find that Etsy shop owners who have seen some initial success are actually most vulnerable to creating new products based on hunches. Why? Because as you build your shop, get into a groove in sourcing your components and products, and start to see some success, it's easy to get overconfident and think your ideas are golden. While delightful and fun, this can make you overly confident when testing out new products and ideas and making purchasing decisions.

The Value of Research

So, how exactly does one gather data and research the chances of success on Etsy? First let the keywords guide your path. (You can review SEO and keywords in Chapter 2!)

Remember, you're ideally looking for those golden high- to mid-volume keywords with low- to mid-volume competition. Tools like eRank.com and Marmalead.com can help you identify those keywords. The goal, especially if you're just getting started, is to send quality, beautifully presented products out into the Etsy universe that won't get completely lost in the melee of competition.

And you need to know that people are searching for those products. Because even the most beautiful, high-quality product won't sell much if nobody is looking for it. So, when you get a hunch for an amazing product, check your instincts by doing a little research into keyword volume and competition.

The Value of Iterating Small

Even if you've identified the perfect keywords, ecommerce can still ride on a lot of variables. So, whether you're new or established, you should always start small with a viable test to plumb the market and your audience, e.g., don't make 1,000 snakeskin wristlets in preparation for your golden idea. Instead, make one or two and see what happens.

Be willing to forgo a "great deal" on bulk supplies or the appeal of shaving a few more cents or dollars from your profit margins to take a risk. More often than not it will bite you in the butt. Why? Because whether or not a product sells can hinge on some subtle and mysterious factors—including imagery, marketing, advertising, quality, color, season, and even what happened that week in the news.

Protect your shop and your investment by keeping the jury out on new ideas or products until you've tested them. This can be done in a few ways:

- Put out a "limited offering" to encourage interested customers to purchase while supplies last and allow you to gage interest quickly.

- Outsource production of the new idea or product with a production partner (more on that next) who is already set up to make this product and is willing to let you buy smaller quantities. Your margins might be small, but you won't be stuck with a bunch of products you can't sell.

- If the product can be made or put together quickly, try creating a mockup or realistic image of what that product will look like, and advertising it BEFORE you purchase the components to gage interest. If you see lots of positive feedback and a few sales, that's a good indication you have a winning idea. If you get crickets, you can send me a thank you note.

- Create a small Facebook group or email list of repeat customers that have given you positive reviews on similar products and serve as "beta testers." These beta testers offer honest feedback and stay on your list, in exchange for a free product once in a while as a thank you.

Drop shipping and Production Partners

Do you have to make everything yourself because you sell on Etsy in a handmade marketplace? Nope. But you do need to be upfront about that fact and work with production partners and drop shippers selectively. Because at the end of the day, it's you who will be on the hook for customers with bad reviews or complaints that can hurt your shop. Let's start with a couple of definitions.

Drop shipper: Someone who produces a product for you and ships it to customers as if the product has come directly from you. Some Etsy owners use drop shippers exclusively, especially those who create apparel and accessories like bags and iPhone cases. Basically, a customer will buy the product from you, you give the order (and the customer's address) to the drop shipper, and the drop shipper sends the item to the customer (with your return address on the label). A good drop shipper is invisible. Your customer shouldn't ever know they exist (unless they look at the information on your listings about production partners, since you have to disclose this information).

Pros of using drop shipping

The biggest appeal of drop shipping is that it's easy. Some platforms like Printful.com are even quite streamlined and automated, so you can actually integrate your Etsy shop and fulfill orders automatically whenever one comes in. This can be a great way to test the validity of a new product or a new Etsy shop without investing a ton in your own equipment or production space. Drop shipping can also be a good way to test out new product ideas without fully committing. You can use drop shipping to sell items your customers might love that you aren't interested in making yourself (like iPhone cases, for instance).

Cons of using drop shipping

If something goes wrong, your margins are so small that you're probably going to lose money on the sale (unless it was the drop shipper's fault, but even then you might have a very annoyed customer on your hands who just wants a refund instead of a replacement). Not to mention the pride factor. Some customers want stuff made by YOU and feel a little annoyed if (after reading your awesome "about" story) they notice you're using a drop shipper to create your products.

TIP: Spend some time really getting familiar with drop shipping. Because an "oops" on your end, (e.g., selecting the wrong brand of shirt to send out) is a much more costly mistake than if you had produced that product on your own. If you have to send out a replacement, you'll likely lose money on the order. You'll also want to make VERY sure that any images you upload are high-resolution and don't contain barely-visible stray pixels. I've made that mistake a couple of times, and I've had to send out a replacement when my customer got a shirt with a little pixel splotch on it (which was totally my fault). Double and triple check ALL your work when you drop ship.

Production partner: A production partner helps you make your product (rather than making the entire thing). There's a bit of gray area here, since you're not required to list EVERY product component you include as a production partner. However, if a hefty portion of your product is made or created by someone else, list your production partner (you'll have the opportunity to explain your relationship with that production partner in a blurb when you list them as a partner on Etsy).

For instance, if you sell earrings in your shop that are primarily concepted and created by someone else (but you package them up and maybe add your own special touch to the ear wire) that shop or person should be listed as a production partner. However, if you use felt or linen for sewing projects, you don't need to list the fabric store as a production partner. It's all in how much of a role that partner plays in creating the *finished product* that your customer buys. Etsy wants its customers to have transparency in sourcing and creation. People feel betrayed when they think they're buying hand-knitted wool slippers but are actually buying slippers made from machine-knit wool from a factory in Arkansas.

Pros of Using Production Partners

There are endless benefits to using production partners. They can make your life easier, help you expand your product offering, and help you stay relevant to customers without requiring you to spread yourself thin learning new techniques or buying new equipment. Just make sure you stay honest about where you source your stuff and who helps you create it.

Cons of Using Production Partners

There's not a lot of cons to using production partners, as long as you're honest. However, you'll always have the folks that want to buy directly from the person who sheared the wool, wove the wool on the loom, and stitched it into their product, and these customers probably won't buy from you. But that's okay.

Stuff We Learned the Hard Way

The most important lessons I've learned the hard way over the years when it comes to supply chain and quality are as follows:

Failing to realize that drop shipping was a thing and how it could help me test out new grand ideas without breaking the bank to invest in new equipment.

Feeling confident that I was getting a steal of a deal on my supplies—without bothering to do my homework on whether or not that hypothesis was true. For a while, I was purchasing my supplies at WAY higher prices than I should have been. I didn't ask about discounts (I didn't know you could!), and I didn't shop around much because it was a pain in the butt. When I finally did, I kicked myself.

I've always tried to sell the BEST quality stuff I possibly could, but I've learned over the years that sometimes my customers have different ideas about what is most important to them. For instance, I was selling a more expensive sweater in my shop for a while that required special care. Most people didn't listen and washed it the wrong way (and damaged it). They were happier with a slightly lower quality item that was easier to care for. Evaluate quality through your customer's eyes, not yours.

CHAPTER 19

Selling through Your Own Site–Pattern by Etsy

For the vast majority of Etsy sellers, their shops are side hustles that bring in a little "fun money" and nothing more. For these sellers, Etsy's main platform is enough. But this is not you. I know because you're reading a book on how to turn your Etsy shop from hobby to business. This chapter talks about expanding beyond the standard Etsy shop—to Etsy's Pattern. Pattern is a great next step into the wide world of ecommerce that allows you to consolidate all your orders within the Etsy dashboard but gives you more freedom in what you sell and how you display your products to the world.

In the final chapter of this book, we'll talk about other ecommerce platforms totally beyond Etsy. But for now, let's focus on Pattern. Because it's such a natural, easy first step as a foray into ecommerce beyond Etsy.

Here are the pros and cons of adding a Pattern site. It won't be for everyone, but it's a great way to test how well your shop might succeed off Etsy's platform without the overhead of running two shops on two separate platforms.

Each of Pattern's features comes with pros and cons, e.g., having your own domain is awesome but brings extra costs. And customization is great, but there are definitely limits. Let's explore the different pros and cons to adding a Pattern site in depth.

Pro: Your Own Domain

This is the biggest benefit to adding a Pattern site—you can now sell from your own domain, a custom URL with your brand name, as well as through Etsy's platform. And on your end, sales from both sites flow through Etsy. That means you can still print labels, manage convos, and do everything, with a Pattern order exactly as you would with a straight-up Etsy order.

Selling through your own domain (ours is www.fourthwaveapparel.com) lends credibility to your shop because customers see that you're professional and established enough to have a legit web presence outside of Etsy. It also helps Google and other major search engines recognize your shop as an online store in its own right, separate from Etsy. Another perk of having your brand name in your URL is that your brand name becomes associated with the product you sell. Kleenex = tissue. Fourth Wave Apparel = awesome screen printed feminist shirts! That's what we're working toward, anyway.

Having your own domain can also give you an edge for running ads on Facebook or Instagram since you can place a "pixel" (a tracker essentially) on your Pattern site to gauge how well your ads are performing. You may find that different audiences respond more favorably to a traditional website than Etsy as well, depending on your product!

Con: Extra Costs

Owning your own URL does have a few downsides, though. For one, you've got to purchase the domain separately through a *domain name registrar* for a yearly fee. Etsy doesn't help with this step, nor offer much guidance on how to do it properly. And there are like a million companies out there that want to sell you a domain, so it can seem overwhelming. Most of these companies offer *web hosting services* (which you do NOT need to sell with Pattern), so you really have to go into the process knowing exactly what you're after: namely, JUST a domain purchase through a **domain registrar**.

I'll say it again because this is key: To create a Pattern site, you *only need a domain*. Etsy provides all the hosting services through its platform.

So, unless your business plan involves hiring a developer to build you a completely unique site later on, buy your domain from a *registrar* rather than a *hosting service*. Domain.com and GoDaddy.com are probably the most popular registrars out there and are great options. We use NameCheap.com, which is perfect for us. If you DO decide to use a hosting company (BlueHost, InMotion, GreenGeeks…), go into the exchange with the mindset you use when renting a car. They'll try to upsell you at every turn. Don't let them.

The only real reasons to go with a web hosting company rather than just a registrar is if you think you might want to start a specialized WordPress site (one with extra integration options that uses WordPress software but not WordPress hosting) alongside your shop. Or if you want to eventually hire a web designer to make you a website from scratch (or build a site yourself). Both of these options require third-party web hosting. If, however, you think you may want to leave Etsy and Pattern for Shopify or Squarespace, you still won't need web hosting because both companies provide it through their platforms. Even if you want to build your own site using a website builder (like Gater, Weebly, or Wix just to name a few), you don't need web hosting because all of the most popular site builders offer hosting with the monthly fee.

Pro: Pattern is Super Easy to Set Up and Use

Once you have your domain name, setting up Pattern is delightfully simple. I've worked on sites on a number of different platforms from Wordpress and Wix to Shopify and Squarespace, and Pattern is hands down the easiest I've ever set up and used. This is largely because Etsy fills in your Pattern site automatically with listings from your Etsy store. You simply choose a template and *BAM!* your Pattern site is up and looking pretty darn good

Con: Minimal Customization Options

The downside to simplicity, as one would expect, is that you don't have much power to personalize your Pattern site. The actual HTML and CSS are totally untouchable with a Pattern site. You've got the option to choose from ten themes, and once you pick one, you're mostly stuck with the layout and look of the theme unless you pick a different one. Within a theme, you can change the font, text color, and the color of certain sections of the page, like the header, and you can toggle the search feature and visibility of your reviews on or off. That's pretty much the limit in personalizing the look of your page.

Pro: Your Branding, Not Etsy's

On your Pattern homepage and all of your listing pages, Etsy's branding is completely absent. The only evidence that your site has anything to do with Etsy is a bit of text at the bottom of the page that says "Powered by Etsy." (You'll see the same notice on sites powered by SquareSpace or Shopify). Having your brand front and center lends a lot of legitimacy to your shop as an online store in its own right rather than just one of thousands of Etsy stores.

Con: Bumpy Checkout Process for Customers

The checkout process in your Pattern site isn't exactly seamless, and here's where Etsy's branding DOES show through: Once a customer clicks "checkout," they're forced to *leave your domain* (boo!) and checkout through a payment processing site with Etsy's URL and Etsy's branding. Customers even have to register as an Etsy guest or login to their Etsy account to complete the purchase.

Pro: More Freedom to Sell Items that Don't Fit Etsy's Rules and Regulations

Once you get your Pattern site up, you have the option to choose where each listing is displayed—Etsy only, Pattern only, or both channels. This is especially helpful because Etsy allows sellers to sell items on Pattern that are not allowed in Etsy stores, like resold items and services like photo restoration, tailoring, and consulting. You still can't sell anything from the "prohibited" list, of course, but Pattern definitely gives sellers more freedom.

Pros: Integration with Marketing, Social, and Analytics Platforms

For nearly the first year of its existence, Pattern offered options to integrate with third-party services (like MailChimp), but many of them either didn't work or were listed as "Coming Soon!" Seriously irritating for those of us early adopters. By 2020, however, sellers can connect their sites to Mailchimp, a free (with paid tiers) email marketing platform, and add Google Conversion Tracking, a Facebook pixel, and Pinterest verification.

I'll give you a brief overview of what each of these options is good for to help you decide if they'd be helpful for you.

- Mailchimp integration: Integrating your Pattern site with Mailchimp allows you to create **pop-ups** within your site asking customers to sign up for your mailing list and gives you access to Mailchimp's **targeted email tools**. Basically, these tools allow you to set automated emails to go out to customers who abandon their carts and target emails about specific products to customers who have bought similar items before, among other things. For Pattern listings, Etsy sends out "thank you" emails about purchases with the same custom message included in emails sent out for Etsy shop sales, but none of the other targeted emails (abandoned cart discounts, etc.) are sent to Pattern customers.

> **Warning!** If you already are doing email marketing successfully, there's no obligation to integrate your Pattern site with Mailchimp. In fact, it's probably more work than it's worth to try to integrate an already established Mailchimp account with a new Pattern site. Because Mailchimp limits free accounts to one "audience," and Pattern wants to create a new one during the integration process, you either have to upgrade or delete your Mailchimp audience (while saving the emails in an Excel file or something) and essentially start over, which means losing all your analytics reports from previous campaigns.

- Google Conversion Tracking: This is a free service offered by Google to specifically track conversions, a term that means the number of people that buy your stuff out of all the people that see it. Once you know how to use the data, conversion tracking can help you make smart decisions about which listings to promote when and how best to market your products.

- Facebook Pixels: Like Google Conversion Tracking, the Facebook Pixel analyzes what's happening with purchases on your site. It tracks information about customers like demographic information, what they look at and how long, and what they end up purchasing with the end goal of focusing your Facebook ads toward the right group of people. If you have an active Facebook account and run ads, and especially if you're a verified business on Facebook, the pixel can do incredible things for your sales by showing your ads only to people who are most likely to purchase what you're advertising.

- Pinterest Verification: Connecting your Pinterest account to your website helps you become a Verified Pinterest Merchant, which gives you special privileges in the Pinterest community. For one, your account will have a special badge that lets viewers know you've been vetted and are a legitimate company. And Pinterest also gives advertising perks to its Verified Merchants like better and more frequent ad placement targeted to viewers who Pinterest believes would be interested in buying your products.

Con: Limited Ability to Integrate (Beyond Integrations Above)

Beyond the integrations mentioned above, Etsy doesn't allow Pattern sellers to connect their sites to Google search console or use any external analytics or marketing packages. You can't install add-ons or plug-ins like you can in Wordpress. There's no option to integrate with an Instagram account or other social channels beyond FaceBook and Pinterest. In other words, you're stuck with the limited selection Etsy offers in Pattern's "Marketing" shop section.

Pro: Etsy Customer Service (for Sellers)

Etsy has improved its customer service for sellers a lot over the life of the company. They now have a chat feature (YES!!) that sellers can use to get help and answers to problems quickly, and the customer service reps are polite, helpful, and knowledgeable. And Etsy has always used the Etsy forums very effectively for troubleshooting and for letting customers know when they're having a problem on the platform that affects sellers. What I'm saying is when you run into a problem setting up and running your Pattern site, there's fast and reliable help to be found.

Con: Slow Technical Support

While Etsy's communication is top-notch, unfortunately, their technical support, especially when it comes to Pattern, is still lacking. I think that Etsy may have stretched itself a little too thin when they decided to add Pattern and compete in the ecommerce platform market. Technical issues that come up don't get fixed very quickly, and there are some display problems in certain Pattern templates that the engineering team doesn't seem inclined to ever get around to fixing.

Since Pattern was offered to sellers as an option in 2016, sellers have found that their "Add to Cart" button is routinely broken (our customers were recently unable to purchase anything from our Pattern site for more than ten days—eek!). Hopefully, as Pattern grows (if it grows), Etsy's engineers will prioritize it more, but for now, slow fixes and some half-baked web coding are a few things to be aware of if you go down the Pattern route.

Pro: Minimal Costs

Etsy's Pattern site is free for the first month and costs $15 a month after that, which is less expensive than other options on the market (Squarespace, Shopify), and you only have to pay the $0.20 listing fee once for items listed on both Etsy and Pattern. Etsy has also recently eliminated transaction fees on items sold through Pattern as an extra incentive to sellers.

Con: You Still Have to Pay Shipping and Payment Processing Fees

Etsy still charges shipping fees and payment processing fees for items that sell on Pattern, so make sure to factor in these costs in your monthly budget for Pattern.

Things We Learned the Hard Way

When I decided to add a Pattern site, I'll admit I believed the process would be as simple as checking the button listing all my products on both my Etsy shop and my Pattern site. But it turns out that a shop optimized for Etsy search is very different from a site optimized for Google search. (And you want to focus on Google SEO rather than Etsy SEO on your Pattern site.) Below, I'll list some differences along with suggested solutions.

Titles: Etsy search rewards listings with longer titles made up of strings of relevant keywords. Google's search algorithm actively punished this behavior (called keyword stuffing).

Solution: Within each listing, check the box (found just under the description) "Edit my title and description for my Pattern site." This will allow you to edit your title and description specifically for listings displayed on your Pattern site. It'll take some time, but it's worth it. Not only will it allow your listings to rank higher in Google search, but shorter titles also look better on the Pattern site.

Descriptions: Descriptions on Etsy are largely for customers since Etsy's search algorithm doesn't consider them when deciding where to rank a listing for a given search. But Google's search algorithm does consider the first 150 words of the listing description.

Solution: Modify the first 150 words of your Pattern description based on keywords that customers might search for in a Google search (make sure to still use natural language though—no keyword stuffing!). This is a good place to include "handmade" and related keywords that are obvious to customers on Etsy's platform but might make your listing stand out in a Google search. There are some decent free "keyword volume tools" and "google rank checker tools" you can use to find the best keywords for getting your Pattern listing to rank in Google search. Paid tools like those from Moz.com are more accurate but probably not worth the price.

Troubleshooting: As I said above, troubleshooting even significant problems with your Pattern site can be difficult and time-consuming. The technical support team doesn't seem able to keep up with support requests, making Pattern somewhat unreliable as an ecommerce platform.

Solution: An Etsy shop alone can take you a long way. It's not necessary to ever have a Pattern site also. But if you do decide to use Pattern, I'd suggest it not become the main source for your sales. If you want to expand into having your own online store and perhaps leave Etsy behind, you will want to consider a platform whose whole existence is centered around making sure your ecommerce site works all the time. Some of the most popular of these platforms are discussed in the next chapter. Onward!

CHAPTER 20

Etsy vs. Other Ecommerce Platforms

If you're reading this book, you're likely already an Etsy seller or are strongly considering opening an Etsy shop. So I'm not here to pitch Etsy to you (any more than I already have, anyway). We've made it pretty clear that we're fans of Etsy as an ecommerce platform and have had a lot of success there. But I know that many Etsy sellers have questions about what else is out there in the world of ecommerce. So, as we wrap up, I want to give you a quick overview of the type of business that does well on Etsy (and on Etsy plus Pattern) so you can either feel confident that Etsy is the right place for you, or you can make the leap elsewhere.

So, let's jump into an overview of several of the other big-hitter ecommerce platforms and what they have to offer, specifically, SquareSpace, Shopify, and Amazon. After that, I'll also recommend some third-party integrations that can make your life SO much easier if you decide to sell across multiple platforms.

Etsy

Long story short, Etsy is an ideal selling platform for anyone who makes their products by hand. It has a reputation as an online market for boutique-style, mom-and-pop shops selling handmade items. Customers shop on Etsy knowing prices will be a bit higher and shipping times a bit longer but that they'll be able to find totally unique, high-quality handmade goods.

Because of Etsy's policies aimed at supporting small sellers, you can still make money even if you sell very few items and even if your shop is more of a hobby than a job. Etsy's seller platform is also very easy to use even if you're not tech-savvy, and Etsy will take care of advertising for you also.

Takeaway: Etsy is ideal for handmade-centric, smaller shops where the seller often strives to make personal connections to customers through unique, creative products.

Etsy Plus Pattern:

Selling on Etsy alone is great, but it can be discouraging when customers don't remember your Shop Name because you're "just another Etsy shop." Adding a Pattern site can add legitimacy and is a great tool for branding. Not only is your company name all over your homepage, but it's also the website address that customers type into Google search or the URL bar to find you, meaning they can get to your shop directly. And because your Pattern shop is basically your already-created Etsy shop displayed differently, setting up your Pattern site is incredibly simple. (If you haven't already, check out Chapter 19 for more info on this process and the advantages of a Pattern site!)

Squarespace

Squarespace is another excellent ecommerce platform aimed at helping small businesses market and sell online. It may be a good option for a seller who feels she's outgrown Etsy and wants more freedom, someone who wants to sell services in addition to (or instead of) products (Etsy doesn't allow the sale of most services on its platform), or a seller who prefers to sell in person—for example at boutiques, craft fairs, or trade shows.

One of the main strengths of Squarespace's platform is how incredibly image-focused it is. Squarespace websites tend to be eye-catching and serve very well as online catalogues of the beautiful products you're offering at your next in-person event and that customers can browse before your next trade show. Squarespace templates also allow sellers to advertise in-person events in ways that are sure to catch customer's eye.

Squarespace also has excellent integration with social media platforms, so if you're already advertising on FaceBook and Instagram, and your photography is one of your shop's best assets, it may be a great fit for you.

Like I said above, Squarespace's template options and integrations make it a great option for those selling services rather than products, largely because the platform was created with service-focused businesses in mind. The majority of templates are aimed at meeting the needs of lawyers, restaurants, hair stylists, etc. So, if you want to sell, say consulting services alongside your products, Squarespace is an excellent option for that.

Squarespace is the most expensive ecommerce platform mentioned in this overview ($30/mo for the platform plus $9/mo for shipping integration, which is really necessary if you're selling products), so you definitely don't want to try it if your business is just a small side hustle. Because it uses a third party for sales (Stripe) and shipping (ShipStation), actually fulfilling orders for a SquareSpace shop is more cumbersome than it is in other ecommerce platforms.

It also takes substantially more time to set up and maintain. There are a variety of template options, and building the site is fairly user-friendly for the non-technical person, but it does allow sellers to make changes in the website code—specifically the structure (HTML) and the aesthetics (CSS), so it may be necessary to learn some basic coding at some point.

Shopify

Another platform to consider if you want to expand beyond what Etsy offers someday is Shopify. Shopify is by far the most popular ecommerce platform on the internet. It's clean, contemporary templates are ideal for selling products, which was why Shopify was created. Shopify's ecommerce tools are definitely its best feature. Customers can pay online through Stripe and PayPal and in-person through Shopify's Pay-on-site iPhone feature. And Shopify comes with shipping tools that make calculating shipping costs and printing labels easy and even give sellers shipping discounts up to 60%.

A basic Shopify account costs $30/month and includes everything you need to sell products online, including easy social media integration for marketing purposes. As with Squarespace, selling on Shopify isn't a step to take if your business is a side hustle. And like Squarespace, sellers can modify the website code, so some technical skills may end up being necessary.

Shopify's excellent customer service is one feature that makes it stand out among other ecommerce platforms. The platform is known for its responsiveness and customer support. So, if you're worried about taking the jump to a new ecommerce platform and would love some extra help, Shopify is a great option.

Amazon

This chapter wouldn't be complete without mentioning Amazon. Because of its size and reach, Amazon is a great platform for ecommerce. A lot of sellers do very well selling on Amazon.

That being said, it's hard for me to recommend Amazon to Etsy sellers. Amazon's business model and reputation are just so different from Etsy's, and the company is known for some borderline unethical practices toward its sellers, stuff like forcing sellers to have really low margins in order to even rank in search, unexpectedly lowering the percentage sellers keep from each sale, and even worse, stealing a product idea and selling it under "Basics by Amazon" for less than the original. Also, Amazon is so well known that there are actually apps out there that track the best prices and ratings on its products. Competition is fierce.

Customers come to Amazon expecting to find fast shipping, lower prices, and brands they can't find in their local stores. They're not necessarily coming to Amazon for handmade items, and they may not be willing to pay extra for these types of products.

Sellers who often do well on Amazon are drop-shippers who sell tens of thousands of their product at lower profit margins and people who sell very niche items customers can't find anywhere else (specialty tools or hardware, for example). It's worth noting that for broad-market items (for example, clothes or household items), Amazon prioritizes its own products over third-party listings.

Amazon also rewards sellers with very short shipping times. Amazon offers 2-3 day shipping on most of its products, and third-party sellers are expected to offer similar shipping times. This means keeping a stock of product on hand all the time or using Amazon's "Fulfilled by Amazon" tool, which allows sellers to send products to Amazon to store and ship out when orders come through.

Like Etsy, an Amazon account is free to set up. Amazon just charges sellers transaction fees when items sell, but no listing fees. If you take advantage of all the "extras" Amazon offers, however, (like warehouse space or advertising), the costs can wrack up quickly. If you want to give selling through Amazon a try, make sure you read over their "Sellers University" information *very* carefully.

Why Not Just Use ALL THE PLATFORMS?

Some sellers do sell on multiple platforms! But, as you can imagine, this can get expensive fast. Not to mention, a logistical game of Tetris in how you spend your time and resources. The companies that can do this and still make a profit usually have a different business model than your average Etsy seller. The biggest difference is scale. Some sellers spend a lot of money selling on many different platforms and advertising like crazy, and it pays off because they sell tens of thousands of products. Even if their product margins are lower (as in the case for drop-shippers), they still make plenty of money to cover the platform and advertising fees. Think about it this way: these sellers are moving so much product that the fixed Etsy fees and $30-$40 a month for Shopify and Squarespace are easily covered with plenty to spare.

Those of us who sell on Etsy, on the other hand, often make the stuff we sell ourselves, usually by hand, which means selling 10,000 [insert your product here] in a month is out of the question without some significant restructuring and hiring (which can threaten to change the vibe of your shop). The average Etsy seller needs to sell far fewer products but with higher margins, and we can't afford to waste our profits selling on multiple platforms or advertising across the internet.

Does that mean Etsy sellers who start selling a lot of product regularly need to jump ship or add a second platform? Not necessarily. But it's definitely something to seriously consider. As this chapter has discussed, different platforms cater to different business types and different "levels" of scale, and Etsy simply was not created and is not set up to handle businesses that sell very large volumes of product regularly.

There is, of course, nothing wrong with either end of the business model spectrum. Whether you sell a few items for more or lots of items for less or are somewhere in-between, it's a good idea to recognize the model that fits your business because it'll impact which platform(s) you pick and how you go about advertising and even interacting with customers.

Easing Expansion with Third-Party Integrations

Let's say you DO decide to expand your web presence. That's awesome! Selling across multiple platforms is an incredible way to get your products out into the world and to brand your shop as a serious and growing business. It also means more sales and more income (woot!). But taking the leap onto even one additional platform besides Etsy can be so daunting. Now, you have to manage sales and fulfillment, listing uploads, customer service, etc. from two different platforms, often *doubling* the amount of time you spend on the often less pleasant aspects of running a business. And that's not even taking into account the time you need to spend learning how a new platform works.

The good news is that you're not the first person to have this problem. It's been solved. And the solution is ***integrations***. Integrations are tools that will automate different parts of your business for you or help two separate apps or tools work together more seamlessly. Think of some shop-related things that you'd rather not spend your precious time doing, say, posting to Instagram daily. There's an integration for that. Purchasing shipping labels? There's one for that too.

I couldn't list all available integrations here even if I wanted to. The really important thing is for you to understand the benefit of integrations, so that when you run into a process that's taking you far too much time, you can check the web for automation tools to solve your problem. That being said, here's a list of a few (out of hundreds of) super useful third-party tools you can use to automate your business processes across multiple platforms. Many of these tools integrate specifically with Etsy, while others integrate with useful platforms like social media.

- **ShipStation:** This service integrates well with all of the major ecommerce platforms including Etsy (and Pattern). It pulls shipping information for your customers from all of your sites and allows you to purchase shipping labels in big batches rather than getting labels for each of your platforms separately.

ShipStation is most useful if you have an Etsy shop AND use another ecommerce platform like Shopify.

- **Later:** Through Later, you can schedule social media posts across multiple platforms. You just need to spend an hour or so once a week choosing or creating content, and Later will post for you at your pre-scheduled times, meaning your audience will see you as highly engaged, but you don't have to be glued to your social accounts all day everyday.

- **MailChimp:** We talk a lot about this email marketing tool in Chapter 11, but it's worth mentioning here as well. You can create a MailChimp landing page that offers willing subscribers a coupon code for your Etsy store. Then, you can send marketing emails out to these customers and increase your Etsy shop traffic (and sales).

- **Facebook Pixels:** If you place a Pixel onto your ecommerce site, FaceBook will track the behavior of your customers so you can target ads directly to them on your social media accounts. Pixels give you a lot more information about who's actually buying your stuff and lead to much higher conversion rates for your ads.

- **Survey Monkey:** Customers love to give you their opinions, and Survey Monkey is a great tool for creating questionnaires that you can send out to see what your customers like and don't like about your shop. You can even integrate Survey Monkey with your MailChimp account, so the surveys look like official emails from your business account.

- **Zapier:** This is the mother of all integration tools. Zapier is a service that integrates integrations—basically, it connects tools and sites that don't already work together. Let's say you want the answers to your survey questions to flow seamlessly into a Google Sheets spreadsheet so you can sort the data. But Survey Monkey and Google Sheets don't work like that. Zapier will integrate them for you. The service now has 300+ options for "Zaps" and is adding more every day.

Takeaway: With ecommerce integrations, you don't have to struggle through the onerous tasks of running a business. There are tools to help you out. Stop burning the midnight oil and put more of your processes on auto-pilot.

GET OUT THERE AND ETSY!

slaps you on the butt

Okay team. Before we break this huddle and you go build your Etsy empire, I just want to say this:

You CAN do this. You absolutely can. Take it a step at a time, listen to tried and true advice, listen to your own data, iterate small, don't be afraid to grow (smartly), and never EVER let anyone tell you that you have a "little hobby." Etsy is an incredible platform filled with potential and it's only going to grow. Because of shops like yours and mine.

I spent way too long undervaluing my ability to run my own business. I saw myself as a mom from Idaho with a "fun side hobby" for far too much time. And I know from talking to many Etsy shop owners and clients over the years that others often feel the same way.

But people who craft, and people who create art have what it takes. I know this to be true, and I love what I do in helping other artists and crafters and makers see their own potential to follow their passion and do what they love for a living.

So, get out there and do the thing!

Like we mentioned at the beginning of the book, if you'd like to enroll in the University of Etsy (by yours truly, CraftRanker!) as a companion to this book, you'll find more than 90 in-depth instructional videos and worksheets that enhance and reinforce book learning and help you apply what you've learned here about starting a successful Etsy shop. These standalone video courses are $247 at full price on our website. We're offering them as a learning companion to our readers at a price we don't advertise anywhere else (19.99).

You'll find that offer here:

www.craftranker.com/etsy-university

Printed in Great Britain
by Amazon

10226226R00159